BAXTER HATHAWAY, Ph.D., University of Michigan, is Professor of English at Cornell University, where he directs a program in creative writing and teaches courses in language and modern poetry; he previously taught at the University of Montana and the University of Wisconsin. He has been a recipient of Hopwood Awards in both fiction and poetry, has published a novel, and has been Editor of *Epoch, a Magazine of Contemporary Literature* since 1947. Dr. Hathaway has written several books on language, writing, and the history of literary criticism, including *Writing Mature Prose,* published by The Ronald Press Company. He has also published many articles and reviews.

A Transformational Syntax

THE GRAMMAR OF
MODERN AMERICAN ENGLISH

BAXTER HATHAWAY
CORNELL UNIVERSITY

THE RONALD PRESS COMPANY • NEW YORK

Library of Congress Catalog Card Number: 67–11889

PRINTED IN THE UNITED STATES OF AMERICA

For Sherry

PREFACE

I have intended this book to serve as a textbook for a course dealing with the structure of the English language today—the kind of course on the upper-class or graduate level that I believe most English majors should elect whether or not they intend to be teachers.

I have written this book in order to present an outline of the kind of transformational grammar upon which I believe the study of grammar in our schools should be based. This kind of transformational study relies heavily on the work of Noam Chomsky and his co-workers at the Massachusetts Institute of Technology but departs from it in certain significant ways. I surrender the pretense to the writing of precise rules for the generation of all grammatical sentences in English and the elimination of all sentences that are not grammatical. I am content to suppose that complex structures are generated out of basic structures in terms of a relatively small number of transformational principles, while the number of fine variations in the application of any one of the principles is so great that mechanical exploitation of them is unprofitable for most students of language.

In order not to multiply rival technical terms any more than necessary, I have adopted many of the terms used by Professor Chomsky and by Professor Paul Roberts. Since, however, I have spent a quarter of a century in developing a "depth" or "process" grammar that has much in common with transformationalism, I have been loath to surrender a vocabulary with which I have been long familiar. I am also deep in debt to the structural linguists for many of the ideas in this book. We need now a synthesis of the widely divergent approaches of the past thirty years. Needless to say, if I distort or fail to understand any concepts of other grammarians, the fault is in no ways theirs.

I wish to thank my fellow members of the language section of
the Planning Institute of the Commission on English that met in
Ann Arbor in the summer of 1961—particularly Professors Fred-
eric Cassidy of the University of Wisconsin, Priscilla Tyler of the
University of Illinois, and W. Nelson Francis of Brown University—for re-directing and re-vitalizing my long-standing concerns with language. I am grateful to the Grant-in-Aid Fund of
the English Department of Cornell University for assistance in
the preparation of the manuscript of this book. And I am in-
debted to students in my language classes for materials I have
used from papers they have written, especially to Mrs. Catherine
Detweiler and to Thomas and Katherine Hanna.

BAXTER HATHAWAY

Ithaca, New York
January, 1967

ACKNOWLEDGMENT

Special acknowledgment for permission to reprint copyrighted material is hereby made to the following publishers.

The Dial Press, Inc.: From James Baldwin, *Another Country*.

Dodd, Mead & Company, Inc.: From H. G. Wells, *The New Machiavelli*.

Harcourt, Brace & World, Inc.: From Alfred Kazin, *A Walker in the City*; Eudora Welty, *A Curtain of Green*.

Harper & Row, Publishers, Inc.: From Vardis Fisher, *Children of God*; Martin Mayer, *The Schools*.

Harper's Magazine, Inc.: From Bernard DeVoto, "New England, There She Stands."

Harvard University Press: From Jerome S. Bruner, *On Knowing*.

Houghton Mifflin Company: From Irving Babbitt, *Literature and the American College*; John Livingston Lowes, *Essays in Appreciation*.

Life.

The New York Times: © 1953–1966 by The New York Times Company. Reprinted by permission.

The New Yorker.

W. W. Norton & Company, Inc.: From Anthony Burgess, *A Clockwork Orange*.

Charles Scribner's Sons: From F. Scott Fitzgerald, *The Great Gatsby*; Ernest Hemingway, *The Gambler, the Nun and the Radio*.

The Viking Press, Inc.: From Graham Greene, *Across the Bridge*; James Joyce, *Grace*; D. H. Lawrence, *Shades of Spring*; John Steinbeck, *The Red Pony*.

CONTENTS

A Transformational Syntax

1

INTRODUCTION

WHAT SYNTAX IS

This book is about that part of the grammar of modern American English known as syntax. No hard and fast boundary lines can be drawn for the territory covered by syntax, but in the main it begins with words already formed and ends with sentence structures. The structuring of words is the territory of morphology; the structuring of units of discourse larger than the sentence is the territory of rhetoric. Grammar is usually said to include morphology and syntax, but not rhetoric. The grammarian who concerns himself with the syntax of a language thus takes as his province the ways in which words attach to each other or to a context to form phrases or clauses or sentences—that is to say, meaningful utterances, whether these are expressions of emotion, reasoned declarations, questions, commands, or exclamations. Meanings are communicated not only by the dictionary items that we call words but also by the complicated systems in line with which words fit together to form larger structures.

When we adhere to our workaday habits of thought, we assume, as if instinctively, that words isolated from a context have distinct meanings and that we can check those meanings by reference to a dictionary. We know that a dictionary will list for us more than one meaning for many words and will attempt to anticipate the contexts into which words fit by classifying usages according to "parts of speech" arrangements, which is an act of going beyond morphology into syntax. We may lose some of our

3

initial assurance that we know what the word *fire* means when we think of a range of uses for it, such as *Fire!* (Shoot!), *Fire!* (There is a *fire* in the theater!), the *fire* in the *fireplace*, the *fire* in her eyes, *fiery* red hair, Turn the *fire* on under the teakettle (on an electric stove), He is a *fire*-eater, or His genius exudes a pale *fire*. In comparison with the range of meanings of some words, the range here is a small one, even if it is complex enough to be disconcerting.

We are all aware, at least dimly, that meanings of words may be denotative or connotative, literal or figurative (by a more or less, since words, as symbols, are always in a sense figurative), close to an established central meaning or extended in a particular instance from an established central meaning. But it is natural for us to resist the notion that a word acquires much of its meaning from the context in which it appears, even though that it does should be obvious. We also act as if we know when a word is a word since we operate in writing or printing by a set of conventions that tell us to leave a space between words. Grammarians, however, often have difficulty in defining a word so that all will agree, particularly for that no-man's-land of compounds where usage differs. The meanings of a whole utterance are likely to depend upon relationships that exist between segments of words as well as between words. Compare *He clarified the situation* (segments: *clari-fi-ed*) and *He made the situation clear*. Consequently, the territory of syntax may often spill over into the territory of morphology. Sometimes the syntactic connection is between one word and only one segment of another word, as in *perfect stranger*, in which the noun phrase can be seen as a transformation, or adaptation, of *perfectly strange* by the deletion of *-ly* and the addition of the suffix *-er*. A large part of meaning derives from syntax and not from isolated words.

The termination of the limits of syntax at the limits of the sentence is similarly arbitrary. Can we adequately define a sentence to everyone's satisfaction? The schoolbook definition of a sentence as a "complete thought" is plainly unsatisfactory, since a whole book can likewise be described as the expression of a complete thought. What one speaker or writer may express in one sentence another may express in two or more. Where one writer says, "Our objection to his silly motion is that government intervention encourages hatred of dissident groups," another may say, "We object to what he moves. What he has moved is silly. We believe that when a government intervenes in a situation

some citizens are encouraged to hate groups that are dissident."
In the first instance we have one sentence and two clauses, in the
second three sentences and nine clauses. It can be argued that
syntactic relations do not extend beyond a period as a mark of
punctuation, or in speech to a terminal dropping of pitch to the
lowest pitch level; but such a distinction is arbitrarily imposed
since it entails the ruling that personal pronouns like *he, she, it,
they, them* or demonstratives like *this, that, these, those, such,*
or any of these words in their functioning as near-nouns, adjectives, or determiners, are related in idea to their referents but not
syntactically. In comparative linguistics this kind of distinction
is often hard to make. In English we can ordinarily say that a
relative pronoun like *which* is capable of expressing a syntactic
relation. When we find a writer writing: *He had a lot of trouble
with the natives. Which is more than can be said for Carpenter,*
we are hung up on a dilemma. If the realm of syntactic relations does not extend beyond a period, either *which* must be
treated as a demonstrative and not as a relative, or the use of the
period between the two units does not follow any normal system
of marking sentence ends. When two complete clauses have a
semicolon between them instead of a period, without a connector, we have a case of two syntactic governments—that is,
syntactically two sentences, particularly if the terminal of each
shows a rise in pitch above the normal level and then a drop
below it (a 3–1 pitch contour). By use of parallelism or balance
carrying beyond the limits of one sentence, by repetition or
orderly alteration of key referential terms, or by such devices as
listings, classifications, or partitions, a speaker or writer may
signal meanings that are structural rather than lexical over an
extent far greater than a single sentence. Rhetoricians, consequently, sometimes refer to the syntax of paragraphs or whole
passages. Although syntax is the term we use in reference to
the signaling of structural meanings within the limits of sentences,
we cannot neatly and inflexibly confine the study of syntax within
such tight limits.

GRAMMAR AS THE DEVICE FOR FORMING
PREDICATIONS

To the average speaker and writer of a language, the definition of "grammar" as the description of his language's syntax and
morphology combined is not likely to be very meaningful. In

popular parlance "grammar" is a collection of "rules" learned at some time or other in the process of education for distinguishing "correct" from "incorrect" speech. It has, in this sense, some kind of God-given connection with a universal logic of phrasings even though paradoxically American children who have been subjected to extensive drills intended to teach them "correct grammar" uniformly report that grammar begins to be meaningful to them only after studying a foreign language, in which the so-called "universal logic" of grammar demands forms that are different from those of modern English. What the student of a foreign language comes to realize is that, whether he knows it or not, he has been forming a set of habits from early childhood by means of which he can take the raw material of sensation and thought that his mind furnishes him, can process the raw material, and can display it in symbols and structures so that other people in his speech community who have formed similar sets of habits can decode his meanings. He learns this from studying a foreign language because he learns that the encoding principles of the new language are more or less systematic but are not the same as his own. What he learns is that there must be an overall system, or systems, by which his own language can be described, just as the foreign language has its describable system, or systems, and in learning the systems he has been learning its grammar. If the grammars of all languages adhered closely to a "universal" grammar, he would have less to learn than he does in mastering his foreign language. He might, indeed, still have much to learn, for even if the morphology and syntax of the two languages were identical, the vocabulary items of the two languages, the articulation of sounds, and even the rhythms given utterances might differ, and these differences would have to be learned before mastery of the new language could be achieved. But foreign languages that are hard to learn are those formed on unfamiliar systems of morphology and syntax.

In the evolution of a language, sound changes and differentiation of vocabulary usually go hand in hand with changes in the morphological and syntactic systems. Certainly no sharp line can be drawn between aspects of a language pertaining to vocabulary or sound systems and those pertaining to grammar. Many modern linguists, perhaps most of them, insist that the spoken language is the real language and that written forms are merely artificial ways of recording the spoken language. In the spoken language, grammatical distinctions must be conveyed by sound or the absence of it, and any evolutionary shifting in the articulation of sounds is bound to have its effects upon the signaling systems. But when we speak of the grammar of a language we refer to the systems by which the relationships that exist among words or parts of words are signaled. The phonology of a language is thus only indirectly part of the grammar of a language. A Spaniard may use a certain word because the contacts of his ancestors were with Moors, whereas a Venetian would use a different word to refer to the same thing because his ancestors did business with Byzantines or Germans; but if Spaniard and Venetian used their different lexical items in a quite similar grammatical structure, their languages would be considered closely related. The grammar of a language is its systems of structure by which relationships among words or parts of words are built up to create meanings.

Pointing to a cat and saying "cat" does not convey meaning if the intent of the speaker is only to indicate what sounds are used to refer to that animal in English. Anyway, not much meaning. The meaning is more complex when we point to a tiger and say "cat," for we are now effecting a communication that might take place between one adult user of the English language and another. The adult user of the language does not have to be told that a cat is a cat, but may profit from the statement that a tiger belongs to the cat family or that an apple tree is a kind of rose bush. When we point to a tiger and say "cat," we are creating a "predication," a movement of meaning, in a sense that learning the word for a thing in a given language is not a meaning. A grammar of a language is eventually a description of its devices for forming predications or combining them into larger predications. Normally we think of a predication as a subject phrase of some kind followed by a predicate phrase of some kind, and we proceed to describe complex grammatical structures as manipulations of this basic principle. This procedure will be particularly true of this present grammar, since the attempt here will be to illustrate the principal deployments or transformations of basic predicational patterns.

At the beginning we need to see clearly that human beings have other ways of creating meanings than that found in the linking of a subject to a finite verb form. Meanings, in all languages, have to be "two-parted" (subject and predicate), but an actual utterance may consist of only one part—a subject or a predicate—if the other part can be inferred somehow from the environment or context. Thus, when you point to a tiger and say "cat," the subject-part of the predication exists in the environment (the thing pointed at) and the predicate-part is expressed in words. The implication is: "A tiger is a cat." The expression "Him no good" is not standard English, but it is a predication in which both subject-part and predicate-part are verbally expressed. We can, furthermore, imagine a language for which this way of expressing this kind of predication would be standard. If we reject this expression in a description of modern English grammar, we do it because it lacks a formal predicator—a finite verb. In speech we recognize the predication implied in "Mighty pretty girl!" (that girl is mighty pretty), provided that the intonation contour (the pattern of pitch, stress, and pauses) is right, and cannot reject the form as a way available in English for the making of a predication. The grammar of a language is largely the description of the resources of a language for handling predications.

When we say we can imagine a language (or a dialect of English) in which the expression "Him no good" illustrates a standard way of making a predication, we are practically saying that it is possible to describe the grammatical features of any language or dialect that actually can be shown to serve the needs of a speech community for the communication of ideas, information, attitudes, or feelings. For if it does serve the needs of the community it must contain signaling devices that the members of the community understand and can duplicate. Many of us are offended by the notion articulated by avant-garde relativists among modern linguists that no language can be said to be better, nobler, or more beautiful than any other language. We often equate the power of languages, by an easy substitution, with the economic power of the societies that use them, with the artistic achievements related to them, with the complexity and stability of the political structures found in their societies, or with the literary monuments that they exhibit from past or present. In a similar way, it is a common failing of New Yorkers to believe that they are wiser, better, and more sophisticated than small-town dwellers, as if the size and complexity of their city were of their own doing. But the New Yorker is partly right, and likewise the user of a language that Shakespeare has also used knows that he has at his command countless cliché utterances that were original creations of Shakespeare's mind, not really attributes of the English language, any more than a statue by Phidias is an attribute of the marble from which it was made. All grammatical systems may be equally capable of complex development but not all are equally developed.

Language is not only a dictionary full of words and a grammar. Intermediate between the two is the vast corpus of learned phrases, which is what the child first comes in contact with, and which he is never entirely capable of going beyond. It has become commonplace to say that children learn before the age of six to respond accurately to most of the grammatical signaling devices of their native language. A better description of their situation is that they have learned the import of a large body of phrases—phrases rather than words or abstract grammatical patterns. The baby who learns to say "ball" before his first birthday and "Where is the ball?" before his second is learning phrases in both instances. Once he begins to substitute items in the frames (*Where is Mama? Where is the cat? Where is Dolly?*) he has begun to recognize similarities between one phrase and another and to have a sense both of the identity of words and of the abstract patterns that we call the grammar of a language. But the learning of phrases continues to be the bedrock of the process, even though with time the area of abstraction toward the two poles of words and grammatical patterns grows and grows. The grammarian knows that ultimately usage is king and that usage is more dependent upon the clichés of phrasings than upon the simplifying force of analogies between one phrase and another out of which grammars emerge. It is not the word-horde itself that a Shakespeare enriches (although expansion of vocabulary may be one of the by-products of his efforts), nor grammatical structures. What is passed on principally is a large storehouse of imitable phrases.

KINDS OF GRAMMARS

It is because grammarians cannot ultimately claim the primacy of structures over phrasings that the strategies exhibited by grammarians differ one from another. Languages change. This is one of the inescapable facts of life that any grammarian must face. As decades and centuries go by, human societies undergo subtle shifts of attitude; styles of living alter in adaptation to differences in technology or intercommunication; new dialects are formed or old ones are absorbed into new standardized forms. By hindsight it can often be shown that language changes are regular, that is, follow marked directions, even over centuries, without human reason having much control over the process. It is as if society is a great animal stubbornly pursuing an end of its own, of which the sentient cells that are the individual human beings are unaware. Since both sound changes and changes in morphology and syntax exhibit some orderliness of pattern, the grammarian is almost invited to make predictions about the future on the basis of the drift from the past. But if he gives in to this temptation, he turns away from simply describing the language that he uses and begins to prescribe for it. He begins to assert what the grammar of his language "ought" to be, rather than to content himself with telling what it "is." One convenient division of grammars is into descriptive grammars and prescriptive grammars.

For the past century, advanced grammarians have intended primarily to be descriptive in their approach to the English language. The grammarian who "describes" a language pays little attention to value judgments, to questions of "better" or "worse." He does not necessarily believe that an "ideal" language can possibly exist. He turns as often as he can to actual examples of living speech or writing and tries to form what generalizations he can from the evidence that he gathers. He prides himself on his inductive method and on his "scientific" approach to his subject matter. He often pays more attention to the spoken forms of language than to the written, believing that he has to catch his speakers when they are performing naturally, i.e., unselfconsciously. More than the speaker, the writer is likely to reflect the influence of false, pre-scientific authorities. The writer often may tamper with his native habits of speech or give in to arbitrary notions about what is "better" or "worse" in the construction of utterances; furthermore, he may indulge his own whims and do anything he wishes, like the avant-garde poet who declares his independence of the linguistic mores of his society. The real language, the descriptive grammarians say, is what the speaker who is enslaved by his society uses.

Descriptivism is more than a century old, as has been said, but we should quickly add that until recently most descriptivist grammarians did use the written forms of language as sources of evidence. Otto Jespersen's *A Modern English Grammar* and the large grammars of Poutsma and Kruisinga are good examples of this kind of descriptivism. More recently, particularly since the publication of Trager and Smith's *Outlines of English Structure* (1951) and C. C. Fries's *The Structure of English* (1952), the large group of grammarians concerned with what is called Structural Linguistics have gathered evidence almost exclusively from the spoken language, and have tended to call fellow descriptivists like Jespersen, Poutsma, and Kruisinga traditionalists, as if their use of written records allied them more to a pre-scientific past than to an enlightened present.

Believing that the written language is only an artificial way of recording the real language, which is the spoken language, the structuralists have made somewhat extensive investigations of the systems of syntactic signaling to be found in spoken languages. Up to a point, the effects have been salutary; but the structuralists have spent so much time with the sound aspects of language (with phonetics and phonemics) that they have had little chance to be exhaustive describers of syntax. By an error of procedure, they have paid more attention to the kind of speech used on the street and in the give-and-take of practical affairs than to the kind found in an oration or Congressional debate. It is true that when Adlai Stevenson addressed the United Nations the speech forms he used exhibited a development and elaboration of naive patterns and that this development and elaboration were the result of academic training. But also the corpus of evidence of the structuralists has been heavily weighted with the kinds of structures that relate concretions to one another, not abstractions. For this and many other reasons, the syntax of modern English has undergone a shrinkage at the hands of the structuralists. Many generalizations have been made that clearly apply to only one segment of the language we actually use, even in speech.

Any descriptive grammar suffers, however, from certain built-in limitations. When the intention is to describe what exists, and the existence of any utterance implies its grammaticality, the number of such existences becomes almost infinite. Descriptive grammars tend to be very long grammars, lost in the multiplication of particulars, or very sketchy ones that indicate that only a small part of the total grammar is being described. We all know from personal experience that when people speak they often create sentence structures that they would not themselves choose to defend. The grammarian who disavows all right to decide what a locution "ought" to be and who must formulate his generalizations only from what he finds in the evidence has no good way of distinguishing between disease and health, between momentary mistake and speech habits that adhere closely to the standard behavior of the speech community. He may have to turn to statistical counts to determine what is standard. And then in a few years he has to repeat the process since language is always undergoing change.

But surely grammarians should never lose sight of the world around them. What is said in the grammars is fanciful if it does not respond to what can be found in the books or newspapers we read, what we hear on the radio or on television, or what occurs in the normal speech of educated men and women. The structuralists of recent years have launched a violent attack on what they call the traditional school grammar, because the textbooks used in the schools have customarily defined parts of speech by "idea" (a noun is the name of a person, place, or thing; a verb expresses action) rather than by structure or behavior, or base many statements upon an irrelevant Latin grammar. The more serious charges against the school grammars are, however, that they are not grammars at all but random collections of warnings or shibboleths (Don't say, "It's me" or "Does everybody have their boots on?") or that they are concocted, over-simplified grammars that cannot account for the grammatical facts of life that any newspaper page can exhibit. A grammarian is faced with the practical necessity of explaining the grammatical systems of his language in such a way that there can be elementary instruction concerning it while at the same time a proper base is being created for dealing with the more complicated aspects when the time comes for them. When the time comes for the more complicated notions, the teacher should not have to start over and undo everything that has been done to date. In their attacks upon the traditional elementary grammars of the schools, the structuralists have implied that the backtracking has been necessary.

By basing their systems upon a set of definitions that are partly notional and partly functional without discriminating between the two, the writers of traditional school grammars have, according to the structuralists, confused the whole picture of the relationship between form and meaning. The structuralists in turn have been accused of not being interested in meaning at all, of putting all their energies into the description of structures without reference to meaning, and not bothering with why some structures operate in a limited range because of their meanings. Does an indirect object, for instance, occur only after certain verbs, the joint lexical meaning of which gives some kind of hint of the nature of the indirect object relationship? Can an indirect object be identified and described by reference only to its morphology, word order, and stress pattern, and be kept distinct from other kinds of objects that have the same structural features? This simple illustration can give no real hint of the complexity of the problem. One kind of compromise is to give a list of verbs after which an indirect object can be found without attempting to describe what meanings these verbs have in common. When too much stress is put upon these common meanings, grammar is turned into a subdivision of logic or study of the nature of thought, or is not treated enough as one of the conditioners of thought.

Over a decade ago C. C. Fries attempted to refute the charge that the structuralists were not at all interested in meaning. Meaning, he claimed, should not be used as the basis of linguistic analysis. Meaning must come from a putting together of structural meanings and lexical meanings. Any lexical item and any structural signal may have more than one meaning.

Although a certain control of specific kinds of meaning seems to me essential for the various parts of linguistic analysis I should like to insist that as a general principle any use of meaning is unscientific whenever the fact of our knowing the meaning leads us to stop short of finding the precise formal signals that operate to convey that difference.[1]

While these arguments are telling, it is still necessary to say that the prolonged search for formal signals, which are in themselves ambiguous, leads to vague, roundabout, and inconclusive descriptions of structures when the descriptions can be greatly simplified by taking into consideration the meanings within the range of which the structures obviously operate. This is especially true of languages that we know well. The structuralist's

[1] C. C. Fries, "Meaning and Linguistic Analysis," *Language*, XXX (1954), 57–68; reprinted in H. B. Allen, *Readings in Applied English Linguistics* (New York, 1964), p. 110.

approach has always been particularly useful for the description of exotic languages, where the avoidance of certain preconceptions about meaning is important. The carry-over of the same machinery to the description of well-known languages is unduly cumbersome, except as a laboratory check on the rightness of basic assumptions. It should not be incorporated into the primary system to be described.

Ralph B. Long has argued persuasively that "language is primarily an activity of the human brain, not of the human mouth and throat or of the human hand." [2] This is to say that language is not primarily speech (as the structuralists have been claiming) or writing, but a system that is organized by the brain. But it is not solely the servant of the rational part of the brain. If it embodies logic, the logic is its own, derived from the speech habits of a whole society-full of creators, and incorporating within itself large quantities of what we can only call unreason.

If the field of grammar has been dominated by the descriptive grammarians for the past century, the preceding three centuries were by and large controlled by prescriptivists. The Renaissance was marked by a rebirth of interest in languages—in questions of style and quality in the use of language, and was a turning away from an emphasis upon logic that had characterized the Schoolmen. Accompanying a revived interest in the study of Greek was a deepening concern for the literary aspects of Latin. The new grammarians were dominated by rhetoricians whose ideas in turn were held fixed to the idea that modern society should strive to return to the splendors of Classical Greece and Rome. Hand in hand with their attempts to purify their own style in writing Latin went a desire on the part of poets and prose writers to chasten and subdue their own vernaculars, to rationalize them, to stabilize them, to create standards for diction from what seemed to them to be the chaos of an inferior society in the preceding centuries. This was in part a war against dialects in favor of an elegant court language for centralized states. The grammarians of Europe from the sixteenth through the eighteenth centuries were well aware that their native languages were not Latin, but they were often influenced by parallels with Latin when they felt it to be their obligation to adjudicate between competing constructions in the interest of good taste and purity. They knew that languages, like political

[2] Ralph B. Long, *The Sentence and Its Parts* (Chicago, 1961), p. 3.

states, rose and fell, suffered constant change, but they hoped
that they themselves were living in golden ages of their own
culture and hoped against hope that their own state would be im-
mortal. Actually, these incentives to prescriptivism came late to
England and the English language. The study of propriety in
modern languages flourished first in Italy and then in France,
accompanied by the founding of academies for the perfecting of
languages. One typical and influential expounder of these doc-
trines in France was Père Dominique Bouhours, whose dialogue
on the French language was printed in 1671. His treatise was
ultimately a defense of French culture, or an attempt finally to
free French culture from the overlordship of Italian culture. He
has the court of Louis XIV in mind when he reasons:

[Change] is the ordinary course of human affairs, and particularly of living
languages. Italian and Spanish have changed in their turn, in spite of all
the stability on which the Italians and the Spaniards pride themselves. Each
of them was at the time of birth only a pitiful jargon, and only by changing
did they become what they are today. It is true that these two languages
developed sooner than the French language, but that does not make them
any better than it. Things that are finished soonest are not the most perfect: nature takes whole centuries to create gold and precious stones. However it is, the Spanish language and the Italian language, which were born
out of the confusion of peoples who made themselves masters of Spain and
Italy, did not languish for long in the feebleness of infancy; they became
somewhat capable almost as soon as they were born, similar in that respect
to rivers that are navigable to their source; in a word, they arrived in a
rather short time at the peak of their perfection; but also they are far from
purifying themselves always more and more like ours and go downhill little
by little; or at least they have fallen off from their first purity, with the result
that they are not so pure at the present as they were in past centuries.[3]

Any grammar deriving from subjective pronouncements such as
these will be by necessity rhetorically oriented, more concerned
with what a language "ought to be" rather than with what it "is,"
distrustful of new forms even while assuming that those of yester-
year are primitive and crude. The attempt is to create a standard language based as much as possible on internal consistency
—and hence rationalized—even if discriminations depend only
on the taste and arbitrary judgment of some self-constituted
authority. At bottom, the authority was the dialect spoken by
the king, just as in earlier ages a king could decide what the

---

[3] Dominique Bouhours, *Les entretiens d'Ariste et d'Eugène* (Paris, 1671), pp.
123–24.

religion of his subjects should be. It is curious that Bouhours could reject as unbearable neologisms in the French of his day such words as *irreligieux, inconvertible, intolérance, clairvoyance, inattention, élèvement, abregèment,* and *inexplicablement.* A grammar based upon rulings such as these is weighted toward usage and morphology, not toward syntax. The modern prescriptivist bothers himself about the uses of *shall* and *will,* about double negatives, about the assignment of parts of speech to words such as *like* and *as.* He questions the propriety of forms like *reliable* or *dependable,* since the meanings are "able to be relied upon" or "depended on" rather than "able to rely on" or "depend on." When he assents to the general proposition that languages change and are not amenable to fixed rationalizations, it follows that he agrees that his discriminations are arbitrary, just as an editor's style sheet is self-consciously arbitrary. Attempting a rationalization of language based upon constant discriminations between "better" or "worse" among competing forms, the prescriptivist usually ends up with an etiquette rather than a science. Few descriptivists, on the other hand, manage to free themselves from the charge that they are actually prescribing the laissez-faire anarchy that prevails when each speaker or writer makes his own idiolect the final authority. The seventeenth-century grammarian made language the product of man's will, not of his habits.

TRANSFORMATIONAL GRAMMARS

There is room here only for a brief explanation of the differences between descriptive and prescriptive grammars, not for an argument on behalf of one against the other. In the last decade a third kind of grammar has been attracting much attention. This kind may be called "theoretical." The terms that most commonly are used for this third kind are "generative" or "transformational." Since this present grammar is fundamentally of this kind, the general explanation of it will be kept skimpy, since the text will illustrate it at length. A generative grammar begins with the assumption that certain universal components are present in the formation of basic patterns of predication—i.e., assertion or communication. Any specific language may have its own particular devices for disposing of these components; the grammar of the language should, however, be thought of as the body of rules for "generating" complex and not-primary structures from the assumed basic structures. If these generative rules are complete for the English language, they will be able to produce any sentence that is grammatical in English and will reject any sentence that is not grammatical in English. It is perhaps unimportant that making the generative rules complete may be an impossibility—unimportant because the important thing is to approach grammatical facts in terms of this process of generation and so to have an intelligible grammar insofar as the rules are complete. It is unfortunate that in their current operational forms generative and transformational grammars seem to be inextricably associated with computer theory and mathematics. The larger implication of this association is that the logic of language is confined to that part of language that a mechanical robot can be programmed to "understand." Some people resent the implication that a thought is a thought only to the extent that it is a machine; what they should resent is the simplification of thought to a *method* of mechanization. The first, early crop of generative grammars already hint at a new prescriptivism founded on the predefined clarities of basic structures and bearing some resemblance to the Basic English advocated by C. K. Ogden and I. A. Richards. The spreading successes of computer theory may be responsible not only for a general antagonism to a kind of theoretical grammar that in itself can be both teachable and finite but also, as a kind of backlash, for an insistence on all the programming paraphernalia which is in no sense an essential part of the grammar.

The "transformational" part of a generative grammar begins with the basic sentence patterns already described. It then shows how non-basic or complex structures can be created by rearrangements or combinations of these basic structures. These altered or built-up structures are explained in terms of processes of transformation. Traditional school grammars and the kind of structural grammar that is based upon immediate constituent analysis are almost always "static" or two-dimensional grammars since in them each structure is to be accounted for in terms of the relationships that exist among the constituent parts in any phrase structure's present form. Thus, if we take as illustration the two units *he pretended to the throne* and *his pretension to the throne,* both traditionalist and structuralist would describe the structures as if they had nothing in common. According to the writer of the traditional school grammar *he pretended to the throne* would give us in parsing, *he,* a personal pronoun, as subject; *pretended* as verb; and *to the throne* as a prepositional phrase modifying *pretended* adverbially. In *his pretension to the throne, his* and *to the throne* are adjectival modifiers of the noun *pretension.* In dealing with these units, the structuralist would emphasize that *his* is a determiner, to be separated on the first cut from *pretension to the throne* in the process of analyzing immediate constituents. The prepositional phrase *to the throne* (a structure of modification, whether adjectival or adverbial) would next be cut, in accordance with the principle of binary division, from *pretension.* According to the principle of binary division, any construction is divided into two constituents at any given step of its analysis. Immediate syntactical arrangements are what are important to both traditionalist and structuralist. This is why both their systems can be called two-dimensional. The transformationalist grammarian, to the contrary, is less interested in an explanation of nomenclature that accounts for the immediate disposition of relationships than in how the present structure has evolved from more basic, simple structures. That *his* in *his pretension to the throne* can be called a determiner or a possessive adjective is less important than that it represents the subject in relation to the verb quality still present in *pretension* and that the whole phrase *his pretension to the throne,* with the noun *pretension* as headword, represents a transposing of the whole set of relationships found in the overt predication *he pretended to the throne* so that this predication can be combined with one or more other predications in forming a complex utterance. By going beyond a description of immediate constituency, the transformationalist grammarian adds the third dimension of process or generation. The result is not a complication of the grammar eventually to be produced but a simplification, since the addition of the third dimension makes possible the application of a new set of general rules or laws, allowing intelligible explanation for what has to remain anarchic when syntax is conceived only two-dimensionally.

At this point, it is necessary to return to the argument that generative and transformational grammars, even though they have been developed over the past decade by men with strong interests in computers and communication theory, are not necessarily dependent upon the kind of thinking or the rituals associated with computers or communication theory. It is, indeed, possible that the development of adequate grammars of this kind has been retarded and thwarted by their contingent association with these disciplines and procedures. The problem is like Charles Lamb's classic case of burning down a house in order to roast a pig. Linguists have an interest in computers in connection with machine translation, and by following this interest they have been able to anticipate many kinds of researches into the structures of language that are desirable and as yet undone. Work on generative and transformational grammars has often been motivated, so far, by the need for a pure theory to accompany the practical inquiries. Use of elaborate formulas, replete with detailed glossaries of abbreviations and distinctive symbols, has made the usual transformational grammar look like a mathematical treatise or a procedural manual in industry. In Paul Roberts' *English Syntax*,[4] for instance, the transformation rule that would generate a sentence such as *We found John studying* appears as:

$$\text{T-Vt}_{ing}: \quad \text{insert:} \quad \text{NP}_1 \ (1) - \text{Aux} \ (2) - \text{X} \ (3)$$
$$\text{matrix:} \quad \text{NP} + \text{Aux} + \text{Vt}_{ing} \ (4) - \text{Comp} \ (5) - \text{NP}_1 \ (6)$$
$$\text{result:} \quad 4 + \text{ing} + 3 + 6$$

Whether or not this apparatus is fruitful in computer study and will ultimately lead to the desired end is somewhat beside the point. It does put a surtax on the student of grammar as grammar, since it asks him to learn an extensive code in which to record his understandings *after* he has arrived at them. The alternative would be to say—Here is the pattern for one kind of sentence illustrating a double-base transformation:

insert: John was studying.
matrix: We found John.
result: We found John studying.

Actually, since a certain ambivalence is to be found in the functioning of *John* in the result sentence, neither the code formula nor the verbal statement is entirely satisfactory. For accurate description only a fluid commentary will be satisfactory. When we say *We found John studying* we do really mean, or can mean, that we "found John" and when we found him "he was studying." When we say *We found his conclusions reliable* we have

4 Paul Roberts, *English Syntax* (New York, 1964), p. 400.

a structure that is almost identical, but not quite, to *We found John studying,* for *conclusions* is not in itself a direct object in the partial way that *John* is. The word *John* has double valence in its sentence—both as object of *found* and as subject of the predication reduced from *John was studying.* In *We found his conclusions reliable,* the object *his conclusions reliable* is a reduction of the predication *His conclusions were reliable* and only that. The word *conclusions* therefore functions only as the subject part of that reduced predication. Noam Chomsky and his followers in the development of transformational grammar have created rules for disposing of this kind of problem by treating *reliable* as if it were part of the verb *found* and calling it a "complement," at the expense of destroying the possible emphasis upon the transformation that can best explain the formation of a sentence such as *We found his conclusions reliable* since the disposing principle plays down the subject-predicate relationship between *conclusions* and *reliable.* The computerized mentality, which can produce satisfactory pragmatic formulas for the disposal of problems in mechanical operations, works at the expense of even more simple theoretical understandings than are useful pedagogically. One of the boasts sometimes encountered in the computer-type of transformational grammar is that the intelligence of the user of the rules is not called upon in the manipulation of rules, and it is this feature of this kind of grammar that renders it ultimately doubtful as a philosophical or educational discipline, since only by allowing fluid understanding to the user of the grammar can complete re-tooling be avoided every time the language changes or varies.

There is no need here to belabor the inadequacies, or possible inadequacies, of the currently popular kind of transformational grammar. It is enough to say that the attempt in this present grammar is to present a transformational theory of grammar that is verbal rather than formulistic, that is based as consistently as possible upon the manipulation of basic predicational structures without much concern for the transformations that are not double-based and with little or no concern for morphophonemic rules. It is also my belief that Chomsky, Bach, Roberts, and others have taken a wrong turn, at least insofar as the application of grammatical theory or rhetorical analysis is concerned (and this is ultimately the business of the schools), by ignoring the polysystemic nature of the English language as we know it. In consequence of this belief, I choose to pay more attention to the ways in which, for instance, analytic structures compete with synthetic structures, or the structures of compounding, in the manipulation of predications, than is customary in the kind of transformational grammar to which we have become accustomed. It is my hope that this kind of approach can be seen ultimately more simple and at the same time more comprehensive than one based on mechanical rules for the generation of sentences.

2

CONTRASTING SYNTACTIC SYSTEMS

WORD ORDER

Languages consist of (1) a bank of words, or word-like segments made up of sounds or letters, that communicate more or less the same meaning whenever they are used in their speech community, and (2) ways or orders of putting them together that carry as much of the burden of communicating as the words themselves do. In fact, the forms of utterances are what determine communication, not the contents of utterances which are what words are. An unsystematic jumble of words can supply the material for many different meaningful utterances, some of which may be compatible with our opinions about the nature of things and some not. Consider, for instance, the possibilities inherent in different arrangements of three particles—*ate, cat, mouse*. If we come to this mass of three words with beliefs already formed about the common meaning of the particles, about the range within which these particles can function (either of denotation or part-of-speech), and about what is within the realm of probability in the world we live in, we can adduce the same meaning for the mass (let's agree that we are speaking of declarative utterances only) no matter how the particles are ordered. Of the six obvious possibilities

Mouse cat ate	Ate mouse cat	Cat mouse ate
Mouse ate cat	Ate cat mouse	Cat ate mouse

only *Cat ate mouse* seems to make sense in the acceptable structures of Modern English. *Mouse ate cat* we discard because in the world we live in mice do not eat cats although they may do so in other worlds than ours, such as Disneyland fantasy worlds. In order to believe that such a statement makes sense, we have to be able to imagine a world in which the meaning is possible. If the mouse has just eaten X-Brand Power Pills, we may suspend our disbelief and consequently acquiesce in the notion that the statement is meaningful. However, even without belief we are aware that *Mouse ate cat* combines the elements grammatically, i.e., in a way that is meaningful to us, even if the meaning is in the area of improbability. This is a word order for subject, verb, and object that we learn to find natural in early childhood, long before we learn consciously what subjects, verbs, and objects are.[1] The recognition of *ate* as a verb presupposes then the recognition of *mouse* and *cat* as nouns, functioning as subject and object. If we were users of certain languages other than English, we might find the word order *Ate mouse cat* or *Cat mouse ate* more in accord with our commonly accepted structures for meaningful communication than *Cat ate mouse*. At least the Frenchman will say *Je l'aime* (which is somewhat like *Cat mouse ate*) where we would not say *I him like*. Unsystematic jumbles of words become meaningful when they cease to be unsystematic and can be seen to conform to a system that we recognize. Structural systems are charged with conveying much of the meaning we get out of language.

Word order is one kind of order, one kind of system by means of which meanings are communicated; but it is only one kind. There is no absolute, natural logic behind whatever happens to be our way of doing things. Any one of the six immediate arrangements of *ate, mouse,* and *cat* could convey the meaning *The cat ate the mouse* in a possible language. Usually within a given language word order is only one signal of relationships out of many kinds of signals. English is a language that once had

---

[1] Since this is not an elementary grammar, many grammatical terms such as these will not be carefully defined in it, or will be defined only when there is need to bring into question commonly accepted definitions of them. Since a verb is a part of speech, an attempt at a definition of it will be found in Chapter 3. Since this grammar is a description of the manipulation of predicational structures, and since we assume that predications (that is, those that do not need a context in order to be grammatically significant) necessarily contain a subject-part and a predicate-part, we cannot go behind the assumption and determine in *a priori* fashion what can and what cannot be a subject-part. Comments on this primary assumption will be made throughout the grammar.

more inflections than it now has—of nouns, adjectives, determiners, and verbs—and it is evident that, as English has sloughed
off inflection, word order has become more rigid and has come to
play a larger role in the communication of the intended relationships among words. But no simple formulas for word order can
be inflexibly applied to Modern English without risk of unreal
prescriptivism. In a sentence such as *The mouse-eating cat
returned home* the predication *Cat ate mouse* has been (or could
have been) transformed into a subject phrase that is a constituent
in a larger utterance. The word order of *cat, ate, mouse* has
been reversed. Word orders that apply to basic sentence patterns do not necessarily apply to complex transformations of the
basic patterns. Can we be sure that a locution such as *This cat
mouse-eats* (by analogy to *baby sits* or *bird watches*) will be
forever alien to the grammar of English? We could, without
much difficulty, construct an imaginary language in which this
ordering of direct objects would be the rule rather than the exception.

SYNTHETIC AND ANALYTIC SYSTEMS

Structures interplay with meanings. It is almost impossible to
discuss one without getting involved in the other. Grammars
describe structures rather than meanings, but structures are relational and relations involve us in meaning. To make *Cat ate
mouse* immediately meaningful, we must as if deny the immediacy and "know" beforehand that *cat* and *mouse* are nouns
and *ate* is a verb. If we had a statement such as *Ate moused cat*,
we could affirm that an "ate" is a kind of elephant that dwarfed
a cat so that it seemed to become mouse-sized. Words normally
thought of as belonging to one part of speech can undergo functional change so that they operate as another part of speech. In
order to know when a functional change has taken place we have
to have common basic understandings, consciously or unconsciously, of the structural systems we use.

One of the axioms of the modern grammarian is that language
is by necessity systematic. It is sometimes falsely concluded
from this axiom that a language like Modern English exhibits
only one system. This is far from true. Most of the Indo-European languages from which English has evolved, or to which it is
related, showed a more marked synthetic syntactic system than

does Modern English. This means, in simplest terms, that languages like Latin, Greek, and Sanskrit, as well as Old English, made much more extensive use of inflection than we do in order to differentiate between aspects of meaning, to make explicit the relationship between one word and another, or to indicate the functioning of a word-unit in an utterance. Inflections, as we usually think of them, are suffixes added to word stems to indicate the precise distinction intended. Sometimes, especially with verbs, several suffixes are strung together in order to complete the act of precise distinction. Consider, for instance, the Latin word *portabantur*—they were being carried. Let us simplify the situation a little and say that this word is composed of the stem *porta* + the suffix *ba* signaling the imperfect tense + the suffix *nt* signaling *they* (i.e., third person plural) + *ur* signaling what is called the passive voice (that is, the verb does not have *they* as its agent but as its ideal object; an "ideal object" must in turn be defined as a subject of a passive utterance that would be the object of the verb in a cognate utterance containing an active verb). The Modern English equivalent, *they were being carried*, is put together in a different way. It is in comparison a more "analytic" phrase, and a language that shows its relationships or makes its distinctions by means of separate function words—auxiliaries, prepositions, or other particles—is called an "analytic language."

Few languages, if any, are completely and consistently analytic or synthetic in their principal devices. This pair of terms is only one way, and an inconclusive one at that, for describing the syntactic systems embodied in a given language. It is hard to draw the line between inflection, that can be accurately described in grammars of languages with which we are quite familiar, and a kind of agglutination of more or less separable parts exhibited in grammars of languages that are more exotic to us. In an imaginary sentence such as *The men go-did-they*, meaning "The men went," can we consider *did* and *they* inflectional suffixes; or to make the necessary distinction must we call inflectional suffixes only those forms that are arbitrarily symbolic, bound forms, never free forms? Many languages make some use of a principle of distinction that involves internal change with or without terminal inflection. Ready examples are *man, men; goose, geese; sing, sang, sung.* Can we draw a line between the principle of inflection and the principle of derivation when we consider these internal changes alongside internal changes effecting functional or semantic shifts, as in *ride, rode, raid, road?* These questions are not meant to be confusing. In order to find an adequate base for a generative or transformational syntax for Modern English we must assume that our language is systematic. We would, however, be starting off on the wrong foot if we ignored certain broad generalizations about the structure systems of languages that can be obtained from comparative linguistics. What is clear is that Modern English, like most languages, is polysystemic. What is not so clear is the boundary area between any two systems. Also, it is difficult, perhaps unprofitable, to attempt an exact definition and classification of the systems—how many of them are there and to what extent do they overlap? Signals of word order do not, properly speaking, comprise a syntactic system; they do, however, vary with the morphological orders with which they interact. In a highly inflected language, signals from word order are less important than they are in a language that has lost its chief inflections, since the inflections indicate the relations among the words and either they or the word order signals become redundant. In Latin the objective, or accusative, ending of *canem* and the nominative ending of *homo* tells us who is doing what in *Canem homo mordet*, whereas in English we have to put our faith in word order alone (provided we get no signals from determiners or agreement of subject and verb) to derive the meaning *the man bites the dog—* which the journalists tell us is an improbability.

The general drift of modern European languages has been away from synthesis and toward analysis. The attack of modern grammarians upon the traditional school grammars has centered on the observation that such grammars have been too much based upon analogues with Latin grammar, so that English has not been described on its own terms or in terms of the systems that have evolved in it. The problems here actually are of two kinds. Nouns, adjectives, and determiners were more highly inflected in both Old English and Latin than in Modern English but the inflectional systems of the two old languages were far from identical. The Old English verb system was, on the other hand, already far more analytical than the corresponding Latin verb system. Much of the confusion of applying Latin grammatical principles to Modern English comes in relation to the description of verb phrases. During the centuries when Latin was the language of learning and scholarship, in England as well as on the continent of Europe, the actual structures of the Latin grammatical system had a palpable impact upon English structures—certainly rhetorically, and the rhetorical features became linguistic realities when they became culturally assimilated. Modern English grammar is not Latin grammar, but it is a falsification of history to ignore the fact that the recasting of English structures on the lines of analogues with Latin was a reality over a period of centuries, especially in the literary language, but with strong effects also even in folk speech. To insist upon the alienness of the Latin analogues is to adopt a partisan position encouraging a return willy-nilly to one segment of the past.

The other problem is that the drift toward analysis was already well underway in Classical Latin and has been continuing in the Romance languages as well as in English. Consequently, it is a mistake to interpret Romance grammars on terms only of the paradigms of Latin grammar and to use grammars made in this way as evidence of a universal grammar. In Modern English our phrase patterns are often relics of an older synthetic system with the inflections that once gave clear evidence of it no longer apparent. The structuralist grammarians of the past three or four decades, calling attention to the fact that inflection has largely disappeared, sought ways of identifying structures without recourse to the synthetic system that once informed them. It is quite evident that except for a somewhat curtailed existence of a possessive, or genitive, in Modern English, the existence of objective, or accusative, forms in some of the pronouns, and the continuation of a few random freaks or sports showing signs of original case endings, as in *why, backwards,* or *days* (as in *I work days*), case endings have no real, evident presence. But it may be to our advantage to assume that they still have a ghostly presence, that inflections still exist with us even though they have become "zero" forms. For what we need is the ability to make distinctions between the synthetic structures that still exist in our phrasal patterns and the analytic structures that contrast or compete with them. As long as the contrasts exist in the patterns, we still have need of a polysystemic approach to English grammar. Consider the following contrasting forms:

I gave *Jim* a book.   I gave a book *to Jim.*
I gave *him* a book.   I gave a book *to him.*

I brought *Jim* a book.	I brought a book *for Jim*.
He passed *them* a miracle.	He passed a miracle *on behalf of them*.
Let's have *us* a smoke.	Let's have a smoke (*for ourselves?*).

The first column gives us forms that would once have been inflected datives. Since we now have no distinct endings on any words to which the name "dative" can be given, we can use the term only to name an assorted group of relations (*not* endings) between a substantive and some other sentence part. Even this usage is not exact, since not all members of this group of "relations" find expression by means of the "dative" case in all languages, and in some languages this particular case can be the repository for other relations. How can we then other than by a polite fiction name a case which in Modern English is marked by no distinct inflectional ending at all? It helps little to know that the particular form *him* comes to us by way of what is called the Old English "dative" in analogy with Latin terminology for substantive cases, rather than from the accusative *hine*. Only for certain pronouns in Modern English do we find a joint case for "objects" of various kinds.

In the second column above we have examples of the analytic forms semantically equivalent to but structurally contrasting with the synthetic forms of the first column. In this column the relations are made explicit by prepositions *to, for, on behalf of*. We should keep clearly in mind here that common analytic particles like *to* and *for* do not have single meanings. They can function to express any one of a group of meanings just as inflectional suffixes can in highly synthetic languages, but the distributions are not necessarily the same in the two language systems. We use the same relational signal for "I gave a book *to* Jim" and "I brought a pig *to* market," although one expresses what we might call the indirect object relation and the other an allative place relation. This kind of overlapping of signals is a simplification worked out by users of a language, either synthetic or analytic, over a course of centuries. It is the meaning of the relationships that is relatively constant from language to language, not the structures used for handling them. We must say "relatively constant" because we cannot be sure that there is a universal logic. Since human beings of all kinds are more or less alike, there may be a universal logic and an identical set of grammatical relations to the extent that human beings are all alike. But some primary logical categories, such as the distribution of time-concepts, are not identically shared by all human beings. We cannot, consequently, speak confidently of a universal set of grammatical relations. The subject-predicate relation is what is most constant in human thought, but even there the structures for handling the relation can differ vastly.

It is possible to create a private language of the synthetic type with a distinct inflectional suffix for each describable logical relationship between a substantive and something else. There would then be as many cases and differentiated case endings as relationships, and no case would do double-duty by functioning for more than one relationship. How many cases there would be in this thoroughly rationalized private language would depend on how finicky we were in separating or putting together relational categories. Without being finicky at all we could subdivide the category of space or place relationships into many types. Grammarians use case-names such as ablative, illative, allative (*from, in, to*) for inflectional cases actually employed in the paradigms of some Indo-European languages, showing a differentiation among relations that are all spatial. A hint of the number of spatial relationships we are conditioned by our society to recognize can be found in our inventory of prepositions of place or space: *from, in, to, out of, by, near, into, at, toward, up, down, behind, before, alongside of, over, under, for* (in the sense of *toward*), *toward, in front of, in back of*—this list makes no pretense at completeness. Some of these are approximate doubles. Thus, the difference between *before* and *in front of* is slight. One case ending in our private language could serve both of these, as if they expressed one and the same thing. Likewise, one case could handle both *from* and *out of* with no loss of precise meaning in only part of the range of meanings attached to these words in Modern English. The meanings of "He was shot *from the cannon*" and "He was shot *out of the cannon*" are much the same; but when we say "He drove *from* Rome to Syracuse" we do not mean precisely that "He drove *out of* Rome into Syracuse."

The very act of identifying a relationship implies a grouping together of instances that are approximately the same. All relationships are in this sense approximations. It is possible to create the private inflectional language we have been talking about and to keep the number of cases finite only because the human mind creates concepts by acts of approximation of this kind. Thomistic logicians distinguished carefully among at least four kinds of causality, but in workaday thinking our phrase *because of* can express most of them adequately. This explicit relational symbol comes close enough to the exact meaning so that we can derive from the context which exact meaning is intended.

In the large mass of primary material on which he based his findings in *The Structure of English,* C. C. Fries found that the number of items representing function words was only 154. Of these 154, the group of items comprising what traditionally we call prepositions (the meanings of which could be expressed by inflections in our private language) made up only one group out of fifteen groups of function words. If our private language had fifty cases it could probably approximate all the relationships that grammarians ever choose to distinguish. The number cannot be arrived at by counting the number of prepositions in our dictionaries both because some prepositions are used in expressing a number of different relationships and because sometimes two or more prepositions express the same meaning.

It is rare to find among actual languages an inflected language with as many as fifteen cases. Finnish, which some comparative linguists prefer to call an agglutinative language rather than one showing true inflection, is one of these. Inflected languages like Latin, Greek, and Old English made regular use of four to six cases and distributed functions differently among them. If Modern English can still be considered an inflected language with at most three distinct cases, the brief must be based on the notion that the reduction of an imaginary fifty cases to fifteen already implies a multiplying of the functions performed by the remaining cases and that the reduction from six to three is comparatively not great, even though we now approach the vanishing point. The change is a continuation of the same process of reduction and a piling up of alternative functions for the telescoped cases. In actuality, even in Latin and Greek relations were often expressed only generally by case endings and then more specifically by supporting analytic devices such as prepositions or by signals of word order. Many prepositions in Latin were followed by nouns in the ablative case, some by nouns in the accusative, and some by nouns in the dative. We need to set aside for the time being the more difficult problems connected with which

Latin verbs governed objects in the dative case, which governed those in the accusative, and which governed those in the ablative. The distinction here was sometimes seemingly notional and sometimes arbitrarily grammatical. The verbs taking dative objects in Latin were often those with prefixes corresponding notionally to those prepositions that might be followed by nouns in the dative case. Lacking the ability in Modern English to make formal distinction by means of inflectional differences between substantives in the dative and those in the accusative, we oversimplify our notional definitions of direct objects and are in no position to realize that direct objects also could be signaled by analytic particles in a language that had drifted farther toward pure analysis than Modern English has.

The items in the contrasting sentences *They provided us with an opportunity to escape* and *They provided us an opportunity to escape* function in much the same way, but we are tempted by our traditional methodology of parsing to treat the two sentences differently. In the first we may call *us* a direct object and the phrase *with an opportunity to escape* a manner phrase functioning adverbially. The second sentence we may paraphrase as "They provided an opportunity to escape for us"—a reading that suggests that *us* in the original sentence is an indirect object, marked as a dative by its position and by its zero inflection (that is, it does not use an analytic particle in signaling its relation to the sentence), while *opportunity* becomes the direct object. In this event, both indirect object and direct object are expressed synthetically (by word order and zero inflection). In the paraphrase of the second version the indirect object is expressed analytically, *for us*. It should then be obvious that, if we were accustomed to think of the possibility of expressing direct objects analytically, we would consider *with an opportunity* in *They provided us with an opportunity to escape* a direct object analytically expressed, using *with* as a signal of the relationship, while *us* would remain a synthetically expressed indirect object. The "manner" concept used in the traditional rendition now becomes merely a polite fiction, an act of desperation to account for an item in an oversimplified system.

A transformational grammar depends fundamentally upon our ability to track identities in sets of relations among changes of structure. This is not easy to do, or perhaps is impossible to do, if we pay too much attention to "meaning" equivalents. The transformational grammarian must keep his eye on structural devices that function more or less identically in the handling of "sames" of meaning and not on meaning alone. But to do this he is crippled unless he realizes that he is dealing with more than one system of structures, often overlapping and often with a vague, ill-defined no-man's-land between them. Modern English is polysystemic, not monosystemic.

How many systems does our language make use of? This is hard to tell, because historically many potentially complete systems have never in actuality achieved completeness. It is hard to find a grammar of any language that is completely isolating, completely agglutinative, completely synthetic, completely analytic, or completely derivational. These terms are useful, but they were created in order to point out drifts in language toward system, not to indicate complete systems. Consequently, they overlap to a considerable degree. We can have recourse to them only when in actual usage we have alternative structures at hand for expressing a certain set of relations. The two most complete alternatives for the user of English are the synthetic system and the analytic.

THE COMPOSITIONAL SYSTEM

If we pay particular attention to the language structures currently being used by advertisers, journalists, some social scientists, and some avant-garde poets, we can be tempted to make the generalization that the century-old shift toward analysis has passed its peak, and that a new syntactic system is rapidly coming into being in these days. This new system is the "compositional"—to use an old term for what is now exhibiting new features, so that the term as it is used here does not mean exactly what it has meant in the past. The compounding of word-items to form included predications, or part-predications, is a principle close to that of agglutination, and is present to some extent in most languages at most times. We have different ways of defining compounds, depending on the closeness or looseness in which the items are bound together. These differences are reflected in variations in editors' style sheets and in the decisions of dictionary makers concerning usages in representing compounds as one word, hyphenated items, or separate words. Here we are not interested in style-sheet etiquette or preferences of rhetoricians.

What we are interested in is the expanded use of noun adjuncts, or the compounding of different parts of speech with or without hyphens, so long as a competing syntactic system is revealed for the handling of predicational relations. For the sentence *The most efficient salt-producing mines were in Poland* we can find an equivalent structure in *Polish mines produced salt most efficiently* (this is only one way of doing it—not a necessary way). This first sentence, which attaches together the key elements of the second by using the structures of compounding, shows opposite word order: *efficiently-salt-produced-mines* instead of *mines-produced-salt-efficiently*. This reverse word order is usual in the kind of compounding that comprises an alternative syntactic system. The transformationalist grammarians have been treating the usual pre-positional adjective as a transform of a predicate adjective. If we were to follow this line, and only it, we would have to consider *efficient* in terms of a syntactic system of derivations—a competing system, not a cooperating system.

These distinctions obviously become too fine drawn to be useful. To work out a polysystemic grammar we have to play a cautious game of looking for provisional constants in the midst of eternal flux. That these several systems do interact and cooperate should, however, be clear. Scrutiny of a phrase like *the last century's frontier scarcity of women* (equatable with *Women were scarce on the frontier during the last century*) reveals *century's* as an inflected noun reflecting a synthetic system, *frontier* as a noun adjunct reflecting a compound system, *of women* as the periphrastic equivalent of a subjective genitive reflecting an analytic system, and the key word *scarcity* as a derivation from the predicate adjective *scarce*. Some study of the relational concepts actually carried by these devices is illuminating (*century's* —a genitive of time-measure; *frontier*—a place-noun, not necessarily adverbial, since the term "adverb" loses its force when the item in question is an adverb neither in its form nor in its function as a dependent on a headword-verb). It is hard to create a nomenclature that is based neither upon form nor function; we think traditionally of time-measure and place as functions that are normally adverbial. Thus Fries would say of *the man in the room* that *in the room* functions adverbially in modifying man. This is tantamount to assigning parts-of-speech names to relational concepts. The result is that terms that rationalize one syntactic system are not really apt for another. In order to have a base from which to operate, we should no doubt assign relations to parts-of-speech areas as they function in the simplest or most basic predicational patterns. But as the kernel sentences are transformed, combined, or included, it is the relationship that remains constant, not forms or parts of speech.

MATERIALS FOR EXERCISE AND FURTHER STUDY

Note on the exercise materials in this book: These are usually suggestions for research projects that a student can undertake on his own initiative, with perhaps a small amount of guidance from the instructor and anticipation of some of the difficulties that may be encountered. The student should be reminded, however, that the instructor may be in no better position than the student is in himself until the instructor has had opportunity to test these proposals. Instructor and student must consequently work out these problems together. These are inductive exercises in which each laborer in syntactical vineyards becomes his own grammarian. The task does not call for the running to some authority to find what the answers should be. It calls instead for going to examples of language in actual use and for the employment of the student's own reasoning ability in ordering what he finds and in drawing general conclusions. This does not mean that the student should not check his findings against the statements made in this text or in other treatises. It does mean that he should not be in slavery to those statements. It is his responsibility to check those statements against the evidence that he turns up. That he will frequently make mistakes is to be expected until he has mastered the theory of a complete grammar. But if the student does not turn his mistakes into rigid dogma, should he prize them simply because they are his own invention, no harm will be done during a period of floundering.

The caution is given several times in these exercises that the student should use his wits in gathering material to assure his getting material from many different kinds of prose, for structures often correspond to the functions they have to perform.

I. Seek out some examples of prose, from past and present, representing a variety of kinds of uses of language (abstract and concrete, familiar and formal, technical and reportorial). From them gather evidence for a description of the word order system of Modern English. Under what conditions does the word order of subject-verb-object not obtain? In Latin, modifiers can be properly interpreted even if they are separated from the words they modify because the inflectional suffixes give the syntactic clues. What evidence do you find in your materials of separation of modifiers and units modified where the nexus is nevertheless intelligible?

II. In order to understand the synthetic system that is still to be found in a reduced form in Modern English, one must first and foremost come to terms with what the classical grammarian calls the inflected genitive. The following list presents a small sample of modern usages, to which additions can be made readily by examining almost any piece of writing. In studying these examples, attempt to provide the analytic equivalent for each (i.e., rewrite *the Yankees' hometown* as *the hometown of the Yankees, Europe's highest living at some of Europe's lowest prices* as *the highest living [to be found] in Europe at some of the lowest prices [to be found] in Europe*). Why is it that it runs against the grain of modern usage to provide analytic equivalents for many of the genitives of personal pronouns? Why is the term "genitive" continued here and not the term more often used in our schools—"possessive"? How many of these genitives belong to the sub-class of possessives? The problems of the subjective and objective genitive are discussed in detail in Chapter 12. Examples are *the king's objections* (derived from *the king objected*) and *his murder* (*someone murdered him*). Some of the instances in the list may be subjective or objective genitives. Can you find them? There may also be examples of specification, degree, or respect. These names are not what is important. More important than them is the recognition of some of the differences of uses to be found in the list. Attempt a rough grouping of the evidence according to kinds, and attempt to add to the evidence from your own searching in outside places.

the Yankees' hometown
their vacations
Europe's cities
Europe's highest living at some
    of Europe's lowest prices
London's businessmen
the bicycle bell's jingling
KLM's 800-mile circle
KLM's new "touring fares"
last year's harvest
the world's largest producers of
    tungsten
the world's best wool
the world's size
the world's aspirations
one of their good customers
our common stock research

our research division
whose intimate knowledge
our financial strength
your fingers
a collector's edition
on the ocean's floor
the ocean's demeanor
the ocean's victims
look your best
our repositories of history
his own career
their victories
their beds
their intentions
our neighbors' intentions
the city's Hungarian community

the city's highest point
Britain's finest hour
such people's favorite drink
their wives
John Smith's wife
our shoes
stood in our stocking feet
workmen's heavy shoes
workingman's store
men's fashions
ten miles' remove
their children's shoelaces
plans for their children's
   schooling
our place
raising their hands
below their ears
an elephant's ears
the U.N.'s membership
the U.N.'s role
the U.N.'s control
the U.N.'s biggest problem
everyone clasped his hands

her resignation
Robinson's resignation
put his hands on his knees
our brethren
mankind's savior
whose faith is
got to their feet
the day's end
the hurricane's eye
the hurricane's extent
His Lordship's goodness
my day's beginning
his new job's demands upon
   him
Rome's legions
West Germany's manpower
West Germany's exports
Scandinavia's gift to the movie
   industry of Greta Garbo
his country's having been betrayed by its diplomats
her grace and beauty

III. Assuredly, *of* prepositional phrases are not all analytic equivalents of inflected genitives, but some are. Reverse the process of Exercise II by attempting to rewrite the *of* phrases to be found in the following materials as inflected genitives. Some of these will resist rewriting because the *of* phrase follows a pre-determiner or near-noun (as in *most of the people*). What other kinds resist the rewriting? Consider the curious construction of the "second genitive" (*a friend of ours*). Under what conditions is this second genitive form used? A speaker of Latin or Old English could say "a mail's stack" or "the letters' pile" but today we can use only the analytic prepositional phrase forms. If you know enough about the grammars of Latin or Old English, attempt to work out the rules for the changes in usage. As in II, find out how many of the phrases here represent variants in the analytic system of subjective or objective genitives. Once you have made a rough classification of the phrases found here, turn to some body of convenient prose and search for supplementary evidence. What kinds of *of* phrases do you find that are not represented here?

hundreds of thousands of individual contacts
dozens of such blocks

the thirty days of fasting
the first sliver of the new moon
a friend of ours

long sleeved robe of gray and white (are *gray* and *white* nouns here?)

the rows of men

the brotherhood of our faith

the dauphin of the kingdom of daylight

lands of our birth

the rows of shoes

nerves of steel

piles of coats

a man of medium height

the representatives of the Middle Eastern countries

descendents of immigrants

a number of Negro Americans

some of whom

most of the people

at the end of the prayers

in the direction of the park

a sign of his success

a quarter of an hour

in the course of the next couple of hours

the session of the assembly

at the completion of his tour

a total of five evenings

the walls of his office

a stack of mail

different problems of enforcement

use of an inner tube

two glasses of port

in the manner of comedy

a view of human existence

the import of his poetry

the Marxism of these writers

panoramas of bold landscapes

the attention of his audience

the master of time and space

the fusion of structure, style, and language

the lack of factual evidence

the behavior of a vicar

the cause of her insanity

an awareness of the wretchedness of the creatures

the freedom of our will

the natural superiority of our talents

a critic of Smart's fable

IV. Return to a study of the examples given in II and III with a view to discovering how many of the analytic or synthetic phrasings can in modern usage contrast with derivational or compositional forms. That is, *nerves of steel* contrasts with *steel nerves*, in which *steel* is a noun adjunct, and hence part of a compound in the compositional system of our language. A *study of Shakespeare* can be equated either with *a Shakespeare study* (a compositional phrasing) or *a Shakespearian study* (in which *Shakespearian* is a derived adjective). That a study of competing systems like these is also a study of competing structures of modification need not concern us much at this point; but since many problems are involved here that you may not be prepared to cope with yet, this exercise should be considered only exploratory at this time.

V. So far the suggestions for further study in this chapter have been grouped around investigations of competing systems as they apply to syntactical relationships of the "genitive-class." Similar projects can be worked out to explore the differences in the structures of the competing systems as they concern the syntactical relations of the so-called "dative-class": indirect object relation, the "for" dative relations (reference, respect), the reflexive dative (I'm gonna get *me* a piece of cake). If you were to work on such a project, you would probably have to confine your attention to the synthetic and analytic systems only, and your study might consist only of comparing indirect object forms with zero inflection and the analytic prepositional phrases that compete with them. Competing compositional and derivational forms should, however, be considered to some extent. You may find that some "dative" relational ideas are expressed by inflected genitives (*John's gift* may derive from *John was given* and from *somebody gave John something* and may relate to *a gift for John* in the analytic system; *John's* is, however, a special kind of subjective genitive).

VI. In synthetic languages, inflections may signal relations such as place, time, degree, agent, extent, duration, and attendant circumstance. These relations are allotted to cases called "accusative," "ablative," or "instrumental." In Modern English, nouns with zero inflections—often called "adverbial nouns"—express these relations without using prepositions. In effect, a phrase like *I came home* can be construed as containing a synthetic form *home* (with zero inflection) competing with the analytic form *to my home* found in *I came to my home*. Other synthetic adverbial nouns are found in *He came Saturday, He remained all summer, He jumped ten feet, He swam ten hours.* What are the analytic equivalents for these? Read through the following chapter on Approximate Relations, and then see if you can work out the rationale of the competition between analytic and synthetic phrasings in the expression of some of these relations.

3

APPROXIMATE RELATIONS

Our notions of grammatical relation come to us finely worked out as they apply to the classical languages of Greek and Latin. Carryover to Modern English is at best haphazard, since our systematic handling of phrase structures is not the same as for the more highly inflected Latin and Greek. The following listing of relational concepts is taken primarily from Latin grammar. It can serve for purposes of reference but should not be taken as definitive. It is a point of departure only. The comments that attend the listing are likewise provisional. These relational categories are at best approximations; they overlap, and there are no-man's-land areas between them. In English they are not to be assigned necessarily to any inflectional case.

Subject-predicate—the basic relationship in any formal assertion

Predicate complement to subject—this is the copula relation; a predicate complement is whatever can complete a copula predication after the verb *to be:* He was a *man,* He was *brave,* He was *at home,* This is *for you.*

Appositive to noun or pronoun—in a transformational grammar this relation is distinguishable from that of predicate complement to subject only in that the copulative verb has been deleted and a transformation has taken place by which the predicate-part of the copula predication is on a lower level of subordination than the subject-part; a closely attached pre-positional adjective (restrictive) would by this definition be an appositive; to obviate this result the pre-positional adjective should be construed as representing a prior transformation; to make the necessary distinctions clear at this time is, however, impossible. (See Chapter 9.)

These first three relations are different in kind from those that follow in that these three are predicational relations. The rest are relations that take place in inflected languages between a noun or pronoun and some other part of the sentence. They may in English be conveyed by units of various kinds.

Possession—associated in our minds with the Latin genitive and with the 's inflection in English; as a relation it does not represent the whole functioning of the English genitive, nor is the genitive inflection the only way of signaling the idea of possession in Modern English: the verb *have* can convey the idea of possession; consider: the man *with* the hat, *John's* hat, the hat *of John,* red-breasted.

Partitive—usually expressed by a genitive in Latin, analytically by an *of* phrase in English; the *of* phrase indicates the larger group of which the referent of the preceding substantive is a member, as in "few *of my friends*"; description of a phrase of this kind as a partitive cuts across and confuses the structuralist's categories of predeterminers.[1] The confusion is the result of different approaches to the same phenomena and need not be broadly disconcerting. (A more complex problem is hinted at by Ralph B. Long when he suggests that most determiners are in effect pronouns functioning as modifiers of nounal heads when the *of* particle is not present.[2] Long's interpretation fits far better into polysystemic grammar than that of Roberts.)

Specification—again associated in Latin with the genitive and with *of* phrases in English, although the inflected form is also found in English, as in *last month's* bills; top *of the mountain* (cf. *mountain top,* in the system of compounding).

Purpose—can be seen most clearly in English in infinitive phrases with the sense of *in order to,* or *in order that;* when preposition and noun express purpose the noun is usually abstract and derived from a verb: I sent it *as a gift,* it was intended *for protection against the cold;* these nouns are datives in Latin.

Indirect object—this relation in English comprises a group of relations for nouns or pronouns appearing between a verb and a direct object that in Latin would take dative endings; in English they have zero inflections or are in the objective case; we speak of true indirect objects (with verbs of giving, assigning, telling—periphrased with *to*) and indirect objects of reference (I located *him* a seat, I lo-

---

1 Cf. Paul Roberts, *English Syntax* (New York, 1964), pp. 19–28.
2 Ralph B. Long, *The Sentence and Its Parts* (Chicago, 1961), pp. 290–315.

cated a seat *for him*) and reflexive indirect objects (we are going to find *us* a new home), both periphrased with *for;* in British English pronominal indirect objects often follow direct objects: *give it me;* in passive transforms true indirect objects can be shifted to the subject function: *he* was given a warning; other kinds of inflected indirect objects sometimes cannot undergo this transformation.

Reference, concern, or respect—in the analytic (i.e., periphrastic) forms, these closely allied relations are expressed by *for, for the sake of,* or *in respect to;* in recent usage this loose relation is sometimes handled by means of the derivational suffix *-wise,* as in *money-wise;* the presence of a "respect" component in a sentence is often a symptom of an oblique sentence structure that is a form of redistribution (see pp. 127–28): *I do not like France in respect to its modern architecture—I do not like the modern architecture of France.*

Agent—in basic sentences the agent-idea is usually conveyed by the subject, but not all subjects are agents; in passive transforms agents are usually signaled by the preposition *by* when they are specified.

Direct object—one of the commonest and yet most difficult relations to describe; it is that noun, pronoun, phrase, or clause that receives the action of a transitive verb; however, some transitive verbs express action only by the grace of analogy, or formally imply action but semantically do not; any verb that in form and meaning can undergo a passive transformation can be classed potentially as an active transitive verb and so can take a direct object. (In keeping with this description, *have,* in most of its many meanings, is not a transitive verb and cannot take a direct object, since passive transforms are unlikely with it, and notionally the sense of "having" seems to apply more to the subject than it does to the object. Nevertheless, in *He has a gun* the word *gun* is so patently a direct object that we should make room for this kind of relationship within the area of the direct object, even if it belongs there only figuratively and in terms of superficial form. Other problems arise in distinguishing between verbs with separable particles that take direct objects and verbs followed by prepositional phrases in which the so-called "object" of the preposition is not a direct object—the difference between "He put on *the clothes*" and "He put the clothes *on the chair.*" If the reading *He put the clothes on* is possible, we realize that we are dealing with a separable particle.)

Extent—this is one of a group of relations that traditionally we have associated with adverbial forms, so that when it is expressed by a noun with zero inflection, we sometimes call the noun an "adverbial noun": *They hiked ten miles;* if we transform this structure to the compound structure *ten-mile-hike* the extent relationship is still present.

Duration—this is like "extent" except that it deals with time, not space: *They hiked ten hours, They hiked for ten hours, the ten-hour hike.*

Degree—in base forms (if we can truly speak of such things) words, phrases, or clauses expressing this relation are usually attached to a headword adjective or adverb as qualifiers and so are much the same as intensifiers (*acutely conscious* as distinct from *very conscious*); since a comparison can be a comparison of the degree of something, this relationship overlaps that of "comparison," especially when expressed by clauses (He knew the answer *as* well *as she did*) or compound structures (*angel-soft*).

Separation—this is the central ablative relation in Latin, expressed in analytic phrasing by *from* and similar prepositions; it is one kind of place relation.

Association or accompaniment—the idea of *with* as a preposition expressing the idea of accompaniment overlaps somewhat the idea of coordinates without formal equality of the coordinates; thus, *he came with me* can be related in idea but not in form to *he and I came;* similarly, *he came home with a cold* can be thought of, in transform grammar, as a putting together of *he had a cold* and *he came home,* or as a redistribution of *When he came home he had a cold;* in such a sentence *with* thus expresses not only an idea of possession but also of association or accompaniment; in an analytic grammar *with* is, consequently, a significant function word, especially as it can also express means, instrument, and manner.

Place in which—one kind of place relation: *at, in, under, over, before, behind, around, within,* etc.

Time—this is a whole class of logically allied relations so central to our apprehension of the world around us that we can readily extend the time concept figuratively to express other relational concepts, especially cause, result, condition, accompaniment, and attendant circumstance: *at, in, during, before, after, when, whenever;* time ideas can be expressed by adverbs, prepositional phrases, clauses, or by other means.

Material—this expresses the notion of the substance or components from which something is made or of which it is constituted: a *stone* wall, a wall *of stone;* the rapidly extending system of showing relations by compounding found one of its first manifestations in Modern English in the use of nouns of material as noun adjuncts. (The term "noun adjunct" is used here and in various other grammars since Jespersen only in relation to the syntax of compounding.)

Accordance—one thing is in line with another, literally or figuratively: *according to*.

Attendant circumstance—this is a loose term for a relation between a reduced and therefore dependent predication and a predication upon which it is dependent; in some contexts the two would be coordinate, but in the structure at hand the one is a detail or attendant circumstance of the other; this is a kind of hybrid relationship in which other relationships can play a part. *The cougar stood at bay, its tail switching.*

Means—expressed analytically by *by, with, by means of.* (Means, instrument, way, and manner are allied relationships; they are the principal "how" relationships.) *He lifted the stone with Jim's help.*

Cause or reason—causal relationships are obvious logically but highly complex; syntactically they are simpler than they are logically since the logical distinctions are not always made explicit grammatically; on the other hand, a wide range of syntactic units can express causal relationships.

Result—this is allied with cause or reason and sometimes uses the same signaling devices as purpose: *so, so that,* infinitives. *He exercised regularly, so that he kept healthy.* He tricked us, *only to discover that he was tricking himself.*

Way or manner—this is an explicit substitute for "thus"; common prepositions expressing manner are *as, with, in;* subordinate clauses expressing manner are introduced by *as, as though,* or *as if;* the three commonest types of adverbs are those of place, manner, and time, often appearing in that order when they are all present in a predication: "We went *there* (place) *quickly* (manner) *yesterday* (time)."

Comparison—this is the comparison of substantive with substantive or predication with predication; conjunctions are *as . . . as, as,* or *like* (increased use recently).

Condition—this relationship is most evident between clauses: *if, unless, provided that.*

Concession—a dependent adversative, either clausal or phrasal: *although, though, in spite of, despite.*

This is merely a working list of relationships among components in a sentence, incomplete, only approximately defined, and only partially adapted from the conditions of Latin syntax to those of Modern English. During a span of 2,000 years grammarians of Latin have written commentaries on these relationships. In the face of this long tradition, the modern grammarian cannot act as if he faces virgin territory. Most of these relationships are between subordinate and headword units, not those found among coordinates. Coordinate relations are for the most part either additive, adversative, or alternative (*and, but, or*). Distinction must be made between coordinate ranking of these kinds and the concept that in basic finite predications (not necessarily in the constructions we shall call transforms) subject part and predicate part are to be considered on the same linguistic level. Coordinates are on the same linguistic level also, but subjects are not coordinate with predicates. A subject part in a predication containing a finite verb is not a modifier of the predicate part, nor is the predicate part a modifier of its subject part. In various transformations of basic sentences one or the other of these primary components can be made the headword upon which the other is dependent (as in *fish-eating tribes* or *the senator's objection to the bill*); but the idea of modification must not be overextended or confused.

A modifying unit is one that bears a describable relation to the unit that it modifies and is grammatically dependent upon. One of the principal aspects of meaning is the establishing of referents and the identities of the referents; hence the distinction between restrictive and non-restrictive modifiers is a real one to the extent that we can make the moving pictures of utterances stand still. In the "still" picture of *Wise girls love diamonds* the noun phrase *wise girls* functions as a single restricted unit of identity in relation to the predicate *love diamonds*. In the phrase *wise girls* we shall discover (pp. 103–7), however, a reduction and transformation of a prior predication *Some girls are wise*. In this prior predication *wise*, it will be shown, is not a modifier of *girls;* it is a predicate adjective. It becomes a modifier when it becomes grammatically dependent upon *girls*. Predicate complements (i.e., completers of predicates) are not modifiers of the subjects of the predicates. Modification is a grammatical concept, not a specific notional one, except that we assume that there is a notional relationship of some kind between modifier and the thing modified. All else is a question of the structural resources of a language and the levels of subordination to be found in a grammatical structure. This is a broader concept of the nature of modification than that which attempts to confine it to the expression of qualities, attributes, or descriptive features. True, if a man is in a room, his being in the room can be considered an attribute of him for the time being, as in the phrase *the man in the room*. Creating a relationship between one linguistic item and another is an act of making one an attribute or a descriptive feature of the other, if the one is made grammatically dependent upon the other. Here is the key to the often-cited distinction between *flower garden* and *garden flower*.

The distinction that has become popular during the past two decades according to which modifiers can be separated into "modifiers" and "sentence modifiers" is grossly inadequate in the face of the facts, depending as it does on a confused definition of "modifier." When we say that a modifier is a related, dependent structure, we are not saying that it is therefore an adjective or an adverb, that all structures of modification must be called either adjectival or adverbial, or that we can divide all grammatical relationships into adjectival relationships and adverbial relationships (even excluding the basic predicational relationships). If the grammar of English employed only a derivational system for showing relationships, we could make such a division. Pragmatically, there may be some advantage in partially confusing forms and functions, relationships and parts of speech, but such an arrangement is only scaffolding, to be torn down when the building is finished.

The grammarian must therefore keep in mind some working list of the relationships that are likely to be found among components in a predication, and then investigate the structural resources of his language for manipulating these relationships.

MATERIALS FOR EXERCISE AND FURTHER STUDY

I. The following passages provide material for a study of the semantic relationships that a grammar must be able to express through structures of one kind or another. In this chapter a list of relationships has been drawn up, but the list does not pretend to be complete. Prepositions and conjunctions are relating words, but in a highly synthetic language many relations are expressed by inflections, not by prepositions. Study the nouns in these passages, particularly those that are objects of prepositions (and not those that are simply subjects, direct or indirect objects, or predicate nouns after copulative verbs). Attempt to ascertain the relationships expressed by the prepositions. Keep score of your findings to determine how many different prepositions can be used to express one relationship, and conversely how many relationships one preposition can express. Check your findings against dictionary definitions for the uses of the prepositions. This is not an easy exercise. Prepositions are particles that function principally in the analytic system of our grammar. You may want to keep score also of the nouns in the passages that pertain to the synthetic and compositional systems.

1. At length as the craft was cast to one side, and ran ranging along with the White Whale's flank, he seemed strangely oblivious of its advance—as the whale sometimes will—and Ahab was fairly within the smoky mountain mist, which, thrown off from the whale's spout, curled round his great Monadnock hump; he was even thus close to him; when, with body arched back, and both arms lengthwise high-lifted to the poise, he darted his fierce iron, and his far fiercer curse into the hated whale. As both steel and curse sank to the socket, as if sucked into a morass, Moby Dick sideways writhed; spasmodically rolled his nigh flank against the bow, and, without staving a hole in it, so suddenly canted the boat over, that had it not been for the elevated part of the gunwale to which he then clung, Ahab would once more have been tossed into the sea. As it was, three of the oarsmen—who foreknew not the precise instant of the dart, and were therefore unprepared for its effects—these were flung out; but so fell, that, in an instant two of them clutched the gunwale again, and rising to its level on a combing wave, hurled themselves bodily inboard again; the third man helplessly dropping astern, but still afloat and swimming.—MELVILLE

2. But although we deny not the existence of the basilisk, yet, whether we do not commonly mistake in the conception hereof, and call that a basilisk which is none at all, is surely to be questioned. For certainly that, which, from the conceit of its generation, we vulgarly call a cockatrice, and wherein (but under a different name) we intend a formal identity and adequate conception with the basilisk, is not the basilisk of the ancients, whereof such wonders are delivered. For this of ours is generally described with legs, wings, a serpentine and winding tail, and a crest or comb somewhat like a cock. But the basilisk of elder times was a proper kind of serpent, not above three palms long, as some account, and differenced from other serpents by advancing his head, and some white marks or coronary spots upon the crown, as all authentic writers have delivered.—SIR THOMAS BROWNE

3. Now what I want you to know is that this cell was intended for only three when it was built, but there were six of us there, all jammed together sweaty and tight. And that was the state of all the cells in all the prisons in those days, brothers, and a dirty cally disgrace it was, there not being decent room for a chelloveck to stretch his limbs. And you will hardly believe what I say now, which is that on this Sunday they brosatted in another plenny. Yes, we had had our hor-

rible pishcha of dumplings and vonny stew and were smoking a quiet cancer each on our bunks when this veck was thrown into our midst. He was a chinny starry veck and it was him who started creeching complaints before we even had a chance to viddy the position. He tried to like shake the bars, creeching: "I demand my sodding rights, this one's full-up, it's a bleeding imposition, that's what it is." But one of the chassos came back to say that he had to make the best of it and share a bunk with whoever would let him, otherwise it would have to be the floor. "And," said the warder, "it's going to get worse, not better. A right dirty criminal world you lot are trying to build." —ANTHONY BURGESS, *A Clockwork Orange*

4. Yeats's success in treating these people as particulars who advance to the status of archetypes is, I think, undeniable. It stems from considerable power of technique and from two other sources. First, Yeats usually works out the analogy between the minute particular and the mythical figure in the context of the poem, and he builds a pattern of these images in the larger context of his whole work. Actually Yeats's poems can be thought of as the manipulation of a limited number of particular symbols, observed and reobserved so that they interlock, poem to poem, to create "bright sculptures." Second, time and place favored Yeats as it most certainly did not favor Blake. In some respects the quirks of history decide the fate of poets. Yeats appeared on the scene in Ireland at a dramatic time. He lived in a true microcosm of history. He was, as W. H. Auden has recently said, one of the last political poets; for in Ireland politics was somehow still related to the individual, and Yeats knew the principal characters of the drama. Blake, who also lived in a violent time, was nevertheless more isolated from his political subject. His allegorical treatment of politics symbolizes this isolation even from the microcosm of his vision. —HAZARD ADAMS

Certain general understandings should result from a careful study of these instances. First, a given semantic relation may be expressed in more than one, or all, of the syntactic systems of the language. Second, one can often not come close to deciding the nature of a relationship without first forming an idea of the parts of speech into which the components of a phrase or clause fall. Third, our ideas of grammatical relationships are built upon notions of relationships found in basic sentence patterns, and we can anticipate that many of our findings here will turn out to be only tentative and will have to be revised once we have seen how basic sentence patterns can undergo transformation and redistribution. Some relationships appear, however, to be more stable and regularly identifiable than others. Time and place relationships are usually particularly clear, unless concrete time and concrete place are extended to logical abstractions that only figuratively can be thought of in terms of time or place. Relations of extent, degree, and duration are often clear and identifiable. Manner, means, and instruments are relations that often are harder to pin down. The prepositions *of, for,* and *with* present many difficulties. Since our main concerns will be with structures, not with these semantic relationships, we should not expect at this point or later to be able to make exact discriminations about relationships. Even vague concepts of relationships do, nevertheless, facilitate the description of structures and make possible a moving from structures to the meaning of structures.

4

PARTS OF SPEECH

DEFINITION BY FORM OR FUNCTION

Language is normative. We are able to communicate with each other because we establish norms of different kinds. Some of these are norms of lexical meaning; words usually operate within a range or area of meanings—either denotative or connotative —and we acquire by habit a sense of the centers of these ranges. As a result we know, as if instinctively, when a word-usage is moving away from or toward the established center. Other norms are those of syntactic patterns, habits we have formed of word order, of intonation contours, or of relational sequences. An intermediate kind of norm is that by which we allocate words as they fall out in any given sequence to certain form classes that we call "parts of speech." Part-of-speech is determined primarily by the way in which a word functions in a sentence, but since we are usually safe in identifying functions by superficial formal appearances, our normative sense sometimes betrays us and we act as if we can assign words to a part-of-speech class by formal appearance only. A -*tion* suffix, for instance, normally signals the presence of the part of speech we call "noun." In a sentence like *They requisitioned ten gross of paper clips,* however, the -*ed* suffix (normally used with verbs and not with nouns) presents evidence conflicting with the -*tion* suffix on *requisition.* According to word order *requisitioned* should be a verb, not a noun. It is in agreement with *they,* a possible subject. Therefore, we decide almost immediately that *requisitioned* is a verb in this instance,

49

even though we may also immediately go beyond this decision and conclude that a functional shift has taken place at some time in the past, in which a form *requisition*, normally a noun, has come to be used as a verb, and, by its ability to fill a verb position and be inflected like a verb, has become in effect a verb. Words cannot be rigidly classed as parts of speech by morphology alone. C. C. Fries has said, "In general, 'position' markers in any particular sentence supersede morphological or form markers." [1] In fact, every sentence that is not totally a cliché has to be "edited" by the communicant—that is, he has to see if the various forms in the sentence actually and consistently fit the roles that he has assigned to them in his quick judgment of how they interact. This necessity of "editing," of operating with and checking upon a tentative intuition of how the parts may fit together, is one of the basic facts of life for the grammarian.

It is a primary extension of the concept of linguistic norms to say that parts of speech can be defined either formally or functionally. Functional definitions are likely to be notional and, what is worse, simplistically notional. The noun class is the name class, the class for "beings." Any word that functions as a static entity is a "being" or a "noun." In contrast to the concept of entity or being is the concept of the finite verb, the active maker of a predication (active as predicator, whether the verb is active or passive). Notionally, nouns are non-finite, in themselves timeless and spaceless abstractions, however much notionally they may be made finite by determiners or modifiers. The finite verb, to the contrary, commits itself by its nature to finite space and time and to its subject even if the idea to be expressed in a predication is almost infinite in scope of reference, as in "All men enjoy God."

However, this basic distinction between "naming non-finitely" and "asserting finitely" is not always as clear as it might be. Discrepancies can occur between appearances and underlying significances; the villain can put on the hero's mask and *vice versa*. In *His loving God implies his hating evil* the naive reasoner can find a basis for asserting that *love* and *hate* are the chief "finite actions" or "finite assertions," particularly if he is allowed to ignore interrelating grammatical forms. Furthermore, the units functioning here as nominals—*his loving God* and *his hating evil*—are units that are capable of being modified in the direction of finiteness as in *his having loved God* and *his having hated evil*. These

---

[1] C. C. Fries, *The Structure of English* (New York, 1952), p. 141.

are, however, "aspect" changes. "Tense" is what a nominal is formally incapable of expressing. We can say *in my former life* but not *in my lived.* All finite verbs, on the other hand, express a finite tense whether or not there is an explicit tense signal. In most verbs in English a common form is used both for infinitives, which are non-finite, and for the present tense forms, except for the third person singular. To determine finiteness in some constructions, it is necessary to test by recasting the suspected verb in third person singular form. Notionally, the so-called abstract-present tense—*enjoy* in *All men enjoy God*—does not express finiteness in time, but formally the verb does.

In order to avoid creating an illogical kind of classification of parts of speech that occurs when some classes are described in terms of their functions and some are described only in terms of their forms or morphology, we must make a basic distinction between certain large form classes (nouns, verbs, and adjectives), on the one hand, and several limited or specialized function groups (such as determiners, modals, or prepositions), on the other hand. The most important distinction between these two kinds is this —that most of the words in our dictionaries belong to the three large form classes, and to the "adverb" class, the special problem of which will be discussed later in this chapter. The words that belong to the function groups occur very often in our speech and writing, but since we use the same words over and over again, the listing of them takes up very little space in our dictionaries. The function words are, for the most part, words that signal relationships. In a synthetic language system their work is often done by inflections or other bound forms; they belong, consequently, more to the analytic system of our language than to the synthetic. By using a small vocabulary of under two hundred words the average user of the English language can fit together a very large number of words that belong to the form classes, and, by means of these function words, create meaningful utterances. If we are to proceed in an orderly fashion, we must keep separate these "structure" words from our large, expandable form classes.

NOUNS

Nouns and verbs are the two primary form classes or parts of speech, in the sense that they are the easiest to isolate and define, to describe notionally as well as formally. Tests can be set up for them, even though not every noun will pass all tests for nouns and not every verb will pass all tests for verbs. Whatever will fill the subject position in a sentence will be a noun or something like a noun (e.g., pronoun or nominal). Nouns can also function as direct objects, as indirect objects, as the so-called objects of prepositions, as predicate complements after copulative verbs, and hence in transforms as appositives. In the structures of the system of compounds they can also assume a variety of functions. They are for the most part capable of genitive and plural inflections. In a large part of their functioning they can be distinguished by markers called noun-determiners: *a, the, this, that, his, their, one, three,* etc.

The noun-determiner class does not comprise a part of speech. Whether these examples are to be taken as pronouns, near-nouns, or adjectives, as demonstratives, identifiers, partitives, or numerals, is not at issue here. The determiner function can be performed by various kinds of units, some of which may be performing other functions at the same time. If a word in question is a noun, the possibility should exist of referring to it by means of a personal, demonstrative, or relative pronoun; or its position in a sentence can be occupied by a numerical or partitive near-noun,[2] such as *few, some, both, all, many, much, most, several, one, two, three,* etc.

Sometimes nouns that appear the same on the printed page as verbs are distinguished from them by stress on the first syllable rather than on the second (*réject, rejéct, cóntact, contáct*). A final test is of concord between subject and verb. These tests provide clues from syntax rather than from morphology, and do not

---

[2] This term is used here in order to avoid a difficulty in terminology that has plagued grammarians old and new. Traditionally in English grammars these have been called pronouns even though they also appear in structures of modification (*few* men, *some* men, *both* men), as a true noun-substitute, or pronoun, does not. The structuralists have tended to call them pre-determiners, but since determination is a function and not a classification for a part of speech, this name is useful only in pragmatic description of certain highly localized constructions. Near-nouns are for the most part indeclinable (that is, they do not have genitive or plural forms like most nouns; genitive, objective, and plural forms like personal pronouns; or plural forms like demonstrative pronouns), in which respect they pattern like noun adjuncts. The lexicon of near-nouns is limited since they make logical and not concrete reference; they can appear between determiners and nouns (those *few* men). In partitive functions they appear as headwords (*few* of the men) modified by prepositional phrases with *of, among,* etc. Ralph B. Long's handling of them as determinative pronouns in a kind of apposition (see *supra,* p. 40) is one of the better ways of dealing with this situation.

lead to the discriminations that can be made by study of derivations.

As we have said, evidence from derivational suffixes provides no sure clue to part-of-speech determinations. Generally, however, it is from such evidence that we make our easy decisions. Since the chief function of a derivational suffix is to shift a word from one part of speech to another, we learn to recognize the significances of the suffixes and the parts of speech with which they are used, even though we may not be quite conscious that certain suffixes are used only with certain shifts. Thus, we may not have clearly in mind that -ness functions primarily as a converter of an adjective to a noun (*tininess, strictness, sickness, stoutness*), as does -th (*warmth, health* [from *hale*], *strength, truth*), and such assorted forms derived from either Latin or Old English seen in *supremacy, justice, importance, violence, independence, absence, bravery, wisdom, freedom, anxiety, necessity, clarity*.[3] The suffix -al functions sometimes as the converter of a noun to an adjective (*brutal, tribal, global*) and sometimes as the converter of a verb to a noun, as in *arrival, refusal, denial, acquittal, dismissal, reversal, approval*. Other derivational converters of verbs to nouns are seen in such words as *departure, delivery, acceptance, amusement, deformity, division, leakage*. Other more specialized kinds of shift from verb to noun are seen in *finder, helper, maker*, etc. (agentive nouns), *applicant, servant, superintendent; practice* from *practise*, *advice* from *advise*, *abuse* [s] from *abuse* [z]. Participles and gerunds—and perhaps infinitives also—should be treated as derivatives from verbs, not as verbs, except when they are components of verb phrases. In their functioning as nouns they should, however, be kept quite distinct from the kind of abstract noun like *collision* or *punishment* if only for their properties of being able to take indirect and direct objects, be modified by adverbial structures, and express voice, aspect, and some moods.

When a verb or adjective is converted into a noun, its grammatical nature is changed from one emphasis to another. It is the same meaning seen as if through a different filter or in a different light. The change is rarely complete. The distinction between non-finite name and finite action or assertion is one of degree or

---

[3] This, and other lists given here for the functioning of suffixes, is taken with some modification from C. C. Fries, *The Structure of English* (New York, 1952), pp. 113–34.

of grammatical frame. Nouns, together with attendant modifying structures, can handle a whole gamut of predicational meanings from the highly non-finite to the highly finite. This can be seen plainly in the workings of nominal forms of reduced predications in a transform grammar like the present one (see Chapter 13). Nevertheless, the basic distinction between noun and verb must be maintained as the basis of any parts-of-speech analysis. The class of nouns is made up of many kinds other than the abstract noun forms that are derived from other parts of speech.

Most obviously nouns are those words that make reference to concrete, physical objects of one kind or another. Most base nouns—those not formed by derivation or functional shift from verbs or adjectives—are of this kind: *dog, cat, man, ox, tree, head, foot, book.* Some abstract terms do, it is true, appear to be base nouns and can be considered so in their present-day behavior (*law, right, evil, force, trend*—the distinctions become exceedingly fine); whether these do or do not represent derivational shiftings from other parts of speech is not always significant in terms of current usage. The traditionalist who defines a noun as the name of a person, place, or thing seemingly ignores the large class of abstract nouns formed by derivational affixes from base adjectives or verbs. The structuralists have on occasion chosen to call all nouns derived from other parts of speech nominals and to save the term "noun" for base forms. Here, to the contrary, we must take care not to ignore the existence of base nouns in our concern with those derived from verbs and adjectives.

Proper nouns—those that name particular persons, places, organizations, or entities of one kind or another, like *George,* the *United Nations, France,* or *Swift and Company*—are not timeless and placeless in the same way common nouns are; nor are they likely to be headwords of semi-finite nominal forms of reduced predications as are abstract nouns made by derivation from verbs or adjectives. Common nouns can be subdivided into pluralizers and quantifiables (count nouns and mass nouns) and those to which the concepts of both plurality and mass are irrelevant (After his arrest, he demanded *counsel*). A very large percentage of the meaningful relations that syntactic structures can signal involve nouns as at least one of the items to be related.

It has been customary to consider pronouns as a part of speech distinct from nouns. This can be done, but the student of grammar is under no obligation to arrive at any set number of parts of

speech. Pronouns are function words, not content words; their
number is strictly limited and their meanings are acquired from
context. We are not much more justified in setting up a separate
part-of-speech class for pronouns than for pro-verbs like *do* in *I
went but he didn't*. Pronouns occupy noun positions in predicational structures. We have already indicated that complex differences exist between personal and demonstrative pronouns on one
hand and numerical and partitive near-nouns on the other. Some
words like *every* do not belong strictly in either camp. Note the
difference between *every boy* and *every one of the boys*. In languages in which adjectives are declined, near-nouns can move
readily from noun-function to adjective-function, and are more
likely than in English to appear simply as adjectives.

VERBS

In our description of parts of speech, only the finite verb forms
or the verb phrases that contain a finite form are defined as verbs.
Since English verb phrases are for the most part analytically composed, auxiliaries have a large role to play in their formation.
Some modern grammarians have tended to treat auxiliaries as
modifiers. Thus, in a verb phrase like *could have been going*,
they have called *going* the headword of the phrase, so that the
auxiliaries *could, have*, and *been* are treated as dependencies of
the headword. However, only the first word in a verb phrase can
be inflected to show person, number, and tense, except that the
model auxiliaries *can, may, might, dare, ought, will, shall*, and
must show only tense distinction, while *be, have*, and *do* show
person, number, and tense. All of the working parts of the phrase
assist in expressing the conditions of finiteness handled by inflection in a Latin verb. Analytic English verb phrases must not be
described in terms of the synthetic Latin forms, but what we must
distinguish are finite forms from non-finite forms. This is not always easy to do or sometimes even important to do.

The problem is the broader one of determining when, in a
polysystemic grammar, a word changes part of speech if it
changes function. In compound phrases like *punch-drunk* or
girl-crazy, punch and *girl* cannot be called adverbs simply because
they are dependent on adjectives; they remain nouns functioning
as nouns can function in this particular syntactic system. The difference between *Peru's* (a synthetic construction) *politics, the*

politics of Peru (an analytic construction), *Peru politics* (a compositional construction), and *Peruvian* (a derivational construction) *politics* is more a matter of syntactic systems than a part-of-speech problem. In all structures *Peru* appears in a dependent unit in a structure of modification, but only *Peruvian* is formally an adjective. We do not usually balk at classing *run* as a noun in *the chicken run* and as a verb in *the chickens run,* or *yellow* as an adjective in *the yellow moon* and as a verb in *moons yellow.* First of all, we can put *run* through its paces as a noun in *the chicken run;* it has a noun determiner *the;* we can recast the phrase in *The chicken runs are dirty,* showing that *run* can be inflected as a noun, even though the phrase *the chicken runs* is in itself ambiguous except for the difference of intonation contour in the two possibilities.

What then happens if verbs are limited by definition, in setting up a part of speech, to finite verb forms or phrases, so that infinitives, participles, and gerunds are not classed as verbs unless these forms help to make up a finite verb phrase? The structuralists have classed the participial suffixes (*-ing, -ed, -en,* etc.) as inflections rather than derivational suffixes and have been very silent about infinitives, as if they do not exist, and in so doing have set up a part-of-speech classification by which verbs can function as the subjects of verbs. James Sledd has shown in his *A Short Introduction to English Grammar* that much of the difficulty inherent in constituting parts of speech arises from the necessity of a double basis of definition—definition by form and definition by function. But the problem with verbs is not quite of this kind, for participial and infinitive forms do not necessarily remain verbs in form while changing function to nominals, adjectivals, or adverbials. The participial affixes can be considered derivational but markers or absence of markers are not derivational affixes to infinitives. Infinitives should perhaps be treated as if they were outside the range of words that can intelligibly be put into form classes. The Latin grammarian, Varro, in distinguishing four parts of speech, made participles one of the four. Here only finite verb forms or phrases will be counted verbs.

Tests for finite verbs are relatively simple. If in any sentence the form in question is capable of tense distinction or the distinction of third person singular (except for phrases with modal auxiliaries for which a tense distinction alone is possible), the form is a finite verb. In addition, there must be agreement between subject and verb. Thus, in *the chicken run* we know that *run* is not a verb because of lack of agreement between possible subject and possible verb. In *the chicken runs* (leaving aside difference of stress pattern), *runs* could be a plural noun or a verb in the third person singular. If the meaning seems to be such that the hypothetical projection to *the chicken ran* (past tense) is possible, we know by test that *runs* is a verb. In declarative sentences verbs usually follow subjects. In the setting up of test frames for verbs it is necessary to use basic declarative patterns, since the order of subjects and verbs undergoes transformations in some questions and negations.

The number of suffixes used in converting words from other form classes into verbs is smaller than with nouns. Both nouns and adjectives can be converted by means of well-known suffixes. Two in particular are used to create instances of the sub-class of verbs known as "factitives"— *-fy* and *-ize*. A "factitive" verb conveys the notion of "make," "cause," "force," or "compel," as in "I *made* him go." When a basic factitive verb occurs, it is usually followed by a reduced predication (in this instance *him go,* so that the structure reveals a reduction of *I forced that he go*). In a sentence like *They romanticized the situation,* we find the suffix *-ize* converting the predicate part of the reduced predication *romantic* into the base of the verb; thus, *They made the situation (seem) romantic* can be transformed to *They romanticized the situation.* In the long run no precise transformational grammar can be written without full involvement on the morphophonemic level. Since both nouns and adjectives can function as predicate complements in reduced predication, both can undergo functional change into factitive verbs by adding *-ize.* Sometimes, of course, the resulting verbs can undergo a semantic shift, as in *realize,* in which the sense of "make real" no longer exists in common usage. Test the structuring of *clarify, beautify, magnify, glorify, idolize, magnetize* (but *burglarize!*), *Bowdlerize.* The *-en* suffix can also act with factitive force as a converter of adjectives to verbs, often with the sense of the comparative of the adjective: *He hardened his heart < He made his heart (be) harder.* Sometimes the meaning is "become." *The room lightens < The room becomes lighter.*

The prefixes *be-* and *en-* occur frequently as converters of nouns or adjectives into verbs: *bewitch, befriend, behead* (*be-* is more commonly an intensifying prefix added to verb bases, as in *bestir, be-daub*), *enable, enrich, enjoy, enrage, entitle.* Distinction between nouns and verbs is sometimes shown by phonetic contrast: *strive, strife, prove, proof, clothe, cloth.*

THE PROBLEM OF ADVERBS

From this long analysis we can see that there are three parts of speech that can be converted from one to another by derivational suffixes: nouns, verbs, and adjectives. But what then about adverbs? The structuralists, following Fries, have distinguished between four form classes (Fries's Class I, Class II, Class III, and Class IV—roughly nouns, verbs, adjectives, and adverbs, except that Fries warned against carrying over concepts traditionally attached to these names). According to Fries, other kinds of words should be described and classed by their functions rather than by their forms and so should be separated into groups of function words. Three of the four form classes provide base forms for functional shifts by addition of derivational affixes—nouns, verbs, and adjectives; but few derivational shifts come from the adverb class, and most of the words we call adverbs are derived from adjectives (*quickly—quick, intensely—intense, regularly—regular*. Adverbs containing a noun base (*away, aboard, ashore,* etc.) usually represent a syncopation of a prepositional phrase (*on way, on board, on shore*); sometimes they exhibit the relic of an inflection (see *supra,* p. 27). We are caught in a crossfire between form and function when we continue to class as nouns or pronouns such inflected forms as *boy's, him* when it is an indirect object, or *home* when it expresses a space relation with zero inflection, while we continue to treat prepositional phrases (from the analytic part of the grammar) as adverbial—since "adverb" now means part-of-speech conceived relationally and not formally. Some base adverbs exist (*often, seldom, then, now, first, last, out, back, up, down, there, thus,* etc.) but the list is relatively short, which means that these few words are practically function words, or analytic particles, since one of the criteria used for distinguishing between form classes and function groups is the possibility for form classes of almost infinite expansion of the lexicon. Hence since most adverbs are derived from adjectives, the adverb class is almost an appendage to the adjective class.

ADJECTIVES

But the existence of a large number of base adjectives and the fact that many nouns and verbs (as well as adverbs) are formed by the addition of derivational suffixes to adjective stems indicate that an adjective form class must be added to those for nouns and verbs among the primary form classes. But in order to do this, we must rid ourselves of the notion that an adjective is essentially a modifier, a dependent unit in a predication. The listing of nouns and verbs among the primary form classes was justified by the need for these classes in constituting subject-parts and predicate-parts in basic patterns of predications. This is a justification by function, not by form. Since, according to the theory of grammar that we are developing, modifiers do not exist in basic sentence patterns, we must consider the predicate complement function of adjectives to be the base on which to justify the inclusion of adjectives as a class among the primary form classes. In this functioning, adjectives are predicators with the aid of copulative verbs (*be*) or copula variants (*remain, become,* etc.). Nouns as well as adjectives can be predicators with the aid of copulative verbs or copula variants (i.e., when they are predicate complements) without becoming modifiers. Adjectives, therefore, are strangely like both nouns and verbs, but are different from both, since adjective forms can be derived from both, and both verbs and nouns can be derived from adjective base forms.

Confusion arises, to the contrary, when the form class of adjectives is defined in terms of secondary functions of adjectives—those in which adjectives are dependent units (i.e., modifiers). Only by vague semantic extension can adjectives, even as modifiers, be said to function always as qualifiers, attributives, or describers, since an adjective as modifier can stand in almost any relationship with a headword noun that a noun and preposition in a prepositional phrase can. Adjectives are functionally either noun-modifiers or predicators. In a transformationalist's basic sentence patterns they are only predicators. The normal test positions for adjectives, according to structuralists, are as pre-positional modifiers of nouns or as predicate adjectives after linking or copulative verbs.

The good man is good.

Since in further reaches of the grammar either of these positions can also be occupied by nouns, the test by position is not definitive. In transformational grammar, where distinction is made between basic predicational patterns and patterns involving putting two or more basic predicational patterns together, pre-positional adjectives are thought to represent transformations. This means that the sentence *The good men are here* represents the reduction and insertion of the predication *The men are good* into the matrix predication *The men are here*. On these terms, then, the only test slot for adjectives in basic sentences is the predicate adjective position: "The men are *good*." The pre-position transform is, however, so normal and widespread and involves so many shadings of relational meaning that we have in the past thought that adjectives function primarily as pre-positional modifiers. In some other languages, the normal position for transformed adjectives is after the noun; thus, *le cahier jaune, Barbebleue*. In English, long adjective units will sometimes be attracted to this position, and in certain phrases that are relics from Norman French (*court martial, heir apparent*) this position is normal. Appositive adjectives, which represent more immediate reductions of copula predications than do pre-positional adjectives, can either precede or follow: "The cloud, *dark* against the mauve sky, was shaped like a lozenge." "*Dark* against the mauve sky, the cloud was shaped like a lozenge." But these illustrations take us into the complexities of transformations and are of little help toward the constitution of a form class of adjectives.

One distinct way in which most adjectives and adverbs differ both formally and notionally from nouns and verbs is in their ability to take comparison. It is doubtful that this operation should be called inflection, although by means of suffixes or functional particles like *more* and *most*, which are like specifications for inflections, adjectives adjust themselves to the meaning required. But inflections are relational and comparison in adjectives and adverbs is not, just as the indication of plural number is not relational. English less than some languages—Romance languages in particular—permits little ambiguity between comparison and degree; we can not use one form like *buonissimo* to mean *very good* and *most good*. James Sledd has ruled that only words that can take comparison by suffix should properly be called adjectives; words like *beautiful* or *native* (these with derivational suffixes) he would call adjectivals and not adjectives. This distinction surely can only confuse us. It should be noted that the meanings of some adjectives do not allow comparison of either the analytic or the synthetic variety (e.g., *unique, tribal*) because of lexical incompatibility of one kind or another, but this fact need not destroy faith in the general observation that one peculiar feature of adjectives and adverbs, in contradistinction to nouns and verbs, is this ability to undergo comparison, either by means of the suffixes *-er* and -*est* (along with some irregular forms) or by means of *more* and *most*. It is true that verbs can be modified by structures of degree or comparison, and that the difference between *more power* and *more powerful* may seem obscure to some. We are faced first of all with the question of correlated phrasal changes, as in *more able* > *more ability* > *more power*, just as in the phrase *perfect stranger* we can imply the carry-over into an alien structure of the relationship found in *perfectly strange*. *More* and *perfect* may in these instances be called pseudo-adjectives, borrowing the appearance but not the full notional reality of adjectives. But since in the definitions of parts of speech we have to walk a tightrope between forms and functions and not reside at either end, the term pseudo-adjective is only a descriptive phrase indicating that the evidence does not all agree. Besides, *more* may perchance be called a near-noun in *more power* since *more of this power* is a possible locution.

With nouns and verbs, we looked to the formal presence of suffixes indicating derivations from other parts of speech as further evidence contributing to the setting up of form classes. We can do the same with adjectives. Significant distinctions among behavior patterns of kinds of adjectives can be drawn in terms of the part of speech from which an adjective is derived. Among suffixes used to convert nouns to adjectives are -*ly*, -*y*, -*al*, -*ous*, -*ish*, -*ar*, -*ic*, -*ate*, -*ary*, -*en* (for materials; less common than it used to be), -*ful*, -*ed* (as in *kingly, snowy, emotional, virtuous, foolish, polar, athletic, collegiate, revolutionary, golden, lawful,* and *wretched;* in compound structures, consider also -*ed* in *hot-headed, rose-breasted, green-eyed*); more like free forms are such suffixes as -*less* and -*like* (*lawless, ladylike*). Adjectives made from verbs include participial -*ing*, -*ed*, and -*en* forms although, as we have said, there is reason to think of participles as forming a separate part-of-speech class; sometimes, however, they function quite simply as adjectives. There is little difference between a pre-positional participle in -*ing* (*flying birds* < *birds fly*) and the kind of adjective using an -*ant* or -*ent* suffix (*observant people* < *people observe*), except that the -*ent* or -*ant* suffixes represent what originally were Latin participial suffixes, the participial sense of which is lost to most speakers of English. Other suffixes used with adjectives made from verbs are -*able*, -*ive*, and -*some* (as in *dependable, possessive,* and *tiresome*). As might be expected, adjectives deriving from nouns and verbs are more likely to operate in a wide relational range in the handling of predicational transformations, reductions, or redistributions than are base adjectives: *preventive medicine* < *this kind of medicine prevents; educational soul-searching* < *education searches its soul* (in the false personification we can see why rhetoricians are disturbed by constructions like this).

By a judicious application of these tests of form, word order, and function, we can create fairly stable boundaries for a form class of adjectives with a value in the creating of predicational structures not far behind that of nouns and verbs. In addition, we can see how dangerous it is to try to insist upon specific functions (such as denoting "quality" or "attribute") for this form class to perform, even though this is the base from which the traditional determinations take off. Adjectives are predicators (predicate adjectives) or, by transformation, modifiers. Modifiers can be many things besides adjectives; nouns (in structures of compounding, or genitives in the synthetic system), prepositional phrases expressing analytically many kinds of relationships, phrases of other kinds (participles and infinitives), and dependent clauses. When these are dependent on nouns as headwords, we are tempted to think that all of them function as adjectives. In this sense, any modifier of a noun is an adjective, at least by definition according to function. But modification is a grammatical function, not a logical one. Perhaps the only logical functions for adjective modifiers are those denoting qualities or attributes. If this is so, then only by the grace of extension of the concept of what can be comprised under qualities and attributes, to almost any discernible relationship between nouns, or between nouns and verbs, will most derived adjectives fit into this form class.

Little needs to be added to what has already been said about adverbs. Nouns used to express oblique relations (the so-called adverbial nouns) are here classed as nouns (but called adverbial nouns) functioning in the synthetic system of English, with zero inflection. Base adverbs are so few in number that without the addition of the derived forms they would lack one of the principal characteristics of a form class—a changing and almost infinitely expandable lexicon. Another way of saying the same thing is to say that adjectives can perform a specialized function by acquiring a distinct marker, usually the derivational suffix -*ly*. Prepositional phrases that seem to express notions traditionally thought of as adverbial can be found as predicators (i.e., in the position occupied by predicate nouns or adjectives), just as the so-called adverbial nouns and base adverbs can: *He was in the room, That was after lunch, He was home, He was there, The motion was downward, The music was everywhere.* But only the relatively small class of *-ly* adverbs derived from a noun base (and these forms are identical with *-ly* adjectives—*daily, hourly, weekly,* etc.) can function there—not *He was furiously, The cost was extravagantly.* Adverbs normally are modifiers of verbs and adjectives. Since qualifiers or intensifiers like *very, quite,* and *rather* can qualify or intensify, and in that sense modify, adjectives, adverbs, and even prepositions (*right to the door, almost to the door*) but not verbs, they should be considered outside the adverb form class, even though there are frequent borderline cases and exceptions. The adverb structure can be borrowed for non-adverbial functions in certain redistributional transforms (*He was evidently a man of honor* < *It was evident that he was a man of honor* < *He was a man of honor; this was evident*); for adverbial structures, like other grammatical structures, are only structures and can be put to many kinds of notional uses. Walter Mitty's fountain pen (in James Thurber's story) was not manufactured to function as a piston in an operating-room machine, but at least in Mitty's dream-life it was able to function in that way. The users of a language determine the range of functions for a grammatical structure, not philosophers defining functions.

The positions that *-ly* adverbs can occupy in sentences are less rigidly determined than those for other parts of speech. We can say *Quickly he came, He quickly came,* and *He came quickly* equally well. Some people will find a slight difference of meaning in these three versions, but if it exists it is one of style and cannot be grammatically pinpointed, for some speakers who intend the same meaning will alter the position of the adverb at will. The few adverbs that in form are indistinguishable from adjectives (*fast, slow, hard,* etc.) are more strictly limited to the position after verbs. Whether particles that sometimes double as prepositions should be called adverbs or function words (*over, out, up, away, in, off,* etc.) is an open question; they either follow the verb or come at the end of the predicate as if they are separable parts of the verbs. In some instances they become in effect post-adjuncts.

FUNCTION GROUPS

The groups of function words cannot be very precisely defined, nor is there any particular point in doing so. It is no detraction to the ultimate orderliness of language that at times there is an overlap between some of the form classes and some of the function groups. Determiners, which can fulfill the specific function of marking nouns (*a, an, the, this, that, his, John's, one, two,* etc.), may from certain angles be considered adjectives, near-nouns, or pronouns; they can carry out more than one function at once. The word devices of the analytic system of English function in general in the function group area, not in the form classes. Verb auxiliaries, as we have seen (p. 25), form a special problem. Prepositions can be distinguished from analytic particles if the prepositional phrase can be isolated as a separate syntactic unit expressing an identifiable relation between the noun, called the object of the preposition, and some other constituent of the sentence.

Sometimes it is difficult to draw a line between subordinating conjunctions and prepositions, especially in truncated, elliptical, or reduced constructions (*after going, before going, when to go, in spite of thinking such thoughts, whether to do it or not,* etc.). An arbitrary distinction can, however, be made on the basis of whether or not the word subordinates a clause or a less-than-clause unit. In the illustrations given here, *whether* and *when* in *whether to do it or not* and *when to go* introduce dependent units that function nominally; they thus function as what the traditionalists have called interrogative adverbs. It confuses terminology to insist that such forms always function as adverbs, but that the units they introduce are transforms from interrogative predications can be more easily established. What we must remember is that the term "adverbial" as it applies to some of these phrases or clauses suggests a parallel between their functionings and the functionings of certain adverbs. The term signifies relationship, not form. Our only real problem in classification is whether to constitute one large function group of subordinators including (1) such particles as *that, why, when, where, whether, if* when these introduce clauses or reduced clauses used in nominal positions and functions, (2) such subordinating conjunctions as *although, because, if, when, after, as if, as,* etc., when these introduce dependent clauses expressing such relations as concession, cause, condition, time, and manner—relations thought of with some reason as being conveyed basically by adverbials, (3) relative pronouns such as *who, which,* and *that,* and (4) conjunctive adverbs such as *however, therefore,* and *nevertheless;* or, to the contrary, to separate these partially similar structural functioning-units into separate groups. A need on a higher level is that of separating conjunctions into coordinators and subordinators. Except for relative pronouns and some conjunctive adverbs—which do double duty between form classes and function groups—all words of these kinds are function words operating in conventional structures that can be identified and tested as such. It is safer to describe these structures in separate groups than to classify them unilaterally on the notion of their functioning. A relative clause is, for instance, notionally capable of conveying the idea of causality (Jones, *who had a good alibi,* was not questioned by the police); we cannot, however, for this reason conclude that *who* functions as the same kind of subordinator as *since* or *because.* We would do better to set up as many different function groups for subordinators as we can describe distinct differences in structural behavior. By this token we should keep separate subordinating conjunctions (*because, when, although*), coordinating conjunctions (*and, but, or, for*), conjunctive adverbs (*however, therefore, in this case*), particles introducing noun clauses whether declarative or interrogative (*that, why, who, what,* etc.), and relative pronouns (*who, which, that, as*). To lump these all together without distinction is to fail to note differences among some of the chief structural devices in the English language.

Other function groups are less important. Certain words attached to adjectives, adverbs, or even prepositions can be called intensifiers or qualifiers (*very, rather, quite, pretty,* etc.). Negators (*no, not, never,* etc.) form a special group. *There* as a "dummy" (as in *There* is a wolf outside) performs a unique function. Interjections can perform a variety of minor functions and do not have the characteristics of form class words; the lexicon here is, however, greatly expandable—a feature not common in function groups. Other function groups serve too highly specialized tasks to deserve consideration here.

NONCE FORMS

It is always difficult, in this act of setting up basic form classes of parts of speech and function groups, to distinguish between normal forms and nonce constructions. It was said in the introductory chapter that a grammar is ultimately subject to the phrases that are learned by the users of the language and become habitual to them. But there would be no grammar if the structures of words, phrases, and sentences were not frequently repeated. We form habits of structures as well as of lexical meanings. When a boy says to his mother, "I wanted to play baseball," and the mother answers crossly, "I'll baseball you if you don't mind me," we recognize an unhabitual use of the word *baseball* (as a verb and with no customary lexical meaning) in the mother's response. This is a nonce-construction—one that is used *ad hoc,* as a lawless expression, for this time only. Actually, of course, nonce-constructions are found in a whole spectrum running from any yoking together of words not usual in the clichés of the language (suppose we substitute *monkey-watcher* for *bird-watcher*) to the opposite extreme of creating patterns that we would never expect to become standard forms, as in *the wait-till-you-see-the-whites-of-their-eyes spirit.* Almost any extension of the use of a structure thus makes the structure a nonce-structure until through habit we feel at home with it. The wonder is that we can accept even nonsense yokings as in "slithy toves" as if they were perfectly normal because we are habituated to the pattern adjective-noun even though the words are now coming to our attention for the first time. The lexical content of the words is less important, in fact, in this distinction between nonce and normal constructions than are the syntactic and the logical relations between components. Thus, our habits may tell us that the *-er* suffix on nouns is usually found in words converted from verbs to indicate "agent." Thus, we can extend almost infinitely such a list as *singer, watcher, writer, teacher* without a sense of doing anything unusual. We feel something less usual when we attach the *-er* suffix to something other than verbs, as in *left-winger* or *polecater.* We would feel quite outraged by a neologism such as *gorgeouser,* meaning "a girl who is gorgeous." This is extension quite beyond the range of our habits, and the usage would be definitely a nonce-construction until such time as it had become familiar through use. In the working out of any grammar it is necessary to ignore the implications of nonce-constructions. The structuralist grammarians, who have taken everything they have found in their raw data at face value, have tried to describe a lot of structures they should have ignored. An example is their attempt to define a subject in such a way that an adverbial particle—a function word —could be used as a subject, as in *The Up is the elevator I want*. This kind of usage should plainly be defined as a nonce-construction and so put out of mind, at least until the functional shift has become standardized through use or through acquiring all the behavior expected of a class of phenomena. We are not much surprised by locutions such as *The Outs ousted the Ins* because we find *Outs* and *Ins* in plural forms, behaving as nouns ordinarily do. Both with *Up* and *Outs and Ins* we find *the* used as determiner.

Parts of speech we have thus defined more on formal and behavioral than on notional terms, even though relationships are notional and it has been necessary to give some hint of the relational range within which the form classes operate. These are notions of the base from which we start, not of the extensions and alterations we allow on the base. In a quite real sense, language is used figuratively whenever extensions are made on the basic patterns. But new habits can be formed, and habits are the ultimate solidity, since they give us our sense of reality. The statement "The clock strikes noon," may seem plain and simple, but is it the clock that strikes something? Perhaps we are looking at an electric clock—does it really strike? Is it noon that is literally struck? And yet we have subject, verb, and object; a meaningful assertion has been made by means of forms capable of conveying it. In grammar it is these forms, either morphological or syntactic, with which we work.

MATERIALS FOR EXERCISE AND FURTHER STUDY

I. Many words function as more than one part of speech without morphophonemic change (such as shift of stress or phonemic change—*cómbat—combát; présent—[priyzént]*) or without the addition of derivational suffixes. Most of the following words can function either as nouns or verbs. Some can also function as adjectives. (In this grammar nouns used in structures of modification are called noun adjuncts— i.e., they are called nouns—rather than adjectives.) How many of these words seem to have been originally nouns, so that the functional shift has been from noun to verb? How many of them seemingly started as verbs, as adjectives? There are no easy ways of deciding these questions, and you should not be too sure of your decisions unless you examine each case very carefully.

spirit	mask	mass
wild	claim	man
mutiny	alert	fear
take	view	fancy
respect	smoke	brain
ease	screen	watch
deal	find	rule
number	attack	cast
figure	book	draw
sanction	balance	value
mock	sport	ally
course	condition	fault
side	weasel	honor
firm	cloud	coin
will	temper	time
hope	posture	patent
wish	leap	turn
result	even	screw
support	praise	hang
limit	prejudice	sign
range	mind	murder
work	remark	load
study	author	exhibit
quarrel	clear	reform
attempt	encounter	comment
point	force	command
favor	risk	light
sober	equal	fill
voice	face	hint
scheme	stand	link
hinge	love	place
question	fit	print
tone	strike	feel
issue	blow	label
cause	judge	cry
start	merit	waste
trick	ground	act
collapse	reason	matter

(That this list of functional doubles or triples was taken from only two and a half pages of an article in a scholarly journal indicates clearly how many of the words we use do undergo functional shifts.)

II. Turn to any convenient piece of prose—book, essay, magazine article—and form a word bank of examples of words with derivational suffixes like those in the following list. What parts of speech are converted into what other parts of speech by means of the suffixes?

monumental	accountable	estimative
exhaustive	institutional	malignant
definitive	anomalously	onlooker
scholarship	sufferance	benevolence
interpretation	rhetorical	craziness
restrictive	resemblance	sensibility
divergence	alternative	misanthropic
critical	conformist	resentment
artistic	denial	discriminate
integrity	rigidity	contradictory
apparent	realistic	sentimentalize
failure	civilization	crafty
demonstrable	reliability	preliminaries
predictable	formalistic	intimidate
sufficiently	radically	particularity
imaginative	statutory	sufficiency
discussion	reducible	signification
constructive	prohibition	choleric
available	morality	frantic
ecclesiastical	community	familiarize
impudent	prejudicial	extemporize
conservative	unsportsmanlike	appropriate
justification	anticipatory	investigate
refutation	polarize	mediated
reversal	navigational	stationary
spectacular	sincerity	loquacious
mediator	ineffective	bountiful
dissociate	proponent	complexity
innocence	general	narrative
possibility	disputation	pitiful
adventurous	vigorous	specifically
occasional	depreciation	projectile
pertinent	referential	legislate
sensational	pithy	incommensurable
correctives	analytical	transitory
difference	characteristic	observational
deservedly	crusty	bulbous
affirmative	comprehension	red-headed
consistency	irresponsibility	beautiful
absurdity	contemplative	
memorializing	descendant	

III. One way of dividing nouns is into pluralizers and quantifiables, that is, into those that can take plurals because they can be conceived as separate objects and into those that present ideas of mass. Another way is to divide them into abstract and concrete nouns. A third way, a division into count nouns and non-count nouns, is a cross between the first two, since it lumps quantifiables and abstract nouns together as non-count nouns. Still another division is based upon the presence or absence of the kind of determiners we call articles (*a, an, the, zero*), depending primarily upon the structures in which the nouns appear. *Brick* is a count noun in *The pile of papers was weighted with a brick.* What is it in *The house was made of brick?* What is the difference between *I like meat* and *I like beans?* Following the same procedure that has already been suggested in these exercises for creating your own grammar inductively, turn to some available body of writing and collect all the examples that come to hand of the phrases in which nouns appear. Work out your own classification of the kinds of common nouns on the basis of your evidence. The following words or phrases may be used as a starter of such a bank of evidence. How many of these are pluralizers? Always? Create contexts for the single words? What articles or determiners can you use with them?

bean soup	inaccessibility
wood-burning engine	piracy
a child's treasure	obesity
that is fool's gold	bunion
pursuit	bottom
archetype	bottom rung
for instance	order
an instance	regulation
the material	ferocity
matter	crocodile
irony	whistle
love	tomb
breadfruit	pastry
youth	stone
mermaid	steel
hatpin	innocence
daydream	sought passage
scissors	burden of proof
mush	top of the ladder
data	top dog
motivation	the mask of art
chaos	love of argument
oath	alert reader

wheat
water
on boggy ground
proof has been limited
limited to assertion and coun-
ter-assertion
this theme of magnanimity
a confession of political duplic-
ity
his lack of independence
the outcome of discipline
mutiny is always deplorable
sees unbridled man as a beast
collision of private morality and
the law
sought exoneration
home base
plea for straightforwardness
the child's bewilderment
both poet and sculptor express
the souls of the blessed
a coincidence in detail
written on vellum
roused high fervor
the high enthusiasm for the
event
to see an occasion
would have interest for them
he had been at work
I love school
big car room and ride
this gave occasion
a field of red earth
he lived upon fish and fowl
house on land belonging to
continuing with difficulty
school of theology
the type of poetry
inclusion of parallel structure
to become commonplace
through repetition
an act of mercy
there is disagreement among
them

a dispute over method
the methods of modern science
without mystification and spec-
ulation
suggestions of greater fixity
materialism is not
the nature of human perception
the forces of nature
conditioned by environment
imposes its pattern on matter or
mind
on the edge of death
a view of culture
ways to health
bird
the rise of capitalism
they wanted to play doctor
separation of capital and private property
syrup
sugar
gasoline
deer
crude oil
beet greens
dries on contact
the instrument of retribution
failure to control industrialism
recognition of genuine distress
the transformation of strips of
tillage into pasture
the Negro slave had no property generally
who made the poor white the
cause of the planter's demise
she represents the Negro family
servant
passing from a warped childhood to a spinster's dream
world
she is both the ungainly peasant woman and frustrated old
maid

IV. Make a research project of your own for the behavior of near-nouns, considering as a starter the description of such phrases as *all boys, all of the boys, each boy, each of the boys, several blackbirds, several of the blackbirds, much mush, much of the mush, much of France, every boy, every one of the boys, a lot of boys, a lot of the boys, some boy, some of the boys, some boys,* and similarly with *both, other, others, few, one, two, the first, the second, the last.* How do these differ from *the brave boys, the bravest of the boys, the most beautiful flowers, the most beautiful of the flowers?*

V. It has been assumed in many recent grammars, especially structuralist grammars, that a clear line of demarcation can be drawn between intensifiers like *very, rather, quite, pretty,* and *-ly* forms that semantically denote intensity, like *thoroughly, simply, terribly, really, barely.* Since we have raised some doubt about the true existence of a separate form class of adverbs, having tentatively entertained the hypothesis that most adverbs in *-ly* were built on adjective (or participial) bases, and so might be considered adjectives fulfilling special functions in transformed or redistributed structures, consider the differences between the *-ly* forms in the following two groups:

1. *entirely too popular, he hardly danced, it matters terribly, a perfectly happy time, really ill, a thoroughly wretched urchin*

2. *swung her train expertly* (the swinging of her train was expert), *said clearly* (saying was clear), *they were irreproachably betrothed* (their betrothal was irreproachable), *he appeared mysteriously* (his appearance was mysterious), *not easily fixed* (fixing was not easy), *he had skipped out blithely* (his skipping out was blithe), *he spoke convincingly* (his speaking convinced), *his performance was surprisingly good* (the goodness of his performance was surprising)

Since you have not yet encountered the analysis of basic sentence patterns and of their transformations, this exercise must perforce be an exploratory one at this time. If you turn to collecting phrases containing *-ly* adverbs from some nearby body of prose, you may well find examples that do not conform to either of these patterns. Try it and see. Notice that the traditionalist would call most of the adverbs in Group 2 above "manner" adverbs. Does the manner relation no longer obtain in the paraphrase (i.e., in *the swinging of her train was expert*)? Does the evidence you have gathered encourage or discourage the need for forming a separate form class for adverbs?

5

BASIC PATTERNS OF
FORMAL PREDICATION

FORMAL PREDICATION

A sentence can be arbitrarily defined as a syntactic government containing at least one formal predication together with whatever modifiers are made to depend on it. A formal predication is a string of words or morphemes exhibiting the necessary formal features of subject-part and finite verb. Since a clause is defined here as any string of words containing a subject-part and a finite verb in concord with it, dependent clauses would qualify as formal predications. The definition of formal predications in this way is intentional, since both dependent and independent clauses can exhibit the necessary form of predication—subject and finite verb. But a dependent clause is not in itself a sentence because it has been transformed from independent status to a status of dependence upon some other structure by being prefaced by some such connector as *that, although, if, after, before,* or by the substitution of a relative pronoun for one of its key nouns or pronouns (except that sometimes relative pronouns or the *that* particle introducing noun clauses are deleted and appear only as zero forms). A sentence, thus, contains at least one formally independent predication. We need not get bogged down in argument about the terminology to be used when two or more independent formal predications are coordinated (with *and, but, or,* or *for*) or are joined together without a formal coordinator by means of a semicolon or comma in asyndetic parataxis. These are questions of local ground rules which do not materially affect the principal discriminations by which we decide what is and what is not a sentence. Thus, the question of whether or not a sentence can properly begin with a coordinating conjunction can be ruled out of court. That is something for someone other than a definer of sentences to worry about.

Similarly, speakers and writers often have occasion to mark off with terminal intonation signals or marks of punctuation a word or group of words that do not have the essential features of a formal predication, present and functioning. As we noted in the introductory chapter, many an actual utterance will imply its subject-part or its predicate-part from the context or from the environment or will supply it in some non-verbal fashion—by gesture, facial expression, or accompanying picture. Language is only one means of communicating meaning. If we have a cartoon representing some known human being—say Napoleon—busily eating cakes cut to resemble the map shapes of European states, with the caption beneath it "Glutton!" the communication is not simple and is part verbal and part non-verbal; we might not agree on which is the subject-part and which the predicate-part of the predication. The very concept of predication is largely based on the use of verbal structures for communicating meaning. It represents the simplification of meaning to the possibilities of a symbolic structure to which the communicator commits himself. In verbal predication an area of total meaning is apprehended at a certain point and the invasion of the area has a certain direction. If we have a picture of a fat boy gripping his stomach in pain, with smears around his mouth from what was perhaps a pie that he has eaten, we are invited to make a verbal commentary paralleling the meaning or meanings that seem to be suggested. But what is the subject-part of the meaning communicated and what is the predicate-part? We cannot even tell how many separate predications are implied in the picture. The definition of a sentence as an independent formal predication with or without attendant modifiers does not rule out the possibility that users of the English language may choose to communicate many of their meanings by forms that are not formal predications. This definition, as we have said, is arbitrary. It starts from a commonly applicable principle and becomes a basis for further discriminations.

In any formal predication there are to be found, explicitly or implicitly, two nuclei—a subject-part and a finite verb. In some languages a single word (a verb with inflection for person) can contain both nuclei: *amo, andiamo, allons.* Only in imperatives do we encounter this situation in English. The structuralist grammarians, who have been unwilling to grant the existence of implied forms, can argue with some reason that a formal predication with two nuclei is as much implied by the assertion "Fire!" (*A fire exists!*) as by the command "Come!" The issue, however, is whether or not a zero morpheme representing *you* can be said to be present in an imperative form of a verb. Some ellipses we all know exist (*I am eating pie, he cake*). Reduced predications, which cease to be formal predications as a result of being reduced, can also contain two nuclei—a subject-part and a predicate-part on the same level of subordination—but do not contain finite verbs (e.g., an absolute construction: *The wind having died in the night,* the boat was becalmed; *wind* is the head in the subject-part, *having died* the head in the predicate-part; the two are nuclei on the same level of subordination). The distinction we need to be clear about is that between formal predication with its two nuclei of subject and finite verb present either in word or morpheme (even a zero morpheme) and predication that does not have this full explicit form even though it may have two nuclei. The main difference is the presence of a finite verb form in formal predication. Before we can proceed with analysis of the reductions or transformations of formal predications, we must first determine the basic varieties or patterns of formal predications that are subject to reduction or transformation.

THE DIFFICULTY OF DETERMINING THE EXACT NUMBER OF BASIC SENTENCE PATTERNS

For practical purposes, arriving at a fixed number of basic sentence patterns should be avoided whenever possible. If a sentence presents us with a basic pattern, we should not be able to show that that sentence represents a putting together of two or more predications or that it can be seen as a rearrangement of parts from a sentence that is more primitive, or more basic, in structure. There are times, however, when, if we consider both structure and meaning, this cannot be done satisfactorily. Consequently, we must consider structure primarily, and meaning or equivalencies in meaning only secondarily, if at all. Differences among basic patterns can be seen to exist almost entirely in differences in the predicate-part of sentences. Variations in subject forms come in the area of transforms, not of basic patterns. The difference in meaning between "Dogs growl" and "Dogs emit growls" is slight. In basic structure, however, we find in these sentences the difference between an intransitive verb *growl* which predicates by means of the verb something that can be said about dogs without requiring a nominal complement called a direct object, and, on the other hand, a predicate in which a verb relatively empty of descriptive content, *emit,* which is transitive, has been used to carry the predication structurally over upon the noun direct object *growls.* This is a difference of basic structural pattern in the predicate-part of the two assertions. But that is all it is. We have no sure way of knowing that *growl* was originally a noun or a verb, and the knowledge would not be particularly relevant to current usage if we had it. When we turn to the more complex problems of transformations, however, the differences between these two basic forms do become important, for an intransitive verb cannot be subjected to a "passive transformation." That is, we cannot subject *Dogs growl* to the same kind of standard transformation that we find in *Growls are emitted by dogs,* in which the direct object has become the subject, the former subject has become part of an agentive phrase after the preposition *by,* and the verb has changed its form to a phrase consisting of the second participle and a preceding auxiliary consisting of the appropriate form of *be.* Furthermore, some differences between *dogs growl* and *dogs emit growls* show up in the transformations of these basic patterns into nominal phrases of reduced predication: *dogs' growling, the growling of dogs* (where the subject *dogs* appears only as a subjective genitive or as its analytic equivalent *of dogs* and no rendition of the equivalent of a passive is possible); as over against *dogs' emitting of growls, growls' being emitted by dogs, the dogs' emitting growls, the dogs' emission of growls, growls' emission by dogs,* etc. (granted that *emission* is not normally used in this range, by happenstance, since many a verb similarly formed will receive this transformation in standard diction).

Another basic difference in the structure of predicate parts can be seen in the option between the use of a copulative verb plus predicate noun or adjective and the use of an intransitive verb.

(Transitives are not excluded from the option, but we need to take one thing at a time.) It has already been said that one of the characteristic functions of nouns and adjectives is to act as "predicators" when these parts of speech are in the position of predicate nouns or adjectives after copulative verbs. The copulative verb *to be* in most of its range is merely a formal sign or assertion of predication, except that it can also assume some of the other predicating signals that can be attached to finite verbs, such as tense, person, number, and perfect or progressive aspect. It can form verb phrases with modal auxiliaries. But these are all formal functional additions to a verb base that is also formally functional, without specific lexical content. In part of its range *to be* has the meaning of *to exist,* which has lexical content—or a shadow of it (as in *There is a high wall on the north side of the garden*). But in the pure copula relation—which *to be* most often signals—the lexical content of the predicate is carried by the noun, adjective, or other unit that follows the copula. As a result, there is often a similarity of meaning but a marked difference of structure between subject + intransitive verb, and subject + copulative verb + predicate adjective. (*Dogs growl* as over against *Dogs are growly.*) We note the frequency in the literary language of periphrastics after copulas lexically doing the work of intransitive verbs (*I was in a rage against him* as over against *I raged against him*). Consider the difference between *This contradicted that* and *This was a contradiction of that.* Presumably, progressive verb phrases can only with difficulty be distinguished from predicates made up of the copula + participle or adjective (*Birds are flying,* birds are *flying,* birds are *in flight*), except that a clear-cut adjective can be qualified by an intensifier. We can say "This book was *very interesting* to me": but not "This book was *very interesting* me." In *The birds are all flying, all* is not an intensifier but a redistributed near-noun or pre-determiner. Even though verb phrases of progressive aspect appear to resemble copulas + predicate adjectives, since the forms of *be* are used as auxiliaries in rendering the progressive aspect, the two structures must be kept separate. Our language, with its heavy use of analytic devices, courts such ambiguities.

An even more difficult distinction is illustrated in such structures as *He was unable to go, This dress is ready to wear, He was willing to put up the money, He was capable of doing anything.* These structures are not all exactly alike. Insofar as *He was un-*

able to go does the work of *He could not go* we can think of it as a periphrasis of auxiliary and verb and can entertain the hypothesis that copula + certain adjectives + infinitives can constitute a kind of verb phrase. What is the relationship between *He was willing to put up the money* and *He would put up the money*, or between *This dress is ready to wear* and *This dress can now be worn?* But what is important is that, however close these parallels of function are, the structures are identifiable and distinct. We see another problem in the parallel between *It appears that he is no good* and *It is apparent that he is no good.* In both *it* is a "dummy" or "proxy" construction: *That he is no good appears (is apparent).* Actually, other structures exert influence on the formation of these constructions. Notice in connection with the phrasing of the preceding sentence the parallel between *exert influence* (transitive verb with little lexical content), *influence* (transitive verb from the former object), and *have been influential in* (copula and adjective).

THREE BASIC PATTERNS

By this approach to classification of basic sentence types, however, we look at difficulties first and resort to simplifications afterwards. The three most obvious basic patterns are:

1. Subject + intransitive verb
2. Subject + transitive verb + direct object (with or without indirect object)
3. Subject + copulative verb (*be*) + predicate noun, predicate adjective, or whatever other phrase or clause or kind of construction can function as predicator after a copula

Beyond the complications already hinted at that can stand in the way of our considering these three as the only basic patterns, certain other patterns should be scrutinized. The question should be: Are other possible patterns merely extensions or highly specialized applications of these three patterns, or should they be listed as separate patterns? Since it has been possible to make a list of these three only by starting at a center of readily observable frequency of occurrence and strong similarity of pattern in spite of local differences, it would be better for us to try to treat variations as variations as much as possible.

The meaning of some predicate parts of sentences containing

intransitive verbs is not complete without an adverbial complement or some construction operating in lieu of an adverbial complement. But can we pay heed to meaning, as over against grammatical structure, to the extent of distinguishing between certain kinds of adverbials that are complements and other kinds that are modifiers, perhaps worked into a basic sentence by early transformation? Consider the principal clause in "After years of wandering, *Ulysses came home."* The expression *Ulysses came* seems to be grammatically as well as semantically incomplete, or would seem to be so in some contexts. In one such as *Ulysses came last night,* the fact that he came home seems unimportant, but now we can imagine an emphasis which would make of *last night* a necessary complement. *Home* represents a "place" and *last night* a "time" relation. If we attempt to create a separate basic sentence pattern in which what some traditionalist grammarians have called "an adverbial object" is considered a necessary complement, can we restrict such complements to place and time relationships, or must we admit the possibility that words, phrases, or clauses expressing other relationships often thought of as basically adverbial can function as necessary complements? In "But Jack *did* get here quickly," the manner adverb *quickly* seems to be semantically a basic component of the predication. If we can admit adverbs expressing an assortment of relations to status of complement, do we need to multiply our number of basic sentence patterns by the number of possible components that can be found together in a sentence that adheres otherwise to a basic pattern: *They arrived* (1) *home* (2) *quickly* (3) *last night?* Surely, in the usual run of sentences that we encounter, a great many such adverbs are not necessary complements but are what can be called either restrictive modifiers of the verb or gratuitous additions (hence included material by some process of transformation). To draw a line between the functioning of particles with verbs when the particles are an integral part of the verb meaning and that of particles that are oblique enough and variable enough to be considered within the range of complements is almost an impossibility (*They held up the bank* as against *He held the glass up;* both positions for *up* can be used in both sentences). We should think of these complexities as disorderly extensions of the orderly three basic patterns. Adverbial complements (if such things exist) can be found with transitive as well as with intransitive verbs (*I brought it home*).

In the formula of the basic sentence pattern of subject + transitive verb + direct object, option was given for the presence or not of an indirect object. By this arrangement a sentence containing an indirect object conforms to the same pattern as one with merely a direct object. This does not entirely make sense, but is a move prompted by expediency and the desire to keep the number of basic patterns as small as possible. It is sometimes said that in English an indirect object never appears without a direct object accompanying it; this is a dubious proposition. In *Johnny, you tell me right now!* one might argue that the direct object—stating what is to be told—is implied in the context, but it at least does not appear explicitly. In *He told me about it* it is hard to believe that *about* is not a preposition, or that the relation of *me* to *told* is any different from what it is in *He told me a story.* In the past, certain purists basing their grammar principally on Latin practice have denied that it is possible to convert the indirect object of an active sentence into the subject of a passive sentence: *We gave Sarah a farewell present* > *Sarah was given a farewell present (by us).* This we know is standard practice among us. In setting up basic sentence patterns, we must not confuse ourselves with transforms unless they can be useful in testing differences in the basic patterns. That indirect objects as well as direct objects can become subjects in passive transforms discourages setting up a separate pattern for them, particularly if allowing for a separate one when both direct object and indirect object are present would entail setting up still another one when a direct object is not present—or the relic of it in a passive transformation. It is also necessary to avoid becoming ensnarled in the problems raised by the parallel functions of inflected and periphrastic indirect objects (expression by word order and zero inflection as contrasting to the prepositional phrase form: *gave to him,* in contrast to *gave him*).

KINDS OF OBJECTS

A great deal of energy—probably too much—has been expended by modern grammarians on the multiple distinctions necessary to make clear the differences between indirect objects, direct objects, and the so-called objective complements. For many reasons, the solution sometimes arrived at—to make distinction only between one-object, two-object, and three-object constructions, without attempt to discriminate among them in any instance—is quite unsatisfactory. The effort here will be to remove the problems relating to so-called objective complements (I considered him a *fool*) as much as possible from the area of basic sentence patterns and to assign them instead to the area of transformations and included predications. In some instances, the evidence does not completely support this disposition. Language, in evolving, is capable of certain hybridizings and "feedbacks," so that certain kinds of constructions that seem to be quite orderly are in the old neo-classical sense "monsters."

In most instances, the unit comprised of so-called direct object and so-called objective complement should be considered as the reduction of a predication, so that the whole unit (*him a fool*) functions as a direct object. The basic pattern among the varieties should be the infinitive phrase having its own subject, as in "I like *little boys to be quiet.*" The clause *that little boys be quiet* contains a verb *be* that has undergone an alteration or transformation found often in dependent clauses from the *should be* of independent clauses: *Little boys should be quiet* > *that little boys be quiet* > *little boys to be quiet.* With *be* a further reduction is possible: *little boys quiet,* as in *I like little boys quiet.* This elimination of the copula infinitive or participle or finite form is a notable feature of reduced constructions of many kinds. Consequently, the standard pattern for this unit of object-objective complement should be interpreted as subject and predicator in what is substantially an infinitive phrase having its own subject, with *to be* optionally omitted if the implied relation is a copula. Thus, the objective complement need not only be a noun or pronoun; it can be any kind of construction that can complete a copula predication:

I found him a *bore.*	I consider this *a great discovery.*
I found him *anxious to be gone.*	I considered it *necessary.*
I found him *in my way all the time.*	This put me *in a quandary.*
I found him *home.*	You make me *nervous.*

Further treatment of some of these matters will be found in the chapter on Infinitives and Infinitive Phrases. The immediate thesis is that this kind of construction needs to be dealt with under the heading of transformations, not of basic sentence patterns. But three things make this solution difficult: (1) the subject parts of these reduced predications can be transformed into the subjects of the higher predications within which the reductions are included; (2) in some instances the subject part of the reduced unit also functions as the direct object of the verb, so that syntactically it has a double valence; and (3) it is sometimes next to impossible to distinguish between an objective complement and what Jespersen called a "result adjunct."

In sentences such as *He was considered a bore by everyone* or *This move was considered necessary,* we are dealing with passive transforms in which the subjects (*he* and *this move*) seem to resemble the direct-objects-made-into-subjects that we usually expect in such transforms. The rendition *That this move was necessary was considered (by someone)* does not seem appropriate to the meaning. But *This move was considered* also alters the meaning. The construction seems to imply a meaning somewhere between the two renditions. Much depends upon the exact lexical meaning of the verb—whether that meaning fits squarely within the range of ideas that can be followed by a predicational object or not. The often-cited, structurally ambiguous *Call me a taxi* ("You are a taxi, sir!") can present *me* either as indirect object, as direct object, or as subject-part of a predicational direct object *me a taxi.* (*He called me an egghead* is a somewhat more than simple reduction of *He said that I was an egghead.* Notice that only under strain can we come up with a passive version of *He said that I was an egghead,* but *I was called an egghead* comes easily.) These complexities reveal the double valence of *me* after *called*—one value as object of *called* and another as subject of the predication reduced from *I am an egghead.* The line is hard to draw between this situation and that of *We saw him reach his hand into the till* (an infinitive phrase object) or *We found him sitting near the lake* (which can be considered a transformation of *When we found him he was sitting near the lake;* in *We found him sitting near the lake studying his geology, sitting* and *studying* are not necessarily parallel and coordinate). The range of what can appear as reduced clauses is not the same in all languages. In Latin, infinitive phrases are used after *dicere* (say) (*Caesar dixit se proficisci*—"Caesar said that he would set out") where we would use a noun clause. In other instances, particularly when a verb was followed directly by an inflected dative or ablative noun or pronoun, the speaker of Latin would have to repeat a referent where the speaker of

English can let the subject part of an infinitive phrase do double duty (*I told him that he should go* as against *I told him to go*).

When we say that in a passive transformation direct objects become subjects, we are not saying that all subjects of passive verbs have come to that position by way of being direct objects of active verbs. Indirect objects, as we have seen, can become subjects of passive verbs. Likewise, reduced predications in the object position can become split in a passive transformation so that the subject part becomes subject of the passive verb and the predicate part is left as retained object. Objects with double valence function in this transformation in general just as subject-parts of reduced predications do. But we have no grounds for constituting a separate kind of basic sentence pattern for sentences with objective complements. These come in the territory of reductions and transformations.

Another kind of problem occurs in making a distinction, if one is possible, between objective complements and "result adjuncts." Be it said that not all result adjuncts express precisely the relationship of result. In *He painted the barn red, red* is clearly adjectival in form, as is *clean* in *He washed the windows clean.* We can understand a possible subject-predicate relation between *barn* and *red* and *windows* and *clean* (*The barn is now red, The windows are now clean*). Chomsky and Roberts, in their transformational grammars, have mandated a rearrangement of terms in handling this construction that makes the adjunct substantially part of the verb phrase: "He *painted* the barn red" > "He *painted red* the barn"; "He *washed* the windows clean" > "He *washed clean* the windows." They give objective complements much the same treatment. For machine operations this handling will no doubt work, but for an understanding of the manipulation of predications in grammatical transformations it is merely obscurantist, and in ignoring the forms that are manipulated it tells us nothing about them. Chomsky and Roberts are presumably justified when the final item resembles a verb particle as in *He held the glass up* (*He held the glass so that it was up*) > *He held up the glass.* In our normal phrasing we are likely to put this adjunct next to the verb if the apparent object is long and cumbersome, as in "He painted *red* that side of the house that faced toward his neighbors." The ambiguity of the construction lies in whether the adjunct predicates something about the verb meaning or about the object. Since in some instances the predication is obviously of the one, and in others of the other, we are in no position to decide categorically, but must describe the construction as we find it, in all its variations. In a grammar based upon the manipulation of predications—their re-arrangements, reductions, and transformations—the whole range of these constructions should be dealt with under the heading of reduced predications, not under that of basic sentence structures.

COPULA VARIANTS AND RELATED STRUCTURES

A quite different kind of problem in the listing of basic sentence types has to do with the handling of sentences with verbs that function like copulas in some respects and yet are not precisely copulas. Examples are *become, remain, grow, get, seem, look, ring, appear, taste, smell, sound, stay,* and some others. These do not all behave similarly. Some, like *become* and *remain* resemble *be* in that they can be followed by either nouns or adjectives as predicate complements (*He became good, He became a hero; He remained good, He remained the stout athlete he had always been*). *Get* and *grow* in colloquial expressions where the meaning is much like that of *become,* are completed only by adjectives unless *to be* is added (*He got rich, He grew to be a substantial citizen*).

Look, seem, and *appear* form another sub-class. What we are faced with in these verbs is a change of function from former impersonal constructions or other usages. The use of *to be* with *seem* is instructive: *His idea seems sound* < *His idea seems to be sound* < *It seemeth that his idea is sound* (the resultant sentence is in effect a transformation by redistribution as well as reduction); *That seems to be a good idea* (*It seemeth that that is a good idea*), *That seems* (?) *a good idea.* The impersonal construction with *seems* was disappearing, however, even in Old English. Usage with *look* is uncertain and subject to much variation. We could possibly set up special sub-classes of basic sentence patterns for each of these groups, perhaps even for each of the verbs; but since in the main they seem to be slight deviations from the copula, we can dispense with separate classification so long as we realize that the copula *be* is capable of these variations. The copulative uses of *taste, smell, sound* (followed by predicate adjectives) are likewise apparent, even though some semanticists might argue that a redistribution is involved here: *The taste of that is good* > *That tastes good.* In general, it is impossible to account for all semantic redistributions in the midst of a description of basic sentence patterns. Thus, we must argue that the verb *toasts* in *This bread toasts well* is an intransitive active verb in form, however much semantically it may be a substitute for a passive. Verbs expressing meanings of feeling, like *feel, taste, smell, sound*, can, in their uses as hybrid copulas, be followed only by adjectives, not by predicate nouns.

Can we define with any precision such a thing as a hybrid construction, particularly as something distinct from a transformed construction, and if we can, should we make room for certain kinds of hybrid patterns among basic sentence patterns? The answer is probably "no" to each part of the question. A troublesome example of the problem alluded to here is found in the structure of intransitive verb + adjective when the adjective seems to function somewhere between a predicate adjective (following *be*) and a result adjunct (bang *shut*, blow *open*, break *loose*). The result adjunct, however, follows a direct object after a transitive verb, but the adjective forms we are now considering follow intransitive verbs and of necessity come directly after them. Note the difference in the use of *open* in "He kicked the door *open*" (result adjunct) and in "The door blew *open*." The lexical meaning of *blew* is dubious. It is wind that "blows." What happens to the door is that it "becomes open." The intransitive verbs that function in this construction are extensional "substitutes" for the copula *be* or for such semi-copulative verbs as *become, remain, stay,* or *get.* The word *blushed* in *She blushed red* means in effect "to become red"; so that the word *red* is actually redundant: *She became red red.* Other examples of this hybrid construction are *come high, come clean, continue cold, fall sick, fly open, go gray, hold true, keep young, lie flat, loom large, make good, prove true, rest easy, ring true, run dry, shine bright, show pink, sit still, stand straight, turn black, wear thin, work loose.*[1] Many of these examples are set phrases and are highly idiomatic. Hybridizing of this kind is a lexical and not a structural matter. We cannot, consequently, set up a separate basic sentence pattern for this construction. Neither can we include it under transformations unless we can think of including lexical equivalents under transformations; this is an impossibility.

[1] These examples are abstracted from a more diversified list given in C. C. Fries, *The Structure of English* (New York, 1952), pp. 135–37.

Finally, distinction should be made concerning the sentence containing what Curme called a "predicate appositive." The predicate appositive does represent a transformation. In the sentence *He died rich*, two predications are implied: *he died* and *he was rich*. The sentence could be recast as *When he died, he was rich* and effect only a structural change. A predicate appositive can be either a noun or an adjective (or perhaps any other kind of unit that can function as a predicate complement after a copulative verb, but this leads us to structural ambivalences): *He died rich* or *He died the richest man in the state; He arrived home broke* or *He arrived home a hero*. Only adjectives can function as complements in phrases like *keep young or lie flat*.

Therefore, even though good reasons exist for expanding the number of basic sentence patterns to some ten to fifteen types, we can, with some relaxation of rigidities, reduce the number to three. These are:

1. Subject and intransitive verb (with possible adverbial complement): *John comes, John comes home.*
2. Subject, transitive verb, and direct object (with or without indirect object or adverbial complement): *He brought the package, He brought me the package, He brought the package home.*
3. Subject, copula, and predicate complement: *I am a man, I am good, I am in a hurry, I am home.*

Out of these and a few variants of these, by means of a variety of transformations (reductions, inclusions, and re-distributions) almost all of the sentences of English can be built.

It will be observed that in these pattern sentences some function words appear that are not accounted for in the description of these basic sentence patterns—determiners like *a* and *the* in particular. In removing determiners from the form class of adjectives we imply that they need not be dealt with under the heading of transformations. The same can be said of modal auxiliaries of verb phrases. So far as basic sentence patterns are concerned, no distinction need be made between *He brought me the package* and *He could have been bringing me the package*. In the exact description of noun phrases or verb phrases accounting would, of course, have to be made for these possible complications, as well as for the use of near-nouns and pre-determiners, for the substitution of pronouns for nouns, or for the use of words from minor function groups such as *yes, no, please, let's, say, oh, golly,* etc. But these matters are not part of our determination of basic sentence patterns.

MATERIALS FOR EXERCISE AND FURTHER STUDY

I. Which of the following word groups are formal predications?

1. since De Greve might have visited the monastery in 1116
2. on his accession to the throne
3. whether to explore the Mission Range or turn south toward Idaho
4. that he be there
5. what there was to expect from the meeting
6. Hugh made him an offer
7. one laughing and one crying
8. him to announce his marriage plans
9. the Sunday school teacher being the first to recognize the danger
10. had we the right to choose or not to choose
11. good work
12. if you will only stop sulking
13. the effect was good
14. why he did that
15. after whose grandfather the town was named
16. in signing away his rights to the farm
17. sailing to the far corners of the earth
18. keep to the right
19. shall we join them
20. where the Shannon reaches the sea

II. Study the functions of the verb *be* that appear here. In which instances is the functioning purely copulative (i.e., signaling predication and no more) and in which instances is there some shade of lexical content (the meaning of *exist*)?

1. I want all the money there is in the world.
2. The youngest was very intelligent.
3. What he really wanted was to be the center of attention.
4. That idea has never been very new.
5. Those signatures had been for years on many similar petitions.
6. This time, however, there was something startlingly different.
7. It was impossible simultaneously to raise the standard of living and increase the means of production.
8. The high school students are increasingly restless.

9. He is up against the same problems.
10. He could not decide what there was to do next.
11. The natives you encounter should be friendly.
12. The creation of large, open interior spaces by the elimination of interior walls had been one of the innovations of the best architects of the preceding century.
13. Dark nights there were, in that part of my life, when it seemed that dawns would never come.
14. We needed to know who the Smiths really were.
15. There's no doubt that too much affection is better than too little.

III. In the following sentences distinguish between direct objects, indirect objects, objective complements, and result adjuncts (or closely related constructions):

1. They found him a good place to live up in the hills.
2. Marat found him an untrustworthy ally in an emergency.
3. George found his twin sister in Cincinnati.
4. We are going to find us a good man as president next time.
5. They then proceeded to run him ragged.
6. The host left the seats vacant for us.
7. My uncle left me an old house in his will.
8. The leaders of the business community thought the scheme harebrained and worthless.
9. The new turn of events presented the evangelists the opportunity they had been waiting for.
10. The *Times* critic called it turgid and unevenly-paced.
11. He described it as turgid and unevenly-paced.
12. His endowment gave the society a new lease on life.
13. He made his son a new slingshot.
14. He made his son a hero in his neighbors' eyes.
15. The counter-move rendered him powerless.
16. He pinned his opponent down in fourteen seconds.
17. The news of the bank failure knocked him speechless.
18. Shall I mark him absent this morning?
19. What can furnish them a better way to redeem themselves than this?
20. The reapportionment scheme allotted the southern counties two additional representatives.

IV. This is a project in attempting to define the nature and range of adverbial complements that cannot easily be excluded from basic sentence patterns. Which of the words or phrases in the following sentences can be identified as adverbial complements of some sort or as constructions functioning in the expression of relations that in older grammars were usually identified with adverbial modification? Identify the relationships. In Chapter 6, pre-positional adjective modifiers will be explained as transformed predicate adjectives; the implication is that their presence need not be accounted for in basic sentence patterns.

In Exercise V of Chapter 4, it was implied that many -*ly* forms likewise represented transforms, in which the adjectives from which the -*ly* forms were derived predicated something about the nominal concepts buried in the verbs or related to them (*he came quickly* deriving from *he came* and *his coming was quick*). Many of these -*ly* forms in surface grammar appear to stand in a manner relation to the verb. This is probably not true of forms that can be called adverbial complements. If such a thing as an adverbial complement exists and has to be accounted for in the area of basic sentence patterns and not in the area of transforms, it will be necessary to distinguish ultimately between adverbs that are complements and those that represent transforms or redistributions. The problem is made the more difficult when we move beyond -*ly* forms and take into consideration prepositional phrases, adverbial nouns, infinitive phrases, and even dependent clauses expressing relational concepts the significance of which might be complementary to a verb. Consider the redistribution of intransitive basic pattern to copula basic pattern in *I came yesterday* (a time adverbial-noun complement) to *Yesterday was when I came*. In studying the following sentences, attempt to separate complementary units from units that may be transforms, but do not be discouraged if your conclusions are not certain ones.

1. He peered into the darkness for some sign of the boat's return.
2. The group visited me every day of the week.
3. Why do you react so violently to my proposal?
4. The wall collapsed soon after the fire.
5. He put his car at my disposal.
6. He jumped a good fifty feet in clearing the obstacle.
7. They prowled the forest the whole night.
8. They did the job thoroughly.
9. We quickly went down the stairs immediately after the crash.
10. This invention can conceivably be called the greatest of its age.
11. The next morning he did the job efficiently with merely a hammer.
12. In the nineteenth century all men were not always equal.
13. The territory was neatly divided up and actually owned by absentee landlords.
14. He lost his grip on the one thing he dearly loved.

15. They distinctly appropriated it for the fiscal year ending on June 30th.
16. The symbolic structure is clearly implicit in the former play.
17. The son pauses to ask the blessing of his mother and father.
18. All things come in the end to him who waits.
19. After the next election his influence extended well into Maryland.
20. Even as a youth he was experienced in sifting historical evidence.

V. Distinction has been made in this chapter between (1) copula-variants like *become, seem, feel,* and *stay* (with sub-divisions); (2) hybrids of copula and intransitive verb; and (3) situations in which predicate appositives (which are transforms) are found. Which of these situations is found in the following sentences?

1. His idea seems to be a replica of one of yours.
2. He arrived full of energy for the job.
3. He became before the end of his life the leading authority on contract bridge.
4. He had sat shut up like that for a week.
5. The sign tore loose during the night.
6. The production job on the new book looked fine to him.
7. I know that you will think that this sounds crazy.
8. He remained in charge of advertising after the merger.
9. He came late to the party.
10. The door burst open and out came the Martians.
11. He grew fat in Transylvania.
12. He kept still at the meeting.
13. The machine continued inoperative for the next week.
14. The dory was snapped loose from the dock by the gale.
15. The situation did not look entirely hopeless.

6

FIRST LEVEL TRANSFORMATIONS

Some of the structural features of English grammar are of the kind that seem to be particularly useful to foreign students of the language and of no great importance to native speakers. The reason is that, though they are very complex and give important signaling of meaning, they come to be understood intuitively very early in life and our systematic analysis of them never quite catches up with the actual subtle distinctions we employ. Of this kind are the first level transformations by means of which we convert basic declarative sentences into questions, negations, and emphatic utterances—utterances that continue to be independent clauses. If a grammarian is trying to create rules for programming transformations for a computer—or is acting as if this is what he is doing in order to create a methodology for himself in the pursuit of precision of analysis—the description of the alteration in structures by which declarative sentences are turned into questions or are negated is as important as any other aspect of the grammar, for the computer becomes a kind of non-native user of English for whom all mechanisms are equally important. To the native speaker, however, the description of these transformations is likely to have value chiefly in the awe we can generate for ourselves and our abilities as we come to an imperfect understanding of the subtle mechanisms that we unconsciously employ. The fact is that in doing something as basic as turning a declaration into a question we have to be responsive to many fine discriminations in signaling; it is easy to form generalizations after scanning only part of the problem, so that the result is half-truth. Some schoolchildren are taught, for instance, that questions always end in a rise in pitch; unfortunately, there are several kinds of questions about which this generalization is not true.

QUESTION TRANSFORMATIONS

One principal way of subdividing questions is into that group for which the answer to the question is likely to be "yes" or "no," and into that group using interrogatives like *where, how, who,* to which the answer is something other than "yes" or "no." Since this present grammar is an attempt at a transformationalist description without having recourse to precise mechanistic transformation rules (on the ground that they are merely encumbrances for the native speaker), the transformations of basic declarative sentences to questions of these two main types will be shown merely by means of certain test sentence frames, and formulas or delineation of the several steps in the process will be avoided.

The simplest way of turning a declaration into a question is to change its intonation contour. The normal declarative sentence shows a 2–3–1 pitch pattern. We normally use four pitch levels, of which the 2-level is the normal level—sea-level, so to speak. In a declarative sentence the pitch rises near the end one level above the ordinary, and then either falls rather suddenly or dwindles off to a level below the ordinary 2-level. In a question the pattern may be 2–3–4 instead of 2–3–1. That is to say that the fall at the end may not occur; instead the pitch may rise to its highest level, above the 3-level. This can be shown by transforming a declarative sentence:

2   2 3 1
Pete is coming here.

This declaration can be turned into a question thus:

2   2 3 4
Pete is coming here?

There are so many variables, however, in a situation such as this that we may not be able to agree exactly about what we do in intoning the sentences. Questions of stress and juncture often interact with those of pitch. What happens to the pitch pattern if the speaker's intention is to put unusual stress upon *coming?*

$$\overset{2}{\text{Pete}} \quad \overset{2}{\text{is}} \quad \overset{4}{coming} \quad \overset{2}{\text{here}} \overset{2}{?}$$

Probably there is a rise to 4 but also a lowering of pitch thereafter. Pitch signals can, no doubt, alone suffice to convert a declaration to a question, but perhaps the signal is only by a deviation in one way or another from the norm. This kind of conversion is found much more often in other languages than in English.

The principal structural transformation in the building of "yes" and "no" questions from basic declarative sentences is the simple inversion of subject and the first item of a verb phrase (1) when the verb is the copula *be,* (2) when *be* is used as a function word in the formation of passive or verb phrases of progressive aspect, (3) when *have* is a function word in the formation of verb phrases of perfect aspect, or (4) when the first item in the verb phrase is a modal auxiliary. When the verb has none of these features, the function word *do* is introduced before the subject in whatever form is appropriate (tense or number) and the verb becomes an infinitive.

1. *You are a menace.* becomes *Are you a menace?*
   He is in a hurry. becomes *Is he in a hurry?*
   They were afraid. becomes *Were they afraid?*
2. *They are threatened.* becomes *Are they threatened?*
   They are being threatened. becomes *Are they being threatened?*
   They were compelled. becomes *Were they compelled?*
   The children were playing. becomes *Were the children playing?*
3. *The ghosts have departed.* becomes *Have the ghosts departed?*
   They have been here. becomes *Have they been here?*
   They have been compelled. becomes *Have they been compelled?*
   They have considered him the best of the lot. becomes *Have they considered him the best of the lot?*
4. *Cats can eat apples.* becomes *Can cats eat apples?*
   The cavalry will arrive in time. becomes *Will the cavalry arrive in time?*
   He ought to leave now. becomes *Ought he to leave now?*
   Children must obey their parents. becomes *Must children obey their parents?*
   I should have been reprimanded. becomes *Should I have been reprimanded?*

These verb phrases, we note, can be very simple or very complex and require in any case the simple inversion of the subject part and the first item of the verb phrase. In an uncomplex verb phrase like *eats* in *John eats hay*, the function word *do* has to be inserted in the formation of the corresponding question *Does John eat hay?* The same is true with verbs in the past tense: *John ate hay* becomes *Did John eat hay?* But when the verb form is passive, shows perfect or progressive aspect, or makes use of a modal auxiliary, either *be, have,* or a modal auxiliary will be the first element no matter how many of these are compounded together. Therefore, complication does not affect the simple principle of inversion. Sometimes, when the headword of the subject-part has long trailing modifiers, these may be separated from the headword in the question transform:

The men who have to depart for night duty at the mines have already eaten. becomes *Have the men already eaten who have to depart for night duty at the mines?* This is, however, more a rhetorical than a grammatical matter. The same separation may be possible on some occasions in the declarative forms. The separation would be more difficult in the illustrative sentence if the predicate were longer, as in *have already eaten a fine turkey dinner,* since there would now be ambiguity of reference for the relative pronoun.

The function word *do* is inserted when these other conditions do not prevail:

Birds fly. becomes *Do birds fly?*
The birds flew. becomes *Did the birds fly?*

Both *have* and *do* can be verbs with lexical content, not function words. When they are such, they act like other content verbs:

I have sixpence. becomes *Do I have sixpence?*
I did it. becomes *Did I do it?*

Have to (*I hafta go*) used in the sense of *must* is sometimes thought of as an auxiliary. It does not behave like one in the question transformation: *I have to go* becomes *Do I have to go?* Similarly, *dare* in *They dare go* becomes, not *Dare they to go?* but *Do they dare to go?*

When questions do not require a "yes" or "no" answer, we commonly find in them an interrogative word of the kinds that traditionally have been called interrogative pronouns or interrogative adverbs. In most instances this interrogative function word comes at the beginning of the question. One notable exception is found when the interrogative word is part of a prepositional phrase, which then moves in its entirety to the beginning of the question (*At what distance was the shot fired? From which window did the killer shoot? At how wide an angle was the shot fired?*). This frontal position is, however, optional, particularly in informal phrasings (*What distance was the shot fired at?* etc.). Since these interrogative words are pronouns or some other kind of substitute word, it is necessary in reconstructing the declarative sentences from which they are derived to fill in the space they occupy with some word of indeterminate meaning or with the essential part of the answer, as in *Pete saw (someone)* > *Whom did Pete see?* or *Pete lived (in Cincinnati)* > *Where did Pete live?*

Again, as with "yes" or "no" questions, we find that certain inversions are in order in the transformations if the verb is a form of *be,* or if the verb phrase begins with the function words *be* or *have* or with a modal auxiliary. Also the function word *do* is brought into use when these special conditions do not obtain, except that *do* is not used when an interrogative pronoun functions as subject of the question: (*Someone*) *saw John* > *Who saw John?* but *John saw (someone)* > *Whom (who) did John see?*

> (*Something*) *caused this happening* > *What caused this happening?*
> *John arranged this meeting* > *What did John arrange?* or *Who arranged this meeting?*
> *This is (some) kind of fish* > *What kind of fish is this?*
> *He can come (sometime)* > *When can he come?*
> *He must go (somewhere)* > *Where must he go?*
> *John is going to town in the morning* > *When is John going to town?* or *Where is John going in the morning?* or *Who is going to town in the morning?*
> *He was sent (somewhere)* > *Who was sent (somewhere)?* or *Where was he sent?*
> *He did that (in some way)* > *How did he do that?*
> *He kissed (one or another) girl* > *Which girl did he kiss?*

Notice the inversion of subject and first verb item, or lack of it, or use of function word *do* in the following assortment:

What kind of husband are you?	*What kind of husband did you catch?*

With whom are you going?   *With whom did you go?*
Who(m) did you go with?   *Who went with you?*

(It is sometimes said that ignorant people use *who* instead of *whom* in some places because they are incapable of distinguishing between a nominative and an objective function for the word. It is a source of some wonderment that these so-called ignorant people will for the most part put in the *did* in *Who did you go with?* and yet will not say *Who did go with you?*)

Which, what, and *whose* as interrogatives can function also as noun modifiers, though imperfectly, as we have already seen. *Which* and *what* become near-nouns in these usages. *Whose* is a genitive. The second genitive used as predicate complement (as in *mine, hers, yours*) is found, with the appropriate inversion in *Whose is this fish?* Other examples of *which, what,* and *whose* are:

Which cities did you visit?   *Which of the cities did you visit?*
Which city is the most beautiful?   *Which city will become biggest?*
Which city can be called the most beautiful?   *Whose little boy are you?*
Whose little boy did I spank?   *Whose fish did the cow eat?*
Whose little boy has he spanked?   *Whose fish has the cow eaten?*

It can be seen from close study of these instances that many finicky transformation rules would have to be written in order to handle precisely and mechanically all of the adjustments in phrasing that are necessary in turning basic declarative sentences into questions. And yet a small number of general principles control the larger number of variations. The most important of these are (1) the simple inversion of subject and first verb item with *be* as function word or as copula, with *have* as function word, and with modal auxiliaries; (2) the use of function word *do* with transitive and intransitive verbs unsupported by auxiliaries; and (3) the absence of these features when the interrogative is the subject or a modifier of the subject. The native speaker makes these adjustments readily and intuitively. The learner of English as a second language might find unduly tenuous all of these minor distinctions in the construction of phrasing.

NEGATION TRANSFORMATIONS

Another kind of first-level transformation is found in the negation of basic declarative sentences. Although it can hardly be argued, as has sometimes been claimed, that *not* is the only legitimate negator in English, it is with *not* that we are chiefly concerned, since *No man is here* and *Some man is here* are both basic sentences, whereas we may need rewrite rules to handle the structure of *The man is not here*. In this instance we do not need one except to assert that *not* is inserted following *is* and to indicate the possibility of contracting *is not* to *isn't*. For in sentences in which the verb is the copula *be*, or in which the first item of the verb phrase is *be* (as in the formation of passives or phrases of progressive aspect), the function word *have* (as in the formation of phrases of perfect aspect), or a modal auxiliary (such as *can, may, must, will, should, ought*), it is only necessary to insert *not* after this first item in order to negate the assertion, and, optionally, in informal styles, to allow contraction to take place. With simple transitive or intransitive verbs, however, in either present or past tense, the function word *do* is again brought into play followed by *not* (again contraction to *don't, doesn't,* or *didn't* is possible). In negations as in questions the function word *do* (or the other auxiliaries in their instances) absorbs the signals of tense and number, while the verb form undergoing transformation converts to the infinitive form. Thus:

He is a thief > *He is not (isn't) a thief.*
He was annoyed by her > *He was not (wasn't) annoyed by her.*
He was singing in the shower > *He was not (wasn't) singing in the shower.*
He was being chased > *He was not (wasn't) being chased.*
I have gone > *I have not (haven't) gone.*
I had heard that > *I had not (hadn't) heard that.*
Pete can swim > *Pete cannot (can't) swim.*
He will be here tomorrow > *He will not (won't) be here tomorrow.*

But when one of these auxiliaries or *be* is not present *do* is inserted and the verb changes to the infinitive form:

He succeeded > *He did not succeed.*
He expects to find you here > *He does not expect to find you here.*
He knows everything > *He does not know everything.*

While we are on the subject of negations, we need to inquire into what happens to the negating particle *not* in reduced predications. One of the best reasons for excluding the object-objective complement construction from basic sentence patterns and not considering the objective complement as part of the verb phrase is that it can be separately negated, or better, that it can render a clause containing *not* without interference to the negation, since in a transform grammar the evidence of change of structure or lack of it is more important than speculations of other kinds. For non-predicative units can also be negated, even with *not: Not everyone was willing to go.* In a sentence such as *She was not very far away,* it can be argued that *not* behaves normally after *was* as the negator of the predication rather than as a modifier of *very far away.* In *Not very far away stood a gazelle,* we find the normal pattern disrupted. Can we believe that this order represents a re-arrangement of *A gazelle did not stand very far away?* Hardly. Another, perhaps better, interpretation would be that the sentence represents a putting together of two predications: *A gazelle was not very far away* and *A gazelle stood.* (Remember our uncertainty concerning the handling of certain kinds of adverbial modifiers in the preceding chapter on basic sentence patterns.) All this takes us out of our depth. But these annoying complexities should remain with us when we scrutinize sentences such as the contrasting *We did not find these answers very satisfactory, We found these answers not very satisfactory, We found that these answers were not very satisfactory, We found these answers unsatisfactory.* The position of *not* before the infinitive in *We found these answers not to be very satisfactory* is standard. To be sure, *I want him not to do that* can be paralleled by the phrasing *I do not want him to do that.* What we are looking at here is in part the ability of the language to negate unambiguously and in part its ability to use double or triple negatives. Is it impossible (un-English) even to negate two parts of one verb phrase, as in *John should not have not been singing* or *John should not have been not singing* or (to carry the principle to absurdity) *John should not have not been not singing?* This problem, of course, is quite different from that of the so-called double-negative: *I don't want no supper.* In our normal phrasing we often have an option between *I consider him not a very good risk* and *I do not consider him a good risk;* in our colloquial phrasing we give the nod to the latter, even though it represents a distortion of the logic of the situation. In *I don't want him to go,* it is not *want* that is negated but *him;* the logic is *not to go.* Only when both the matrix and the included predication are negated can we come face to face with the nature of the situation, as in *I don't want him not to avail himself of his opportunities.* In the more common situation of *I don't want him to go* we hide the reduction of predication in the interest of the more standard pattern representing the first-level transformation of basic sentences.

We find another deviation from the standard transforming in negations in dependent clauses in which the verb can be called a subjunctive. We say *I demand that you not go* instead of *I demand that you do not go.* In *I insist that he not be present,* we should perhaps imagine the presence of *should* between *he* and *not*—a modal to supplant the subjunctive; the construction would then follow the usual pattern.

The verbs of the assorted classes of *become, remain, stay, taste, smell, sound,* which behave in some respects like the copula *be,* pattern like the usual transitive or intransitive verbs in negations and questions:

> *Did he ever become famous? He didn't become famous until later.*
> *How long did he stay at home? He didn't stay there long.*
> *Does this pie taste good to you? It doesn't taste right.*

This fact in itself demonstrates the difficulty of trying to reduce to a minimum the number of basic sentence patterns on the basis of one set of criteria (as, for instance, classing *become* as a kind of copula because it can be followed by either noun or adjective as predicate complement, when even in first-level transformations of questions and negations its behavior is that of transitive and intransitive verbs), without allowing for an extensive gamut of hybrids. Either the number of basic sentence patterns becomes large and so unwieldy, or the transformations of the deliberately reduced number of basic patterns cannot be applied mechanically. But the behavior of basic patterns in transformations should provide checks and balances for our discriminations about basic patterns.

The question now arises: What happens when question and negation occur together? The answer is that practically no new adjustments have to be made, since the two transformations use almost identical devices in operating separately. One exception —the behavior of the first person present tense of *be* (*I am*)—is actually an exception to the simple rule of negative transforms, not of putting the two kinds together, since *am not* does not contract to *amn't* (note the invitation to *ain't*). Thus, we say *Haven't I gone? Shouldn't I go? Must not he go? Can't I go? Isn't he going? Didn't he go? Don't I eat hay?* but the *not* does not precede the subject in *Am I not going?* although we will find it pre-

positionally in *Isn't he going?* or *Aren't they going?* It is true
that without the contractions we are at liberty to move the *not*
after the subjects in the rest of the cases.

A special kind of negation or affirmation is found in that peculiar structure comparable to the French *C'est bon, n'est-ce pas?*
as in *They are teachers, aren't they? They aren't teachers, are
they? They work here, don't they? They don't work here, do
they?* in which the negations seem to affirm and the affirmations
to negate.

PASSIVE TRANSFORMATIONS

Another different and important kind of first-level transformation is that in which basic sentences of the kind employing
transitive verbs are changed into corresponding structures employing passive verb forms. The simple pattern of the change is
that the object of the active transitive verb becomes the subject
of the passive form (in some instances indirect objects can become the subjects), the verb form undergoes certain describable
changes, and the subject of the active verb—if it appears at all
and is not deleted—is expressed as the object of an agentive prepositional phrase. Since in our actual use of language we commonly
use stock phrasings, we are at times unaware of or are indifferent to the specification of the agent in a passive predication. We
may for this reason delude ourselves into thinking that this notion of the derivation of passive forms by transformation from
active forms lacks reality. We are, however, talking directly
about structures, not about meanings. When we say *Ten men
were drafted into the army from this county last month,* only
with difficulty can we specify what agency did the drafting, and
in some kind of ultimate logic it may be argued that this expression never has had, and in no way implies the prior existence
of, an active form. But this is to argue in terms of meaning
alone, not in terms of the evolution of structures. Many verbs
that are active in form may imply, semantically, an action upon
the subject: *This bread toasts well, this car drives easily.* These
sentences represent a semantic, not a structural, shift. Some languages, like Greek, have a "middle voice" somewhere between the
active and the passive that can be put to various uses—uses that
in our different language with our own set of structures we may
express with either active or passive forms. It should be obvious

that in our search for basic sentence patterns we were right in making the active forms basic and in considering the passive forms as transformations, since the passive verb phrases are always complex forms while some of the active forms are simple. When verb phrases are reduced to participles in the kind of semi-predication we call participial phrases, passive participles may seem as simple in form as active participles (that is, *bent* may seem as simple as *bending*), but to say that is to ignore the relative complexity of the processes of transformation through which the constructions have gone. In working out a transformational grammar we must not confuse the equivalencies of structure with total significances.

The passive forms of verbs are constructed in English by means of the appropriate form of the verb *be* used as an auxiliary. As with most verbal constructions using auxiliaries, it is this auxiliary *be* that undergoes change to express the finite conditions (unless another auxiliary precedes it); it changes form to show person, number, tense, and aspect: *I am controlled, he is controlled, they are controlled, he was controlled, they were controlled, they will be controlled* (tense by analytic phrasing, not mood), *I have been controlled, he has been controlled, they had been controlled, they will have been controlled.* If modality is also expressed, the modal auxiliary begins the phrase (modals can express only distinctions of present and past tense, and can combine with other forms to show only some aspects), the *be* remains in its infinitive form (as we have already seen in *they will be controlled: we can be controlled, we could be controlled, we can have been controlled, we could have been controlled, they shall have been controlled, they should have been controlled*). We notice that in the instances of perfect aspect *be* is converted to its second participial form *been* as it usually is in such constructions involving the copula. In passive forms of progressive aspect the first participial form *being* is used to express aspect; therefore, in such phrases we can have one form of *be* used to create the passive and another to express progression: *I am being controlled, I was being controlled.* Duplication of forms of *be* in a conjunction of perfect and progressive aspect is highly unlikely in the paradigm of the passive forms, though theoretically possible: *I have been being controlled, they had been being controlled.* Not all second participles are formed by the addition to the verb stem of the suffix -*ed,* even though this is today their most common form.

One group of the so-called strong verbs makes use of the suffix *-en* (*drive, driven, give, given,* etc.), and those grammarians who attempt a formulistic, mechanical description of the passive transformation have been using the *-en* symbol to represent whatever change is necessary in the verb to convert it to a second participial form. Other odd varieties of second participles are *hit, sunk, spent, sung, lost, sown, sewn.* This second participial form is most commonly used in passive constructions, and there is little justification for calling it the "past participial" form since in none of its uses does it reveal tense. Intransitive verbs do not, however, have corresponding passive forms, and yet have second participial forms used in verb phrases of active perfect aspect (not expressing tense—the form of *have* does that): *he has departed, he had walked.* In such semi-predications or reduced predications as participial phrases or absolute constructions, these second participial forms occur only (with very few exceptions, such as *gone*) with passive signification unless they occur with *having.* We should therefore discard the term "past participle" in English and call this modification of the verb the "second participle" when indicating its form. If we use the term "passive" participle, we refer to one of the two main functions of the "second" participle. When second participles through transformation come to occupy the position preceding nouns normally occupied by adjectives (*controlled experiments*), either the passive sense is conveyed or the word has actually undergone a semantic shift and become an adjective. In nominal transforms of predications, when a verb of a finite predication becomes an abstract noun (*the organization of the company*), the noun is incapable of showing distinction between active and passive, although the gerund form that closely parallels the abstract form is capable of the distinction (*the company's being organized* or *the company's having been organized* contrasting with *his organizing the company*).

We must realize that in the English language the passive voice in its entire paradigm exists only in analytic phrasings, and the fine problems of distinction that arise in connection with analytic constructions are not necessarily the same at all as those that occur in a language with a synthetic verb system, such as Latin. Participles, of either the first or second variety (*-ed* or *-ing*), behave in some ways like adjectives and in some cases should be classed as adjectives. We may rule that *interesting* in *This is interesting me very much* is part of the verb phrase of progressive aspect *is interesting,* while in *This is very interesting to me* it is a predicate adjective since the intensifier *very* is attached to it; we cannot say *This is very interesting me.* The line, however, is a fine one. We assume that *defeated* in *When he came back he was weary and defeated* is an adjective since it parallels the adjective *weary,* but that in *He was defeated by Caesar* it is part of the passive verb phrase *was defeated.* We must furthermore ask if auxiliaries other than *be* cannot function in the formation of English passives. Can the forms of *get,* for instance, operate in that way? *Get* bears some resemblance to *become* (*He got good at tennis*); but where we can say *He got caught by the police* we cannot say *He became caught by the police.* Some kinds of English verb-phrasings defy generalization: *He came to be controlled by some strange power, He grew to be loved by the people, Jonah was about to be swallowed by the whale;* but in this particular group of phrasings we find in all instances passive infinitives in the formation of which *be* combines with a second participial form. The infinitive phrase, however, is part of a larger phrase that can also contain *be* (*Jonah was about to be swallowed*). Observe the active version of the whole: *The whale was about to swallow Jonah, The people grew to love him, Some strange power came to control him.* The phrases *was about to, grew,* and *came to* remain unchanged in this reverse transformation. English possesses many other analytic phrasings that do not follow the usual pattern. To attempt an exact description of the process of transformation in each case would do damage to the entire methodology of the transformational grammarian, who, starting with the most obvious structures, moves as far as he can toward chaos without losing sight of the basic simplicities.

PREDICATE ADJECTIVE TO PRE-POSITIONAL ADJECTIVE

Another important first-level transformation is that by which a predicate adjective in a basic copula predication becomes a prepositional adjective in the normal position before a noun in a subsequent, separate predication. Reference has already been made to this principle in earlier chapters. However, in the present state of inquiry into the nature of transforms, many questions that arise in connection with it remain unanswered or unanswerable. The simple aspect of the principle is that in a sentence like *A good man is here* two predications are contained: *A* (*certain*) *man is good* and (*That*) *man is here*. The predication (*That*) *man is here* is the matrix sentence in the resultant transformation; the predication *A* (*certain*) *man is good* is transformed and becomes an "insert" in the matrix sentence. But to allow the reasonableness of this explanation is not the same thing as to assert that all pre-positional adjectives can best be explained in terms of transforms of this kind. In a phrase like *mental activities* we can, if we wish, with only some strain, presuppose a source-predication: (*Some*) *activities are mental;* but another source-predication is also imaginable: *Minds are active*. *Mental* represents an adjective derived from a noun; *activities* represents a noun derived from an adjective. In *minds are active, minds* is the subject of the predicator *active*. In *activities are mental, activities* is the subject of the predicator *mental*. The most basic form we can find in this situation (without any derivational shifting) is the implied *minds act*. In creating basic sentence patterns we have tried to isolate types without considering the complexities introduced by derivational shiftings; in the long run this cannot be done. When we say, however, that pre-positional adjectives can be interpreted as transforms of predicate adjectives, we are not necessarily saying that, once this principle is established, other more complex transforms cannot come to supplant this relatively simple one. The transformation of *minds are active* to *mental activities* is of this kind. It is a *post facto* substitute for the more normal *activities are mental* > *mental activities*.

If we can distinguish between adjectives that follow the norm of expressing qualities, properties, or attributes of a concrete noun (*bird, house, boy*) and adjectives that move from the center of this norm to peripheral extensions by which any kind of relation is, by grace of the extension, considered as if it were a quality, property, or attribute, especially those that modify abstract nouns (*activity, imprecision, rejection, administrator*), we can by the same token consider most pre-positional adjectives as transforms of the predicate adjectives of our basic copula sentence pattern; but in a phrase like *presidential imprecision* we would do better to take the short cut of supposing that we are looking at a transform of *president is not precise* rather than of (*this*) *imprecision is presidential*. Some purists would object strenuously to the formation of a phrase such as *presidential imprecision,* not without good reason, since we have here a rather extreme extension of the function of the adjective as expresser of quality, property, or attribute. But the syntactical relating of thought items by means of the manipulation of derivational suffixes comes close enough in English to constituting a separate system in our polysystemic grammar that we cannot quickly reject possibilities of this kind. A *Martian space-ship* is not necessarily *Martian;* it can be a space-ship from Mars, one that is going to Mars, one that is taking pictures of Mars, one that resembles a science fiction writer's concept of what a space-ship built on Mars would be like, and so on. And *space-ship* is still a concrete noun. Who knows how many kinds of relation could theoretically be implied by *Martian rejection?*

When we interpret pre-positional adjectives as transforms of predicate adjectives, we automatically exclude from the category of pre-positional adjectives all determiners, pre-determiners, and near-nouns, all nouns or pronouns in the genitive, all noun adjuncts, and all constructions that can be thought of as belonging to the compositional system of English syntax. Some of these may by accident fit well into the adjective pattern—derivation from predicate position (*John's book* > *book is John's*)—but often that imputation of transformation is impossible. Of greater importance is the traditional distinction of adjectives into restrictive and non-restrictive categories, even though this has always been an imprecise division. In any predication the predicate part moves from a more-or-less defined (delimited) subject. Semantically it makes little difference whether the delimitation is contained in a single word (*blackbird*) or is expressed by headword and restrictive modifier (*black bird, birds that are black, birds of black color*). It can usually be said that restrictive adjectives are as much transforms of predicate adjectives as non-restrictive adjectives are, but a difference between the two kinds does exist in respect to the point in time (this is "ideal" time) in which the transformation has taken place. This is to say that there is a difference in priority of transformation between *dead* in *A good Indian is a dead Indian* and in *Behind the bush lay a dead Indian.* In the second *dead* is not necessary to the delimitation of reference; but in the first it has been necessary to restrict the reference of the nouns before this act of predication can take place. So that the distinction we are making is not one of transformation and non-transformation but of precedence of transformation. In general, as we proceed to description of more complex transformations, the principle of distinction between restrictive and non-restrictive modifiers must be kept firmly in mind. It will involve the distinction between "present" and "prior" transformations. Prior transformations can be thought of as "dead" transformations so far as a predication immediately before us is concerned.

A series that is instructive, if still inconclusive, about levels of "presentness" of transformation is the following:

1. *Serene and happy, Mary accepted the invitation. Serene and happy* here is an initial appositive phrase. The two predications—*Mary was serene and happy* and *Mary accepted the invitation*—have been combined by the deletion of subject-part and copula in the first and inclusion of the first as a dependent unit in the second, which is the matrix sentence. The transformation has happened at a late stage of the formation of the "result" sentence.

2. *A serene and happy Mary accepted the invitation.* Only insofar as a referent of a proper noun is capable of partition is such a noun capable of being modified by a restrictive modifier (*the France that I love, old-time America*). Here *serene and happy* may be playing the role of a restrictive modifier, but actually it represents a half-hidden separate predication since there is a clash between the seeming-restriction that it effects and the reality that *Mary is now serene and happy and therefore gladly accepts the invitation.*

3. *He decided to invite Mary. This now serene and happy girl accepted the invitation.* Here we have a real hidden predication, particularly because the third predication *Mary was serene and happy* now has to be reconstructed across the period, which should on general principles separate one syntactic empire from another. We do not find a real hidden predication of this kind every time a synonymous referent is used in a new sentence, since a rhetorician may be at work substituting epithets to achieve his own stylistic effects (*Aristotle said so; the Stagirite was never wrong*—grammatically we need not be concerned that Aristotle is the Stagirite; this substitution of a synonymous term does not constitute a real hidden predication). Precise rules can hardly be worked out for the circumstances within which separate, hidden predications are implied between a subject part in one sentence and the buried predicate part in the subsequent sentence, but we can recognize that certain modern journalistic stylists make frequent use of hidden predications of this kind. The predication, though hidden, is still present and immediate.

4. *Serene and happy girls accept invitations to dances.* This statement may not square with the facts of life, but grammatically

we have *serene and happy* as restrictive modifiers of *girls*. We can rephrase this sentence as *When girls are serene and happy, they accept when they are invited to dances* (we now have three clauses and predications), but in the construction immediately confronting us, the restrictive modifiers represent a prior reduction of predication. "Prior," in this sense, means something a little different from "dependence" or "lower level of subordination," although, when non-restrictive and restrictive pre-positional adjectives occur together, in a noun phrase, the non-restrictive adjectives come before the restrictive and are first cut out in a partitioning of immediate constituents. When a restrictive modifier and its headword become a stock referent to some identity antecedent to the formulation of the sentence at hand (as in *blackbird* or even *red-winged blackbird*), we have a clear instance of prior transformation. But the concept of priority applies here only figuratively as a time concept. The priority is in the steps of the transformation process. It is impossible to distinguish precisely and generally between adjective-noun combinations that have become single lexical units (whether marked as one word or two words)—in which case the implied transformation must be prior to the formation of the sentence at hand—and those adjective-noun combinations that are not stock phrases but that must occur together to determine the identity of the referent. The transformational grammarian is not much concerned with restrictive modifiers, since the problem there is partly one of morphology and lexicon rather than of syntax. A predication may be "hidden," however, when a modifier appears to be restrictive but is not.

ADVERBIAL TRANSFORMATIONS

If most pre-positional adjectives are construed as representing first-level transformations, as one way of adding further predications to basic sentence patterns, we are likely to ask why most adverbs should not also be treated as transforms in a parallel way. In the present state of development of the theory of transformational grammar, the answer to this question is still unclear. We have already seen (p. 79) that some adverbs seem to be necessary predicate complements and so occupy positions in basic sentence patterns. It has also been hinted that other adverbs do in fact function as transforms (p. 63), particularly those like *evidently, presumably, clearly, patently, assuredly,* or *incontrovertibly*:

He was evidently once a clerk < It is evident that he was once a clerk.

He presumably went home < It (can be) presumed that he went home.

(Observe the periphrasis of this passive form that is glossed over in the transformed construction.)

The argument was clearly false < It is clear that the argument was false.

As traditionalists we have always assumed that one function of adverbs is to modify adjectives. When such adverbs are clearly not intensifiers, they may well represent transforms of a kind paralleling pre-positional adjective transforms. In a sentence such as *Dampness causes prematurely gray hair* we are faced with an intricate compression of basic predications. One preliminary recasting of the sentence might be *Dampness causes hair to become gray prematurely*. This in turn can be expanded into *Dampness causes that hair become gray before it is mature* (before the time is ripe or proper). A significant casting of the relation between *prematurely* and *gray* is *The grayness of (their) hair is premature*. We notice that only by the grace of a transformation can we explain *gray* in the original sentence; we can say the same for *prematurely*.

exceptionally fine < fineness is exceptional
provisionally true < truth is provisional
precisely accurate < accuracy is precise

But in *very true*, *truth* is not *very*, for *very* is an intensifier.

In Exercise V of Chapter 4 and in Exercise IV of Chapter 5 some preliminary efforts have been made to isolate and describe another kind of transformation, by which *-ly* adverbs—usually expressing a surface relation of manner—can in a depth grammar be seen as incorporating an included predication with the base adjective (or participle) to which the *-ly* is added functioning as predicate adjective in the source sentence. This is to say that in a sentence like *He arrived promptly* the addition of *promptly* to the basic sentence pattern of subject and intransitive verb can best be accounted for in terms of an implied source sentence *His arrival was prompt*. Since *his arrival* is a nominal reduced predication, this source sentence may seem further removed from a basic pattern than the sentence originally requiring explanation, but the predicate part *was prompt* is the predicate part of a basic pattern. It has been pointed out that *-ly* adverbs derive from adjective bases only; when they derive from participles the participles lose their ability to take objects and they can be modified by intensifiers, so that they are in effect derived adjectives. The relation of *promptly* to *arrived* can thus be seen as the relation between the predicate adjective *prompt* and the subject-part of a copula predication—the noun idea related to *arrived: arrival* or *arriving.* It should, however, be observed that in a sentence like *The spring wind enticingly refreshes,* a possible source for the adverb can be found in a verb coordinate with *refreshes—The spring wind entices and refreshes.* This leads us to our next point.

Some adverbs modifying adjectives are semantically coordinate with the adjectives, or practically so. Can we not, practically speaking, recast *It's refreshingly light and gay* as *It's lightly and gaily refreshing?* Or as *It is refreshing and light and gay?* In interpreting *the strangely beautiful picture* we may well be uncertain whether to recast it as *The picture is strange and beautiful* or *The beauty of the picture is strange.* The actual structure of modification would suggest the latter, but we cannot be sure that the writer did not intend the former. A third, perhaps even better interpretation is *The picture is beautiful* and *The beauty is strange.*

Other examples of adverbs representing transforms of one or another of these kinds are: *regally spacious guest rooms, the rooms are elegantly appointed, famously inadequate solutions to these problems.* Adverbs attached to verbs can likewise represent redistributions, as in *You must interpret them intelligently < You must be intelligent when you interpret them,* or in *He has moved consistently in the direction . . . < His movements in the direction . . . have been consistent.* Base adverbs, as in *He went there, He went to town, He held the picture up,* are obviously not of this kind. What is unclear is where to draw the line between base adverbs that may be considered necessary complements in a basic sentence pattern and adverbs that borrow the form and position as transforms. Manner adverbs are likely to be particularly ambiguous in this respect.

MATERIALS FOR EXERCISE AND FURTHER STUDY

    I. Copy these sentences and determine the pitch contour for each:

      1. What did you say your rich uncle's name is?
      2. You live here, do you?

3. Are you the kid who's been breaking our garage windows?
4. Do you really want me to tell you?
5. What kind of car did Jack buy this year?
6. Didn't you hear what I told you?
7. So Samson was the real hero after all?
8. Why did you tell them all those lies about me?
9. From which bin did he take those eggs?
10. How did you discover how to get here?
11. She isn't going to major in French, is she?
12. Have they ever tried to borrow any money from you?
13. When did the Battle of Hastings take place?
14. Were you trying to insult me last night?
15. Can you meet me in the park this afternoon?

II. Convert these sentences with active verbs into sentences with passive verbs:

1. The police chief gave the detective a new assignment (two versions).
2. The reading public had widely enjoyed Sterne's early writing.
3. The Wilton Company was publishing a fine collection of art books.
4. He declared his desire to paint a picture of the first girl he met in Greece.
5. Unfortunately for Eben, Burmeister provided no literal translation for the poem.
6. Did Nathan ever consider Jonas to be the real offender?
7. Some people who lived at the far end of the valley thought the entire project a waste of good money.
8. The Senate voted for it on July 7, 1956.
9. Whom did the teacher punish for the escapade?
10. Why had he never told us his plans (two versions)?

III. Convert these sentences with passive verbs into sentences with active verbs:

1. The whole of the bill creating the National Endowment for the Humanities has been printed above.
2. It is made particularly clear by this fact that no political maneuvering is without repercussions.
3. It is to be noted that although Kent remains faithful to his lord, his efforts on his behalf are profitless.
4. He was sent an urgent message from the commander of the *Bixby*.
5. All those years had been wasted without the solace of wife and children.

6. Such was her husband's anxiety, that even the judge's heart was moved by it.
7. Milton was led by his memories of Italy to reject all the extreme forms of Puritan bigotry.
8. The room had been decorated with long swinging festoons of orange crepe paper.
9. A more important function of the marriage scene in the play is indicated by the role that Fortunatus assumes in Act II.
10. Why was Banquo murdered by Macbeth?
11. He was caught entering a second story window on Front Street.
12. He continued to be angered by the accusations leveled against him.
13. He got trapped into revealing the secret when she found out about his visit to Rome.
14. He could have been required to fill out an additional set of forms.
15. He remained upset by the stories that Col. Nichols was spreading.

IV. Examine these pre-positional adjectives (ignoring noun adjuncts whenever you can identify them as such). How many of these pre-positional adjectives can be readily seen as transformed predicate adjectives, following the pattern *these habits are pretentious* > *these pretentious habits?* How many of these pre-positional adjectives arrive in this position by some other route? Can you describe the route for the deviants?

many less innovative extensions of the same idea
academic credit
social work
personal fulfillment
the academic relevance of these activities
educational benefits
without adequate study
except for an occasional amateur
their principal endeavor
the social sciences
imaginative thinking
coastal areas
any viable alternative
current dissent
an independent country
additional tryouts

this basic premise
a softer policy
an important part
the important thing
vital interests
any permanent separation
American military policy
major gains
popular pressure
a large war
basic assumptions
American intervention
various aspects
suburban towns
greatest problem
open debate
frank discussion
gaudy chandeliers
the only noteworthy facet

the worst thing
empty seats
a workable integration plan
civil rights
an anti-Semitic remark
an ugly display
elementary schools
primary grades
far small confines
loud demands
entire school districts
doctrinal dilemma
philosophical ideas
individual freedom
respectable ideas
academic freedom
free play
legal document
miscellaneous items
marvelous opportunity
open hearings
congressional approval
a modern new tire
prospective freshmen
for financial reasons
the contemporary writer
systematic irreverence
specific cases
the final versions
a literary legacy
an ambitious man
broad responsibilities
Cartesian habits of thought
a preliminary study
portable cash registers
large increases

a smaller percentage
in early December
the official biography
childish showmanship
creative genius
prolific activity
early romance
wild drinking bouts
scandalous behavior
the necessary perspective
delightful reading
antagonistic attitudes
Anglo-Saxon attitudes
a necessary consequence
healthy signs
a formal public meeting
no quiet little nooks
a nice place
three distinct sections
the circular orbit
complex machinery
experimental devices
nuclear studies
the weird aspect
the piteous Hornet attempts
an impressive attack
interplanetary spacecraft
commercial use
a few critical insights
the artist's traditional separa-
    tion from society
American architecture
equal opportunity
a good laugh
high prices

(The important thing in this exercise is to distinguish adjectives for which the predicate adjective source is impossible or highly strained, not to concern yourself much about the process by which the predicate adjective was formed.)

V. The passages below are taken from the Feb. 6, 1966, sports section of the *New York Times*. They illustrate the rhetorical device of hiding predications that has become a favorite of sportswriters and some other journalists. Institute a search of your own for additional examples. Notice that these examples are not all alike. In most, the subject of a subsequent sentence predicates something about the subject of the preceding sentence. Passages 2 and 10 are distinctly different.

1. Tom Tresh, the healthy Yankee, took time out . . . yesterday to sign his 1966 contract for a "substantial raise." The 27-year-old switch-batter—who led the New York Yankees in "total offense" last year—was rewarded with an increase of $10,000 . . . .

2. Cazzie Russell scored 32 points and John Clawson, a teammate, clipped in with 19 in the second-half today to lead Michigan to a 93–76 Big Ten victory over Indiana. The Wolverines improved their won-lost conference record to 6–1 and 12–5 over all. (This is "epithet.")

3. Jack Kramer, for years the top promoter of professional tennis, returns to an active role in staging the matches in association with the Garden. Since 1961 the former amateur and professional champion has restricted his operations . . . .

4. Enthusiasm out here in Orange County appears to be rising as high as the Angels' 230-foot scoreboard. This A-frame structure, erected in left field at a cost of more than $1 million, will be surmounted by a giant halo, the Angels' traditional symbol.

5. Hiller, purchased from the Giants last May 12 after Ron Hunt suffered a shoulder separation, filled in at second base and appeared in 100 games. He batted .235 and equaled his major league high of six home runs. The 30-year-old infielder played with the Giants from 1961 through 1964 and was one of the batting stars of the 1962 World Series.

6. Regine Heitzer of Austria retained her European figure-skating title today with a flawless free-skating performance. The 22-year-old daughter of a wealthy Austrian businessman was virtually assured of her title when she finished her compulsory figure skating with a huge lead.

7. Last night a crowd of 40,321 shouted and screamed and twice prepared to weep for Bravo. Twice, the 33-year-old Mexican, a former trapeze artist, was hooked by his bull and hurled to the soft dirt surface of the Astrodome.

8. George O'Day, an American yachtsman and boat builder, has completed a series of four lectures before European sailing groups. The 1960 Olympic gold medalist in the 5.5 Meter Class spoke on racing tactics . . . .

9. The Around Long Island Marathon will go around again this year—but not as usual. Instead of starting and finishing at Freeport, L.I., as it did in its first seven runnings, the 234-mile powerboat race will start and finish at Flushing Bay, Queens.

10. A sharp increase in nominations for the $100,000 Sapling and $100,000 Sorority 2-year-old stakes, has led Monmouth Park to predict record-value races when these events are held during the 56-day meeting beginning June 3. The six-furlong Sapling has attracted 746 nominations . . . .

7

REDISTRIBUTIONS

GRAMMATICALITY

The fact must be faced that a transformational grammarian is in no better position than any other grammarian in distinguishing a grammatical sentence from an ungrammatical one. The simple test of grammaticality that Noam Chomsky and others have used is to submit a given locution to any native speaker of the language, who should be able to make the distinction intuitively. Within a large area of obviously impossible constructions all native speakers will agree and would agree no matter what theory of grammaticality they employed. Thus all will agree that *Man dog bit the* does not square with known grammatical order in English, while *The dog bit the man* does. The test of the test comes when we move into no-man's-land where the native speaker's intuition falters and where not all native speakers agree. Intuitions respond only to well-grooved habits; they can tell us what kinds of constructions are frequently encountered in our milieu. We can assume, if we wish, that anything that is frequently encountered is grammatical, at least for the dialect of the speakers. The transformationalist, who starts with simple structures that are undeniably frequent and who attempts to reveal the mechanisms by means of which highly complex structures are created by re-arranging the simple structures or by putting them together, can claim that a structure is grammatical if a procedure can be worked out for its generation. Study of the generative process can be very useful in illuminating the nature of language, but it is not much help in making distinctions of grammaticality, for the mechanisms of generation can be worked out for almost any possible combination of words. The attempt to work out the transformations involved follows the recognition of the fact that the possible combination of words is actually encountered often enough to make description of the procedure worthwhile. It can of course be shown that some procedures are more easily explained than others because they involve less complex alterations of basic patterns. Prescription may follow description; whatever may be easily explained—involving few transformational steps—may seem to be more right, more noble, than whatever is less easily explained. This, however, gets us into areas of taste, of rhetoric, or of expediency. It tells us little of grammaticality.

Some complexities in sentence structure occur, not by the simple addition of new elements, as when certain predications are substituted for key segments in a basic pattern, or are inserted with only a modicum of alteration within a basic pattern, or are externally attached to one, but by a redistribution of elements within a pattern. The passive transformation is, in fact, such a redistribution. The subject-verb-object pattern is still present but with a different arrangement, the mechanics of which can be quite easily described. But not all redistributions of key terms can be handled so easily. Consider this sentence by a sportswriter for the *New York Times*:

> The closest the Phillies came to scoring was when Roberts was thrown out at home in the third on Ted Kazanski's infield roller.

The basic pattern is still very simple: *X was Y* (*closest was this*); but the forms that occupy the basic slots are not simple. A simpler version is: *The Phillies came closest to scoring when . . .* The kind of construction exhibited by *came close* we have already discussed (p. 85); the conversion of the adjective *close* (in its superlative form) to *the most close* in this string is harder to understand, but once understood allows for the redistribution by which *the closest* becomes the subject of a copula predication, modified by the relative clause (*that*) *the Phillies came to scoring*, in which the deleted *that* substitutes for *the closest* (*the Phillies came that* [i.e., *the closest*] *to scoring*); and the adverbial *when* clause is now the predicate complement after *was*. This is a kind of redistribution of terms and functions that is practically anomalous. To describe all the possible varieties of such redistributions would be almost impossible. And it would be almost futile to try to set up criteria by which we could decide whether the sportswriter's sentence was grammatical or not. The distribution of functions among lexical items in the creation of a sentence is something like the problem of a child at a county fair who has only a limited number of coins to spend and an assortment of wishes to gratify: the amount of money he spends at one booth inevitably affects what he can do at another. We cannot specify all of the strategies of redistribution (presupposing that there would be any point in doing so), but we can call attention to the existence of the principle and we can point out a few examples of it.

PREDICATE APPOSITIVES

The incorporation of a predicate appositive within a sentence (see p. 86) can be considered a redistribution. Zandvoort, who calls predicate appositives predicative adjectives and nouns, gives these illustrations: [1]

> *The party arrived safe and sound.*
> *We parted the best of friends.*
> *He left home a beggar; he came back a millionaire.*

Zandvoort, however, makes little distinction between the use of adjectives and nouns in this way and predicate nouns and adjectives, although he affirms that, whereas a predication containing subject + copula + predicate complement has only two nuclei, these have three. He considers intermediate between the two kinds sentences with *seem, become, get, keep, feel,* and *lie,* as in:

> *The situation seemed hopeless.*
> *It is getting dark.*
> *She kept very quiet.*
> *The snow lay thick upon the ground.*
> *Old Jolyon sat alone.*
> *Do you feel tired?*

He further points out that the same construction occurs with some verbs of movement (which practically mean *become*):

> *The dog went mad.*
> *His brother fell ill.*
> *All my misgivings came true.*

[1] R. W. Zandvoort, *A Handbook of English Grammar* (London, 1960), p. 198.

Our provisions ran short.
Morris turned socialist.

These we have called variants of copula predications even though the verbs require *do* in transformations of negation and question. There is an obliquity, however, in his first illustrations, that leads us to consider them transformations:

> *When the party arrived it was safe and sound > The party arrived safe and sound.*
> *When we parted we were the best of friends > We parted the best of friends.*
> *When he left home he was a beggar; when he came back he was a millionaire > He left home a beggar; he came back a millionaire.*

Ralph B. Long, who calls adjectives half-modifiers when they appear in sentences of this kind, recognizes the obliquity that sometimes occurs by treating them as adjuncts of circumstance, but he confuses the picture by classing even predicate adjectives as half-modifiers.[2] Thus he makes no real distinction between the adjectives in *The mountains are very beautiful* and *I finally got the shoes clean* (*shoes so that they were clean*); nor does he distinguish satisfactorily among these, the kind of transform we are considering (*He married young*), pure appositive transforms, and adverbial complements. Two of his illustrations are, nevertheless, interesting. The test of the predicate appositive transform can be applied to *Sigrid was already composing at the age of five* (deriving from *When she was at the age of five Sigrid was already composing*) and to *We ate the chicken cold* (deriving from *The chicken was cold when we ate it*), but two new elements are found in these sentences: *at the age of five* is ambiguously a time prepositional phrase functioning adverbially or (in the source clause) a prepositional phrase functioning as predicate complement (since any unit that can function as a predicate complement can function as an appositive, any such unit may also function as a predicate appositive); in our other illustrations of predicate appositives we found intransitive verbs, but in *We ate the chicken cold* the verb is transitive and the direct object is the subject of the included predication, not the subject of the result sentence. Long points out that in *I never see him alone* we must gather from the context who is alone, *I* or *him*. The difference is between *I am never alone when I see him* and *He is never alone when I see*

---

[2] Ralph B. Long, *The Sentence and Its Parts* (Chicago, 1961), p. 29.

him; again we have a transitive verb with the direct object as subject of the included predication. What here we call obliquity in an adjunct, Long calls a secondary relationship as a half-modifier. Neither of these terms, however, gets at the structural ambiguity found in these sentences. Long points out that in *I saw a dress like that in Hudson's window yesterday* the seeing has not taken place in the store window. We can instead interpret the sentence as a putting together of *I saw a dress like that yesterday* and *The dress was in Hudson's window*, and yet *in Hudson's window yesterday* seems to be comprised of two components functioning adverbially with relational notions of *where* and *when*. Other interpretations are also possible here. We must at least distinguish between a predicate appositive construction that follows a transitive verb and that can be considered a transforming redistribution of the items of two clauses and this ambiguous construction found with transitive verbs where the included subject-predicate nexus is between direct object and what follows it.

However, the difficulty of making some of these finicky distinctions is revealed by a sentence in which James Sledd apparently finds an example of an object-objective complement construction: *The examination left the student a total wreck.*[3] One peculiarity of this sentence is found in the shift of meaning in *left* revealed by the contrasting sentence *The student left the examination a total wreck* (in which we find a clear-cut example of a predicate appositive redistribution of *The student was a total wreck when he left the examination*). What has happened to *leaves* when *student leaves* becomes *examination leaves?* And yet the verb is transitive in both meanings, or seemingly so. The passive transform is, however, impossible in *The examination was left by the student a total wreck,* for *a total wreck* cannot function as retained object since the predicational nexus is between it and *student,* not between it and *examination.* But redistributions that depend upon semantic shifts are very hard to deal with precisely, for transformations can be neatly handled only when the changes are purely structural. Comparisons that are partly structural and partly semantic are bound to be open-ended.

In some of these transformations from which predicate appositives emerge, we need not be confused by the fact that the predicate appositives can also be interpreted as adverbials of manner.

[3] James Sledd, *A Short Introduction to English Grammar* (Chicago, 1959), p. 132.

One of the particular virtues of a transformationalist grammar is that it emphasizes the process by means of which structures come into being and hence is relatively indifferent to the static concepts of relation that seem to come into play at a given stage in the process. This does not mean that the relational concepts are unreal, but that the structures that normally express them can be borrowed for other purposes in a process grammar. As a result, a unit may be said to function in one relation in terms of the present sentence structure and in another relation ín terms of the basic predications from which the present sentence structure has evolved. The following pair of sentences illustrates the two possibilities of interpretation:

> *Water would come from the hose hot and tasting of rubber.*
> *He sat up the whole night wide awake, pondering . . . .*

"THERE" AND "IT" TRANSFORMATIONS

A more mechanical kind of redistributional transformation is found in those sentences that use *it* or *there* as proxies or "dummies" for nominal units of some kind. *It* and *there* are not truly pronouns as they function in these sentences since they merely occupy formally the position of the nominals they supplant so that the nominals can occupy some other position in the sentence. Usually, in order to find the basic sentence pattern from which the present pattern has been transformed it is necessary only to remove the "dummy" and allow the nominal to occupy its normal position once more:

> *There are a lot of people here < A lot of people are here.*
> *It is hard to buy a good horse these days < To buy a good horse these days is hard.*

This is the simple pattern of the transformation. But in many sentences the problem is not so simple. To get at the complexities we need to consider *there* and *it* separately.

The *there* transformation is found most commonly in sentences in which the verb is some form of *be* (or a variant of it such as *seem to be*). Sentences such as *There arrived a new shipment yesterday* or *There appeared a clown in the center ring* are possible but not frequent, especially in the literary language. Since *be* can convey, in addition to its meaning as pure copula (which in a sense is no meaning at all other than a formal indication that a predication is being made), the meaning of *exist* or *have existence*, we should not be surprised to find the *there* construction exploiting this ambiguity. In a sentence such as *There are ten pieces of candy in this row* we may be unsatisfied by any single recasting of the items: *Ten pieces of candy are in this row, Ten pieces of candy exist in this row, (The number of) pieces of candy in this row (is) ten.* By variation of the stress pattern each of these meanings can be communicated. The segmental structure taken by itself allows the ambiguity. The *exist* meaning is shown most clearly in sentences in which no complement follows *be* when the structure reverts to its basic pattern: *There will be no new treaty < No new treaty will be. There must not be any monkeyshines < Any monkeyshines must not be.* It should go without saying that any exact description of the discrepancies here between form and meaning is difficult, if not impossible.

Since *be* is used in English as the auxiliary in the formation of passives and verb phrases of progressive aspect, we can expect to find the *there* transform applied to sentences containing verb phrases of these kinds, although again an ambiguity of structure may be the result. Observe the subtle differences of structure to be found between *There are hardly any traces left of the Norsemen in North America* and *There were hardly any traces left by the Norsemen in North America.* If the grammaticality of either of these sentences is in doubt it is that of the latter. In the former, *left* may be construed as a predicate adjective (but consider *there remain hardly any traces . . .*). *The Norsemen left hardly any traces in North America < Hardly any traces were left by the Norsemen in North America.*

Consider: *There were many kingdoms overthrown by his lust for power, There is a storm brewing, There is coming into being a new kind of political party, There had been programmed for the computer a whole new set of problems.* The interpretation that these sentences contain passive or progressive verb phrases, rather than copula + predicate adjective constructions, is supported by the observation that predicate adjectives rarely occur in *there* transforms without undergoing further transformation to pre-position: *There are few good men nowadays < There are few men good nowadays (?) < Few men are good nowadays.* Another possible origin is *Good men are few nowadays,* but the predicate near-noun *few* has here likewise become pre-positional in the result sentence. In the transform, another possibility is *There are few men nowadays who are good.*

In the following passage (a description of the setting of an indoor track meet), the *there* transform is accompanied by the structural shifting of *informal* to *informality* and of *light glares* and *hardwood gleams* to *glaring light* and *gleaming hardwood,* as a pre-condition to the transform:

> In the afternoon there is the informality of Bacon Cage where the light
> is a watery green from the glass roof and the crowd is smaller—dogs and
> small boys in the majority. At night there is the glaring light and gleaming
> hardwood of Barton Hall . . . .
>
> —Cornell Alumni News

Rhetoricians are likely to object that the *there* transform is used when there is no justification for it—when nothing at all is added by means of the excess structural scaffolding, as in *There are a lot of the pictures painted by Raphael that have religious subjects.* In these cases, a relative clause is created to carry what should be the verb in the principal clause: *A lot of the pictures painted by Raphael have religious subjects.*

In certain idiomatic expressions the *be* of the *there* transform combines with a following adverbial to form a verb phrase of specific content: *There is a notion abroad that he will be the next president* < *A notion that he will be the next president is abroad; A movement is afoot to supplant him* > *There is a movement afoot to supplant him.* In these sentences we find nominal phrases or clauses (*that he will be the next president, to supplant him*) split off from the subjects with which they are in apposition.

The transformations using *it* as a position-filling substitute show many of the same features, but with some significant differences. Usually *it* replaces not a single-word nominal but a clause or infinitive phrase used nominally, so that we are involved with problems of included predications of the kind in which a clause or reduced clause functions in one of the positions that nouns can occupy in a sentence. *It* can also substitute for the kind of reduced predication using *for* + *subject* + *infinitive* (*for him to go*).

> *It is important that you come home immediately* < *That you come home immediately is important* < *You must come home immediately. This is important.* In the first stage of the transformation, one predication becomes a noun clause supplanting *this* as a subject of the other predication (with the introduction of the signaling particle *that* and the change of the verb phrase from

the explicit analytic modal form *must come* to the synthetic form *come*). In the second stage, *it* supplants the noun clause in the subject-position and the noun clause is inserted after the predicate adjective (or the predicate noun or direct object with adverbial modifiers, as the case may be—*it bothered me very much yesterday that you could not be here*).

It worries me how you expect to make a living < *How you expect to make a living worries me* < *How do you expect to make a living? This (question) worries me.* In this case a question is transformed into an interrogative noun clause (see p. 153), included as subject of the matrix predication, and then supplanted by *it*. Interrogative noun clauses appear less frequently in the *it* transformation than declarative noun clauses.

It is good to know that you are my friend < *(for me) to know that you are my friend is good* < *I know that you are my friend. This is good.* In the first stage *I know* is reduced to the abstract (subject-less) infinitive *to know* (this is possible since the subject of the infinitive can be inferred from the context), the noun clause direct object of *know* remaining unchanged throughout, and the infinitive phrase becomes a subject of the matrix predication. In stage two, the infinitive is supplanted by *it* and appears after the predicate adjective.

It is rare for a woman to succeed in surgery < *For a woman to succeed in surgery is rare* < *A woman succeeds in surgery. This is rare.* The modality of the first basic sentence may not be adequately expressed here. The transform procedure is roughly the same as for the other types.

In highly poetic prose the dummy *it* may be used to delay the appearance of a noun (as in *It runs like this, that old nursery tale we all know*), but generally the delayed element is a clause or phrase accomplishing the inclusion of a predication.

The nexus between the included subject and the verb of the matrix sentence is not as cloudy in these illustrative sentences as it can at times become. Ellipses and indirections are sometimes glossed over in the process of transformation. An example can be seen in *It was the same blackguard who opened the door for us now who had stolen Jim's wallet yesterday in the marketplace.* It can perhaps be argued that this sentence is finally ungrammatical, but on what basis can this claim be made? That the transformation achieved in it is not sufficiently common? Shall we recast this sentence as *The blackguard who opened the door for us now was the same man as the one who stole Jim's wallet yesterday in the marketplace?* or as *The man who opened the door for us now was the same as the blackguard who stole Jim's wallet yesterday in the marketplace?* There are hidden predications in the sentence, and they cannot all readily be made explicit at once. We do not have space for listing of all possible varieties of indirection in this kind of transformation, but here are a few samples:

When I finally graduated from high school, it was with the firm conviction that I was a moron.

It was not until years later, when all the members of the original board had retired or were dead, that the scandal broke out.

It is only on the fringes of the area that the worst poverty is to be found (compare with *The worst poverty is to be found only on the fringes of the area.* This sentence provides us with a vivid example of the redistribution of items in a structure).

It was he who told me about the new regulations.

It now takes only one day for an airmail letter to reach Paris.

It was only a year later that he made the important discovery.

It is remarkable how closely the history of the apple tree is connected with that of man.—THOREAU

So it goes in these young countries: telephones, and telegraphs, and newspapers, and advertisements running far ahead among the Indians and the grizzly bears.—R. L. STEVENSON

It is in terms of sociology that human affairs are described.

Clauses introduced by *if* (in the sense of *whether*) are often found in popular usage operating as clause objects of certain verbs (*know, wonder, decide,* etc.). *It* does not supplant these object clauses, but *it* can be found, in a loose and doubtful construction, representing *if* clauses that seem to be more obviously clauses of condition. If usage rules, we need merely to describe this construction, which undoubtedly exists. If we call a construction ungrammatical when the signals of its structure conflict with each other, this construction is ungrammatical:

It would make me happy if you would leave me alone.

If he finds the place all right, it would prove me wrong.

A similar construction is also found occasionally with *when* clauses that resemble adverbial clauses more than interrogative noun clauses:

When Henry won the race, it made our day a success.

It improved our status in the community when Auntie came to visit us.

It functions more often, of course, as the usual retrospective pronoun than as a "dummy." In *Henry won the race; it made our day a success, it* makes a loose reference retrospectively to the whole of the first clause. Stylists might well complain about the looseness of such a reference but they can hardly question its grammaticality. The grammaticality of *When Henry won the race, our day was a success* is similarly unquestionable. What is questionable is the inconsistent blending of these two structural strategies, if for no other reason than that we have a phenomenon that cannot be readily generalized. It seems to embody a misunderstanding or a mistake.

There as a "dummy" appears only in the subject position. *It,* to the contrary, can appear in the predicate part of a sentence as subject of a reduced predication after verbs like *consider, think,* or *find.*

> *I consider it impractical to go around day-dreaming like that.*
> *I think it a good idea for him to come immediately.*
> *The committee found it imperative that the President resign.*

In these instances, *it* is still a supplanter of a delayed subject, but a subject of a reduced predication rather than of a formal predication. The principle of the supplanting remains the same and the kinds of nominal constructions supplanted (infinitive phrases, "for" constructions, noun clauses) are the same. The range of usage is, however, more restricted. In theory it is possible to say *I wanted it to be understood that you would buy the stock,* but many speakers and writers would find such a construction stiff and unwieldy. A judgment like this is rhetorical rather than grammatical.

A reduced predication like *for him to come* can be interpreted in two ways. One way is to consider the infinitive as separable and independent of its subject, which appears in another part of the sentence as the analytic equivalent of a dative. *It is easy for you to do that = To do that is easy for you.* In a highly inflected language such an order and such an interpretation is likely. In English it is more satisfactory to follow the other line of interpretation—to consider *for* as an introductory particle and not separate the infinitive and its subject, so that the unit appears entire as a reduced predication. In constructions using *it* as a dummy, the delayed subject sometimes uses *of* instead of *for* (as in *It was wrong of him to do that,* in which the interpretation *Of him to do that was wrong* is impossible, and the interpretation *To do that was wrong of him* seems more probable, even though *His doing that was wrong* expresses the sense). The unit *of him to do that* is not movable and adaptable to different word orders as is *for him to do that;* its position in the sentence is controlled by *of him* rather than by the positions possible for *him to do.*

The actual construction in some such cases can be betrayed by idiomatic significances. In a sentence such as *It was good of you to come,* the phrase *was good of* has idiomatic force and a particular meaning not found generally in the larger construction. *For you to come was good* does not mean quite the same thing as *It was good of you to come.* Idioms can play hob with general principles of transformation even though they may have come to their present form by way of the transformation principles. In a brief grammar we cannot inquire into all of the possibilities. The separation of the *of* phrase and what is predicated about the object of *of* is apparent in the sentence *It is often said of Ned that he is a snob.* *About* or *concerning* can be substituted for *of* in such a sentence. The noun clause that the dummy *it* supplants can make pronominal reference to *Ned* as the subject-less infinitive cannot.

IMPRECISE REDISTRIBUTIONS

One of the most troublesome redistributions in English is found in the situation in which an infinitive follows a predicate adjective and is seemingly dependent upon it. Examples are:

A good man is hard to find.
That's easy to do.
That's good to know.
That habit is hard to break.

A double valence is apparent in the functioning of the infinitives. By one syntactic hook they seem to be attached to the predicate adjectives, in a dependent relation expressing something like "in respect to." Thus: *A good man is difficult in respect to the finding of one.* This of course does not make much sense, and yet we create compounds in which adjectives and infinitives of this kind are combined and isolated: *hard-to-find objects, easy-to-perform processes, hard-to-break habits.* On the other hand, by another syntactic hook, the subjects of these sentences can be seen as the objects of the infinitives: *To find a good man is hard* (*difficult*),

To do that is easy, To know that is good, To break that habit is hard. In the original sentences, the meanings of the adjectives apply less to the nouns than to the infinitive phrases; hence a false predication occurs when the noun alone is taken as subject.

The double valence is not found, however, in other sentences that seem to be structurally identical to these:

The hot dogs are ready to eat (to eat < to be eaten).
The children are ready to eat (ambiguous).
We are prepared to spend a million dollars.
They were unable to do anything.
Their forces were insufficient to plug the gap.

According to one interpretation of this construction, the combination of copula and predicate adjective (in instances like these) is a special kind of verb phrase, or at least a periphrase of one (*these suffice > these are sufficient, we can do > we are able to do*), and to search for an ulterior reality in the interrelationships is pointless. Even in this interpretation, however, the infinitives that follow can best be explained as expressing a vague relation of *in respect to: the hot dogs are ready (in respect to) their being eaten, the children are ready (in respect to) their eating or their being eaten,* etc.

Linguistic items that come at the end of predications and that can be interpreted roughly as expressing the relation of *in respect to* are often symptoms of a redistribution. Such patent clumsinesses as *I didn't like him as to the bad habit he had of cracking his knuckles* (where the more direct expression of the object of *like* is *his bad habit of cracking his knuckles*) or *The situation worried me because of its instability* (the use of the casual phrase here is not necessarily clumsy in itself, but what *worries me* in a somewhat more precise logic is the transformed predication contained in "the instability of the situation"—*the situation is unstable* —and not "the situation" itself. We cannot expect that even expert writers will always find, or want to find, the "right" (in the sense of the most precise, direct, or logical) subjects for their sentences, but as grammarians we need to conceive of a general principle of redistribution in terms of which a "right" subject finds expression as an adjunct of "respect" in a belated position in a sentence. Even a relatively simple sentence like *She is lovely in spirit* can be considered a redistribution of *Her spirit is lovely.* What is being talked about—the whole (*she*) or the aspect of the whole (*her spirit*)? However, the range of variations in "respect" re-distribution is so great that few vaguely comparable sentences are exactly alike either in structure or in relational significance, so that any attempt to describe precisely the transformations by which they are produced would probably be futile. A sentence like *In some speech communities some utterances are exactly alike as to form and meaning* can easily (and perhaps profitably) be recast as *In some speech communities both the form and meaning of some utterances are exactly alike.* When both whole and aspect occur in the predicate the situation is quite different. Thus in *I scolded him as to his treatment of his wife,* better diction would give us *I scolded him for his treatment of his wife,* in which the phrase *for his treatment of his wife* gives the reason for the scold-ing; it states the end or goal of the scolding. The "respect" rela-tion is, or often seems to be, a catch-all, vague and ill-defined, and sometimes useful because it is just that. To the stylist it is not always advantageous to pinpoint the specific aspects of wholes. Witness: *People can be brilliant or clever or stupid, as to their wits; warm-hearted or cold in temperament; vicious, confused, or virtuous as to their conduct.* The specific *wits, temperament,* and *conduct* could be the subjects of the assertions.

Consider these alternatives: *That is easy for him (for him* would be expressed by an inflected dative in Latin); *He does that easily* (as close as we can come to a basic sentence pattern); *That is done easily by him* (a passive transformation). These show two kinds of redistribution.

In a palpable percentage of redistributions, sentences with transitive or intransitive verbs are converted into copula predica-tions. This is to move from one basic sentence pattern to another, so that there is no gain in complexity in this conversion taken by itself. The complexities found in copula predications are those inserted into the subject and predicate complement parts, since *be* is sufficiently without specific content to relate almost anything to anything.

> *Traveling in Europe was an exciting experience for us.*
> *Bullying was the least of the ill practices current among us.—*
>   Huxley (cited by Poutsma, I, pt. 2, 840)
> *Having you here is a distinct pleasure for us.*

In the following sentence, the basic pattern of subject-verb-indi-rect object-direct object is usurped by a string of words whose content would suggest a quite different structure:

*This signal achievement not only gave Al Lopez' Tribe a clean
sweep of the three-game series but . . .*

Compare this structure with *Al Lopez' Tribe* (the Cleveland Indians baseball team) *swept the three-game series clean.* Structures exist for us, ready to be used within the limits of their capabilities. When one basic sentence pattern is taken over by a string
of notional relationships usually expressed by another basic sentence pattern, we cannot firmly call the act a redistribution, since
we have no clear-cut way of knowing what strings of notional
relationships are basic to what patterns. We need to keep the
complex vagueness of these problems in mind as we proceed, but
we cannot afford to continue at this level of vagueness and indeterminacy. This chapter has at best marked off some of the
outer limits of grammatical inquiry.

MATERIALS FOR EXERCISE AND FURTHER STUDY

I. As we have seen, the kind of construction in which a copula is
followed by a predicate adjective and an infinitive is a highly ambiguous one and may represent a redistribution of more than one sort.
Given here are sentences illustrating at least five varieties of redistributions that all end up with this surface pattern. These five varieties
are: (1) the construction with *it* as substitute subject for the delayed
infinitive (*It was good to get home* < *To get home was good*); (2) the
construction in which the infinitive has double valence (*A good man
is hard to find* < *To find a good man is hard*); (3) the construction in
which the unit of adjective + infinitive represents a verb periphrasis
(*He is able to do it* < *He can do it*); (4) the construction in which
copula + adjective is equivalent to verb + adverb (*He was quick to
tell* < *He quickly told*); in indicating this difference of form, we must
not assume at this point which of these two forms is closer to a basic
sentence pattern; (5) the construction in which the infinitive functions
only in the relation of respect, or seems to do so (*we are ready to eat*).
Determine which of the following sentences belongs to which of these
types. Try to find or to create sentences of your own illustrating these
types. Can you discover still other constructions that make use of this
ambiguous pattern?

1. He has been unable to generate enthusiasm among the minor-
   ity groups for his reform program.
2. Seventeenth-century France is one of the great cultures that
   seem quite impossible to encompass.
3. It's a very hard job to get.
4. They performed in a way that is fun to watch.
5. I was very anxious to see how it worked.

6. He's very nice to watch when he's playing tennis.
7. He says he's not ready to go home yet.
8. Why should you be so set to have me out of here?
9. The girl behind the counter was prompt to tell me that I wanted something for nothing.
10. Anyone as easy to beat as he was should never play poker.
11. That's a mighty fine way to be acting, I must say!
12. The bondservants were free to travel if they had their masters' consent.
13. The parson for one was happy to hear that Jed was getting out of town.
14. The annual recitals she staged for her pupils were always wearisome to sit through.
15. It is smart to ask for more than you hope to receive.
16. All such eventualities are glorious to anticipate.
17. Jackie was prone to do all sorts of things his mother did not approve of.
18. The daily news of the world's doings was in those days always terrible to scan.
19. It was delectable to envision the rewards that came the way of good children.
20. He was prompt to remind me of all my shortcomings.

II. These sentences illustrate the rearrangements of structure brought about by the use of *there*. Point out differences in meaning of *be*. In each case describe the transformational steps leading to the end product.

1. But there is another Newark: a vast sprawl of Negro slums and poverty, a festering center of disease, vice, injustice and crime. —JOHN O'SHEA, *The Atlantic Monthly*
2. There was one nice thing about the way they did it.
3. If the representatives of the people betray their constituents, there is then no recourse left but in the exertion of that original right of self-defence which is paramount to all positive forms of government, and which against the usurpations of the national rulers, may be exerted with infinitely better prospect of success than against those of the rulers of the individual state.—ALEXANDER HAMILTON, *The Federalist*, No. 28
4. But is there any one of these qualities which would prevent his doing doubly as well in a career of honest, upright, sensible, prehensible, and comprehensible things?—E. A. POE
5. There is no faintest trace of snobbery in Edward . . . .—GEORGE MOORE
6. There is not in the whole world a book that I have not read.
7. There are moments when the bow scrapes wildly across the strings.—HELEN WADDELL

8. There are more of them to live near to than of the pigmies.
9. Are there any near-sighted ornithologists in the house?

III. In the *it* redistributions shown below, are the substitutions discrete; that is, can the unit for which *it* substitutes be put in the place of *it* and create a clear sentence? For what kinds of construction does the *it* act as substitute?

1. It is this Newark, this prospering industrial, commercial, and transportation center, that is best known to Americans.—JOHN O'SHEA, *The Atlantic Monthly*
2. . . . it often appears that the white business and residential communities prefer things that way.—JOHN O'SHEA
3. It is the irony of Addonizio's political fate that despite his liberal record and his campaign promises of social justice, he became the first Newark mayor to have to use massive police force and psychological repression against civil rights demonstrators.—JOHN O'SHEA
4. It was a fancy of that far-off time in which he spoke to hope that nations which "understood" each other would therefore live in harmony, and that if all conducted themselves rationally, they would encounter no irreparable conflicts of self-interest.—ERIC LARRABEE, *The Atlantic Monthly*
5. Furthermore, if we think of the century that preceded the eighteenth in England, when one monarch lost his head and two their thrones; when science and superstition, when Rome and Canterbury, when Divine Right and unspeakable wrongs bloodily collided; or if we think of the century the eighteenth gave way to, that yoked reform to respectability, that belched steam and smoke, that bounced with invention and clanged with discovery—if we look before and after, it is to come back to an era whose perspectives seem harmonious and proportions manageable.—LOUIS KRONENBERGER, *The Atlantic Monthly*
6. It is impossible that all these remonstrances and reproofs should not affect me . . . .—MATTHEW ARNOLD
7. It is a matter both of wonder and regret, that those who raise so many objections against the new Constitution should never call to mind the defects of that which is to be exchanged for it. It is not necessary that the former should be perfect; it is sufficient that the latter is more imperfect.—JAMES MADISON, *The Federalist*, No. 38
8. We often hear it said, of this or that proposition, that it may be good in theory, but will not answer in practice.—E. A. POE
9. For if sparrows and sweet peas are incompatible, it may be said with equal truth that the daisy is the grass's greatest enemy; and worse than daisies are dandelions.—GEORGE MOORE

10. It is difficult to think in a garden where amorous birds are going hither and thither, so amorous that one cannot but be interested in them.—George Moore

11. It is significant that the Dominicans, in the first austere years of the order, forbade the brethren to read the classics, though they might look upon them, say, for an hour; and in the *Metamorphosis Goliae,* the great debate between Pallas and Aphrodite, it is the "cowled folk," *populus cucullatus,* who rush in and force silence on the poets.—Helen Waddell

12. . . . it is helpful initially to realize the limitations which circumscribe whatever prophetic achievements he does attain.—James McConkey

13. It is the implication of such a comment in Forster's writings that causes Austin Warren to say that the novel form, more than the drama, is most compatible with such a person as Forster.—James McConkey

IV. Basic sentence patterns are forms or structures. They are not in themselves archetypes of meaning. In our study of parts of speech, we saw clearly enough the difficulty of classifying words as parts of speech without concern for function. Complexities find entrance into basic sentence patterns by means of involutions of predicational meaning within words, as we shall later see at length in Chapter 12 on Noun-Headed Reduced Predications. We cannot come to terms with the kind of redistribution of items in basic sentence patterns by which one basic pattern is converted into another until we have had time to master some of those means of infolding complexities—if, in fact, we can do it even then, since the description of transformations should not allow the substitution of dissimilar lexical items (such as *knows* for *is aware of* as opposed to structural change to a base-word as in *knows, knowledge*). In our description of basic sentence patterns, we have considered both *This interests me* and *This is very interesting to me* as basic predicational forms. But we have not said that one cannot be converted into the other. That this can be done in a variety of ways the following parallel phrasings will show. These show ways of changing copula predications into predications with transitive or intransitive verbs, or the opposite. Try to formulate the varieties of these redistributions that are commonly encountered, using these illustrations as a pilot. Can you add to them?

1. he pursues the trinity / he is in pursuit of the trinity
2. she represents to him a goddess / she is representative to him of a goddess
3. he loves his mother / he has love for his mother (How does *has* function here?)

4. he worships at all three temples / he is a worshipper at all three temples
5. his vision of reality is much less stable / he sees reality with much less stability
6. his own concern is with the task of reconciling physical with transcendent reality / he concerns himself with the task of . . .
7. he is too poignantly aware of the dual separation / he knows too poignantly the dual separation
8. such an integration is in contrast with / such an integration contrasts with
9. one who has suffered / one who has been a sufferer
10. his distrust of reason is a distrust of absolutes / he distrusts reason because he distrusts absolutes
11. these characters convey to us the sense of / these characters are the conveyers to us of the sense of

V. Rewrite these sentences, turning the copula patterns into transitive or intransitive verb patterns:

1. Scandals in Hollywood were a coincidental concomitant of the growth of entertainment films.—BOSLEY CROWTHER
2. The election in 1962 of Newark's present mayor . . . was proof of the strength of applied Negro political power.—JOHN O'SHEA
3. His was the solid support of the business community.
4. Addonizio's most inspired and daring act of political initiative was his declaration during the summer of 1964 of an all-out war on poverty and ignorance.—JOHN O'SHEA
5. It is estimated that between $55 million and $60 million worth of construction projects are now under way in Newark.—JOHN O'SHEA
6. What if our urgent want now is, not to act at any price, but rather to lay in a stock of light for our difficulties.—MATTHEW ARNOLD
7. Our familiar praise of the British Constitution under which we live is that it is a system of checks—a system which stops and paralyses any power in interfering with the free action of individuals.—MATTHEW ARNOLD
8. . . . for allegory is at war with the whole tone of his nature. —E. A. POE
9. . . . for a knowledge of the literature of the world was necessary for the writing of the article I had in mind.—GEORGE MOORE

VI. Noam Chomsky, in his introduction to Paul Roberts' *English Syntax,* calls attention to the difference between *John impresses Bill as incompetent* and *John regards Bill as incompetent.* The functioning of the analytic particle *as* can be confusing in both these instances. What is clear is that in the first sentence the secondary predicational nexus is between *John* (the subject of the primary predication) and *incompetent* (which is a kind of predicate appositive)—*John is incompetent;* whereas in the second sentence the secondary predicational nexus is between *Bill* (a direct object in double valence) and *incompetent* (an objective complement): *John regards Bill to be an incompetent.* We may define a predicate appositive as a complement in a secondary predication whose subject-part is in the subject part of a superior predication. According to this definition, a predicate appositive can be an adjective, a noun, a participle, even a prepositional phrase (see Chapter 9); and it may differ from other kinds of appositives only because it is placed in the predicate part of a sentence and the primary predicator intervenes between it and its subject-part. It will be found therefore that predicate appositive constructions represent a transformation of some kind. In the sentences following, attempt to find the source sentences and to work out transformational paths by which these results are reached.

1. He had the power of making us listen to his voice, amazed at the flow of significant sound.
2. I can't stay in a place like this all night cold sober.
3. Think of what will happen if you get caught fishing out of season.
4. They come up mounted and on foot and in wagons, to enter the yard and look at him and then go on to the front where Lion lay.—WILLIAM FAULKNER
5. . . . to keep yourself from having to find out what this boy was born knowing and fearing too maybe but without being afraid. —WILLIAM FAULKNER
6. . . . and still McCaslin came on not fast but steady.—WILLIAM FAULKNER
7. He went to bed a coward and woke up brave.
8. He hit the sack a coward and raised himself up again brave.
9. The devotion that had so assisted her father and that had been so lavished on her idle husband fell, a heavy weight, on her two children.—LOUIS AUCHINCLOSS
10. He took the insult lying down.
11. He went into the woodshed afraid of what he would find.
12. . . . he could sit unmolested in his grandfather's cool library.— LOUIS AUCHINCLOSS
13. He was born and raised in a backwoods county of Missouri, the son of a blacksmith and part-time preacher.
14. A little boy came down the tow-path whistling, a red-haired, freckle-faced urchin, shoeless and not noticeably clean.

8

DEPENDENT CLAUSES

Basic sentence structures are complicated most simply by the addition to the principal predication of dependent predications of one kind or another, rather than by the rearrangement or redistribution of the component parts of the principal predication. Transformation by redistribution can of course take place in dependent clauses or phrases as well as in principal clauses. Dependent clauses are full formal predications, each containing a subject and a finite verb agreeing with it in the full range of possible verb phrases, with the exception that in some dependent clauses modality is not expressed by modal auxiliaries but by simplified forms that we may call subjunctive forms even though they hardly represent a full range of inflection. Inasmuch as we are mainly concerned with the syntax of transformations, we are interested in the mechanisms by which certain clauses are subordinated to, attached to, or are included in matrix clauses as well as in the functions that they perform in relation to the matrix clauses or to items in them. Although often dependent clauses differ in form from principal clauses only in that a connector added to them renders them subordinates, there is no implication that they are necessarily to be placed higher on a scale of levels of subordination (linguistic levels) than non-clause units, since they can be dependent upon reduced predications, semi-predications, or even upon single words. The chief varieties of dependent clauses are relative clauses (often called adjective clauses since syntactically they are attached to nouns or pronouns and are seemingly dependent upon them), the so-called adverbial clauses (so called

135

either because their syntactic connection is with verbs or adjectives or because they perform functions that are loosely thought of as adverbial), and noun clauses (which fill positions in sentences usually occupied by nouns and perform nominal functions).

RELATIVE CLAUSES

The relative clause provides one of the chief mechanisms for making one predication a dependency of another. The dependency is owing to the nature of the relative pronoun which effects the subordination. The most common relative pronouns are *who, which,* and *that,* together with the inflected forms of *who* (*whom, whose*). These relative pronouns have triple functions: (1) they are proxies for nouns and pronouns and therefore perform functions within their own clauses that have been performed by the nouns or pronouns that they supplant (that is, of subject, direct object, indirect object—usually with the analytic particle *to*—objective complement, or so-called object of a preposition); (2) they are pronouns and therefore refer to antecedents outside of their own clauses, usually to identifiable nouns, nominal phrases or clauses, or pronouns, but sometimes, with more dubious propriety, to part clauses or reduced predications; (3) they signal the subordination of the clauses in which they appear to some unit outside of their clauses (usually the relative clause is technically dependent upon the antecedent of the relative pronoun, whatever kind of unit that may be). It is the relative clause that is dependent on the outsider, not the relative pronoun itself, for the relative pronoun merely signals the dependency.

Since *who* and *which* also function as interrogative pronouns in interrogative noun clauses, some grammarians refuse to recognize the difference between relative and interrogative pronouns and call *who* and *which* relative words even when they appear in independent questions. Thus, they minimize the functioning of a relative pronoun as a signaler of subordination. On a few occasions it is difficult to distinguish between a relative clause functioning adjectivally and an interrogative clause functioning nominally, since the noun clause may be considered to be adjunctive and the relative clause may be considered to be adjectival only by extension or by the grace of analogy. Consider the surface similarity of "His interpretation, *of which I am very fond,* ended the quarrel" and "His interpretation of *which text a reader should choose* was sound." The dependent clause in the first sentence is a non-restrictive relative clause; the dependent clause in the second sentence is an interrogative noun clause that functions as object of the preposition *of*.

When *which* functions as modifier of an object of a preposition within its own clause, the form of relative clause and interrogative noun clause may be identical: *Flint Central, from which high school he graduated, was located in the heart of town. I do not know from which high school he graduated (From which high school did he graduate?).* The first of these is a relative clause, the second an interrogative noun clause.

When a question is transformed into an interrogative noun clause, *do* is deleted and the word order returns to that of a declarative clause. In terms of the overlap we can explain the appearance of clauses that seem to be derived from interrogative clauses in positions of noun modifiers: *the town where I was born; the reason why I did this; apples, whatever kind of tree they come from, are . . . .* The functioning as noun modifier is not, however, a significant feature in the definition of a relative clause. Likewise, dependent interrogative clauses do not necessarily always function as nouns. Certain kinds of relative clauses, notably those using *that* as relative pronoun, cannot be said to derive from questions. So, in spite of the overlapping, we would do well to keep separate as best we can the two kinds of clauses.

A significant test of the distinction between noun clauses made from declarative predications, which use *that* as introductory particle, and relative clauses in which *that* appears as a relative pronoun is to ask if the *that* functions as a noun or pronoun would function in the dependent clause. The forms of the following dependent clauses show the contrast:

his belief *that all men are mortal* (a noun clause in form, whether it is functioning adjectivally or not, since *that* functions in it only as an introductory particle; some grammarians call this kind of clause a noun clause in close apposition; it can also be argued that *his belief that all men are mortal* represents the transformation of a predication *He believed that all men are mortal,* by reduction to a nominal phrase, in which the noun clause direct object remains unchanged—so that the clause should still be called the object of the reduced predication).

his belief *that interests me most* (a relative clause since *that* functions as subject of *interests*).

A relative pronoun comes either at the beginning of its clause or as near the beginning as its function within its clause makes possible. This is to say that in the process of transforming an independent predication into a relative clause two changes may be necessary. If a predication is to become a relative clause, it is theoretically necessary that it have some item in common with the predication to which it is to become subordinated. The predications *I met a man at a dinner party yesterday* and *This man had red hair* have the item *man* in common. Therefore, it should be a simple act of mechanical transformation to subordinate one to the other by converting one of the two into a relative clause. The results will be *at a dinner party yesterday I met a man who had red hair* or *A man whom I met at a dinner party yesterday had red hair*. We notice that the forms of the relative clauses are not identical. Since *man* becomes the subject of the relative clause in the first sentence, the only internal change that is necessary is the substitution of *who* for *this man*. The relative pronoun takes the place not only of the noun but also of the determiners and restrictive modifiers in the noun phrase, except that the behavior may be different when there are pre-determiners; that is, only the equatable part of the noun phrase is converted. In the combining of the predications *Some men love wars* and *A few of these men even like to fight in them,* we find that the pre-determiner *a few* (which we have called a "near-noun") further narrows the field of reference. *Some men* and *a few of these men* are not equatable; in this case, if the second is to be subordinated, the phrasing will be *a few of whom*. A fallacy is revealed here in the structuralist grammarian's tendency to treat pre-determiners as dependent parts of a noun phrase.

In the second of the sentences (*A man whom I met at a dinner party yesterday had red hair*), *a man* functions as subject in one clause and as object in the other. If an object is converted to a relative pronoun, it becomes *whom* in formal writing and speech (but often remains *who* in informal uses). The word order is then changed and the relative pronoun is brought to the beginning of the clause. The order varies somewhat when the relative is the object of a preposition. The standard formal principle is for the entire prepositional phrase to be given the front position (*from whom I have borrowed this book, from a few of which this verse has been selected, after many of the analogues of which this rule has been fashioned*). It can be seen that when a prepositional phrase modifies the object of a prepositional phrase the relative pronoun may be well buried within its clause but still be pushed as far toward the front as it can go. This principle applies only to *who* and *which*, not to *that*. Of these three, only *who* has distinctive genitive and objective forms. When a prepositional phrase comes at the end of a clause to be converted into a relative clause, the preposition may on occasion not be brought forward, particularly in informal uses. An old-fashioned puristic rule was: Never end a sentence with a preposition. This happens when *that* is the object of a preposition in a tail-end prepositional phrase, or when *which* or *whom* do not carry the preposition of which they are objects along with them to the beginning. Winston Churchill's scorn for the stuffiness of *up with which I will not put* is a case in point. Other examples are: *that I borrowed it from, whom I lent it to, which I was heading toward*. *Of* prepositions (which are likely to occur in partitive phrases, phrases of specification, or in other phrases that usually modify nouns) are less likely to occur at the end of clauses in this manner than are prepositions in phrases usually thought of as adverbial, but even those after pre-determiners sometimes are found at the end: *a kind that I have several of, a dessert that I will have none of*. *Of* in *that I have spoken of* belongs to the kind of meaning called adverbial (by a dubious shift of terminology from form to function), signifying *about* or *concerning*.

When relative clauses of this kind of which we have been speaking are further reduced to infinitive phrases, the relative pronoun is often deleted, with the result that the preposition is left without its object: *antiques for which we can bargain > antiques to bargain for; heights that the ambitious may want to attain to*. The object is present in the noun or pronoun upon which the infinitive phrase depends but not within the dependent unit itself. The same principle is at work when the relative pronoun is deleted from a relative clause when the relative pronoun would be either the direct object of the verb in its clause or the object of a final prepositional phrase: *the girl (whom) I gave the ring to; the animal (that) we saw running across the road*. The particle *that* introducing noun clauses used as direct objects is also often omitted: *I knew (that) he had an onion in his pocket,* but since this particle does not function as a nominal in the dependent clause, its omission cannot account for a stranded preposition at the end of the clause.

In the spoken variety of some American English dialects, the illusion is created that relative pronouns used as subjects are deleted, but what happens presumably is that a pause takes the place of the articulation of the relative pronoun: *Jones, . . . saw me coming out of the tavern, got angry right away. This man . . . was my buddy took me on his shoulders.* This kind of signaling is hard to represent in written English.

The use of *as* as a relative pronoun occurs more often in out-of-the-way dialects than in the standard language: *Them as favors this motion stand up* (those who favor). On other occasions, when *as* seems to act as subject of a dependent clause, it might be better interpreted as connector introducing an elliptical clause of comparison: *His overweening pride, as is seen in his rejection of the offer, almost destroyed him.* It is possible, however, to call it a relative pronoun.

The relative clause, no matter what its relational function seems to be, is by position and syntactic attachment a modifier of (that is, a dependent of) a noun, pronoun, or some other kind of nominal unit. A dubious exception to this generalization may be the kind of relative clause in which the relative pronoun refers to a whole predication—both to subject and predicate parts—particularly when that predication is the independent clause upon which the relative clause is dependent (*He splashed around in the bathtub, which got his mother all wet:* the reference of *which* is to the "idea" in the verb *splashed,* or more precisely to the whole formal predication *he splashed around in the bathtub*). In this situation the relative clause may be described as a sentence modifier, or as a modifier of a whole clause conceived as a substantive by a re-orientation in the mind. Some may argue that such a construction is, or ought to be, ungrammatical. The fact of the matter is, however, that pronouns of other kinds (notably *this, that,* and *it*) often are made to refer to whole predications, either formal or reduced, and that particles in non-restrictive phrases can also be found in structures of modification in which the formal headword must be reconstructed, mentally, out of an existing clause structure. That constructions of these kinds are frequently created, even by good speakers and writers, can hardly be denied, but the construction nevertheless runs counter to our usual expectations. It is the stylist's problem to decide how much confusion he will deliberately invite.

Relative clauses always follow the headword referred to by the relative pronoun, but not always immediately, for sometimes other modifiers of the same headword intervene, and sometimes whole predicate parts may intervene when these are short: *A man came here yesterday who had never been here before; The soldier died bravely, who in his childhood had always been a coward.*

In our attempt to build sophisticated sentence structures, it is the non-restrictive relative clause that should particularly attract our attention. The transformational principle is the same for both restrictive and non-restrictive kinds, except for a difference in intonational contour (or punctuation, in writing). The noun modified by a restrictive clause is likely to lose primary stress to the verb in the dependent clause since the dependent clause is an identifier of the noun, and there is no more than plus juncture between the two:

The màn who cáme here yèsterday| is my úncle, as opposed to the non-restrictive *My úncle, who câme here yèsterday, . . .* Distinct juncture can be felt before and after a non-restrictive clause. Some pause may follow a restrictive clause to indicate the end of the whole noun phrase. There is a rise in pitch in the modified noun before a non-restrictive clause but no terminal fall below the ordinary level; the same rise and return is felt at the end of the inserted clause:

2 3 2 2   3 2 2   3 1
My uncle, who came here yesterday, gave me a dollar.

This rise in pitch does not occur before restrictive clauses but may be felt at the end of them.

2   2   3 2   3 1
The man who came here yesterday gave me a dollar.

These are differences in signaling to indicate differences in the structuring of sentences, for the restrictive clause "comes naturally" since it materially aids in the identification of the nominal. The use of the non-restrictive, on the other hand, implies artful manipulation of materials and more-or-less conscious architecture. The transformation of predications and inclusion of them within the frame of a matrix sentence, such as is found in the formation of non-restrictive units, is more a feature of the literary language than of structures used on the street where unconnected brief utterances or easy coordination are more common. Since one of the justifications of grammatical analysis in the schools is the bringing about, at a fairly early age-level, of a comprehension of the more elaborate and sophisticated structures of the literary language, which are not necessarily naively absorbed in childhood, understanding of the workings of non-restrictive clauses is particularly important, even if the controlling concepts are rhetorical rather than grammatical.

Descriptive clauses that are not necessary for the determination of identity are not restrictive and yet may be punctuated and intoned as if they were. What is important in creating relative clause structures is utilizing the point of intersection of two predications—that word or item that occurs in both. This common item is transformed to a relative word in whichever of the predications is to be subordinated. Highly sophisticated uses of this transformation are shown in the following sentences (which I reprint from my *Writing Mature Prose*, pp. 63–64):

1. The last tall masts have slipped out of Salem Harbor, and Hawthorne's ghost is more peaceful in the Custom House than ever those living ghosts were among whose dusty papers he found an initial bound with tarnished gold.—BERNARD DEVOTO
2. He wore patched trousers held by suspenders made of sheeting; a calico shirt that was almost as black as the rich soil in the forests northward; a ragged hat through the holes of which his uncombed flaxen hair thrust up in tiny golden sheaves, and shoes so worn that they barely kept to his feet.—VARDIS FISHER
3. They were so competent in the recognition of theory that they felt strangely at home in a world most of whose citizens lived by theories without knowing it.—MARK VAN DOREN
4. This life did not count at all save as a preparation for an eternal one, entrance to the happiness of which was possible only by following certain rules of conduct.—JAMES TRUSLOW ADAMS
5. But the immediate development with which we are concerned begins in 1525, almost a century before the Jacobean version saw the light.—JOHN LIVINGSTON LOWES

The practical stylist needs to achieve coherence and "flow" as he coerces a whole flock of predications into some semblance of traveling order, within the possible limits of grammatical transformations. The grammarian can point out how useful relative clauses are in this combining of predications.

THE SO-CALLED ADVERBIAL CLAUSES

The mechanisms for attaching the so-called adverbial clauses to basic sentence patterns, or to other dependent units, are even simpler than those for relative clauses. For the most part, all that needs to be done in effecting the attachment and subordination is to put the appropriate connector, called a subordinating conjunction, at the beginning of the clause to be attached, and to insert the clause at one of several possible points of the matrix sentence. These clauses are usually called adverbial clauses, not because they are precisely adverbs as we have defined the form class of adverbs, but because they express relations that we loosely and inexactly come to think of as expressed by adverbs in basic or near-basic sentence patterns. Similarly, we loosely and inexactly think of modifiers that can conceivably be said to express qualities, attributes, or properties as adjectival units, particularly if the modifiers are dependent upon nouns or pronouns. This terminology is inexact because it confuses forms, functions, and relations indiscriminately. The point of syntactic connection of these so-called adverbial clauses is usually either with the verb of the superior unit, or vaguely with the predication as a whole, or with an adjective or adverb (when the clause expresses relations of comparison or degree). With the exception of place and time clauses (which can be attached to nominals denoting place and time), these clauses can be dependent on nominals only when the nominals have been transformed from verbs to that form and function, in which case it can be said that the dependent clause still relates to the verb qualities remaining in the transformed locution. Thus we can find transformed phrases like *his acting as if he were royalty, his elimination from the contest because he had had too much to drink,* or *his desire to compete for the prize while he was still young.* In these the items upon which the clauses depend function formally as nominals but the relational functioning is with the verb ideas contained in the transforms. It is necessary to avoid a terminology that applies only to a static situation and ignores transformations of sets of relationships or that confuses forms and functions. However, for purposes of rough distinction, the term "adverbial" is still useful. These clauses, like adverbs, can occupy several possible positions in a sentence, while relative clauses are more rigidly held to a position following the nominals they modify or are dependent on. Some kinds of adverbs can shift position more easily than others. It is within the range of grammatical possibility to say *Quickly he entered the room, He quickly entered the room,* and *He entered the room quickly. Quickly* is a manner adverb in these sentences. We can less easily shift a clause of manner to the beginning or insert it between subject and verb: *As if he was in great haste he entered the room, He, as if he was in great haste, entered the room.* These orders may be found on occasion, but the more natural order seems to be *He entered the room as if he was in great haste.* Clauses of result almost necessarily follow verbs. Causal clauses, on the other hand, can be front-shifted very readily—so readily in fact that we sometimes tend to consider any front-shifted dependent unit (such as appositive or participial phrases) as an expression of a causal relation. Clauses of time, place, condition, and concession appear frequently at the beginning of sentences but are not limited to that position.

The group of relationships that we figuratively call adverbial by shifting the meaning of the term from form to relational function consists, with some lumping together of allied relationships, of (1) time (*as, before, since, until, when, while, after,* etc.), (2) place (*where, wherever*), (3) condition (*if, unless, provided that*), (4) concession (*although, though, while, even if*), (5) cause (including reason and some kinds of purpose: *because, since, as, inasmuch as*), (6) result (*so that, so . . . that, such . . . that, that*), (7) purpose (*so that, in order that, that*), (8) manner (*as, as if, as though*), (9) degree (*so . . . that, as . . . as, as . . . as if, more . . . than, less . . . than*), (10) comparison (*as . . . as, so . . . as, more . . . than, less . . . than*). Some illustrative sentences are:

> *The moving van arrived before he had time to prepare the house.*
> *Where the birds fly I shall fly also.*
> *If the moon is really made of green cheese, our dairy farmers should be opposed to attempts to reach it.*
> *In reality the world is composed of grays, although it often seems to be either black or white.*
> *Since you have already convinced me, you don't need to argue any more.*

He hit the pole so sharply that it toppled over (note the overlap with degree).

He had an extension phone put in so that he would not have to walk so far.

He performed the piece as he had been taught to do.

He hit it so hard that it cracked.

I am bigger than you are.

These are not discrete logical categories. Subordinating conjunctions, like most function words, tend to have central lexical significances, some more than others, but in the long history of these words coalescence, extension, and simplification have often taken place. We observe that in our daily thinking we naturally assume that causes precede effects in time, with the result that we may express causal connections by means of time connectors: *When it rains the sidewalks get wet, When she entered the room he quickly departed.* Conditions can be expressed by time connectors, particularly when the time is abstract time: *When(ever) heat is applied, the gases expand.* The implication here may also be that the condition is the cause of the result. The idea expressed in an adverbial clause may conceivably be coordinate with the idea expressed in the principal clause. In earlier centuries speakers of English used more paired conjunctions than we do today: *Although I have cast thee away, yet do I love thee.* The pairing practically amounts to coordination. Degree and comparison are often two aspects of the same thing. Result differs from cause mainly in terms of which clause is subordinated; result clauses rarely are found at the beginning of sentences. These grammatical categories are constituted more upon the conjunctions and the range of forms within which the words can be used than they are upon logical categories, even though there is some overlapping of the two kinds of categories.

These so-called adverbial clauses can sometimes be further reduced by a transforming of the verbs in them to participles or to infinitives and by deletion of the subjects (usually by ellipsis since the subjects appear elsewhere in the sentence):

Although he did not wish to appear greedy, he could not resist taking the last piece of cake > Although not wishing to appear greedy, he could not resist . . .

As if he would deprive him . . . > As if to deprive him . . .

Since in many instances subordinate adverbial clauses parallel prepositional phrases both in relationships expressed and in function words used as connectors, differing only in that the subordinating conjunction introduces a clause and the preposition is followed by a nominal object, distinction between a prepositional phrase and a reduced adverbial clause is not always easy. In some instances, however, the connectors are not the same in the two cases. Thus, we say *Although objecting, he* . . . , but *In spite of his objections, he* . . . , in which the first is a reduced adverbial clause and the second a prepositional phrase with a predication reduced to a nominal phrase as object of the preposition. *When going* (a reduced adverbial clause) contrasts with *on going* (a prepositional phrase). Since *after* and *before* function both as subordinating conjunctions and as prepositions, this distinction is impossible in *after going* or *before going*. Purpose infinitive phrases can be thought of as reduced purpose clauses except that the purpose infinitive often appears without connector: *I went there so that I could see him* > *I went there to see him* or *I went there in order to see him*. When the subject of the infinitive differs from the subject of the superior clause, *for* can act as connector: *I went there for him to see me*. Interrogative noun clauses using *when* or *how* as question words can similarly be reduced to infinitive phrases: *I don't know how to do that, I did not know when to go*. Unless these infinitives are abstract and agentless (*When to go had not been decided*), the reduction is possible only when the subject of the infinitive is the same as the subject of the superior predication. In a reduction such as *I was uncertain when to go,* can we decide with any certainty whether the reduced phrase represents an adverbial time clause or an interrogative noun clause? Does *was uncertain* constitute a verb phrase functioning as *did not know*?

There are in English a few special devices by which one clause can be related to another, in connection with one or another of these so-called adverbial relations. Two of these provide variations of conditional clauses. The conditional relationship can be expressed by a construction in which an imperative verb begins the clause that would express the condition, and in which *and* connects the two clauses apparently coordinating them: *Ask me no questions and I'll tell you no lies, Let him try it once and he'll find out what trouble means*. The other variety, which likewise omits the subordinating conjunction *if*, involves the transposing of the order of subject and verb auxiliary in the dependent clause: *Had I asked him* . . . . *If I had asked him* . . . . The inversion can also occur with copulas but not with simple present or past tenses of transitive or intransitive verbs; the condition expressed is usually contrary to fact: *Were I honest, I would repay the debt.* John Locke illustrates the construction thus:

Whereas, were the capacities of our understandings well considered, the extent of our knowledge once discovered, and the horizon found which sets the bounds between the enlightened and the dark part of things, between what is and what is not comprehensible by us, men would perhaps with less scruple acquiesce in the avowed ignorance of the one, and employ their thoughts with more advantage and satisfaction in the other.

That following words normally adverbs or other forms than subordinating conjunctions can act as a subordinating conjunction. *Provided that, now that,* and *seeing that* are examples. *However* can introduce a curious kind of concessive clause: *However much they try to fool us, they will be the ones to be fooled; However violent they have been in the past, they are gentle enough now; However we interpret the facts, we are forced to agree that* . . . (*Although we may interpret the facts in different ways, we are forced to agree that* . . .).

Special problems arise in connection with the split conjunctions that express relationships of result, degree, and comparison (*so . . . that, such . . . that, as . . . as, as . . . as if, so . . . as, more . . . than, less . . . than, -er . . . than*). These conjunctions usually split over an adjective or adverb; *such* as a near-noun combining a significance of degree and a pre-determiner function is an exception. It can be argued that only the second item in the pairs is a conjunction, the first being an adverb of degree, an intensifier, or the particle achieving comparison of an adjective or adverb. Some assorted examples are:

He was *so* fat *that he could not stand* (He was fat to such a degree that the result was that he could not stand).
The men worked with *such* (an) intensity *that the job was finished overnight* (so much of an intensity > so much intensity > such intensity: *such* is a near-noun functioning in the ambiguous role of noun or adjective like other near-nouns).
Jake is *as* clever *as you (are)* (can be called either degree or comparison; the deletion of the verb in the dependent clause is common in English, even though, or perhaps because, the remaining *as you* resembles a prepositional phrase, except that a nominative form is called for when distinction is possible).
She looked as refreshed *as if she had just gotten out of bed* (a hy-

brid between degree and manner or possibly comparison and manner: her fresh appearance resembles what her appearance would have been had she just gotten out of bed).

I am not *so* strong *as you* (An old rule, rarely followed, is that *so* is used instead of *as* after a negative).

This car runs *more* economically *than that (does)* (*more*, the analytic particle effecting comparison, can be called the first element of a clause of either comparison or degree; here the split is over an adverb).

He gave me *more candy than I wanted* (*more* is here a near-noun: *more of candy*).

He came *less* quickly *than I expected* (a curiously elliptical construction; *less* is here a particle of negative comparison).

He gave me *less* candy *than I wanted* (*less* is a near-noun).

He is a bigg*er* fraud *than I thought (him to be)* (the *-er* morpheme of comparison functions as the first item in the clause of degree of comparison).

He is rich*er than I thought*.

He is rich*er than I (am)*.

It can be seen that the syntactic mechanisms of these clauses are more subtle than those of other kinds of so-called adverbial clauses and that to create transformational formulas for all of the variations would be more difficult. The position of the *as* and *than* clauses is rigidly fixed after the adjective, adverb, or noun, although other modifiers may sometimes intervene: *He is richer in the kind of worldly goods that make entrance into heaven difficult than I am.* Combinations of result and degree or comparison clauses are possible: *He is so much richer than I am that his brand of thinking is alien to mine.* We would have to spend much more time on these problems to work out all of the possible complexities.

SEQUENCE WORDS

The subordinating conjunctions introducing the so-called adverbial clauses must be kept distinct as a class from connecting words of a different kind whose functions seem to run parallel to theirs. These (words like *therefore, however, thus, nevertheless,* and *consequently*) can be called "sequence words." Traditionally they have been called "conjunctive adverbs." That they express logical connections between clauses can hardly be doubted, but only by great extension of principle can some of them be called adverbs. They do not effect subordination of one clause to another; consequently, the connections that they indicate are logical or semantic rather than syntactical. The only syntactical problems they present are their relations to the clauses in which they appear. These relations can range from close to distant, and the position of the sequence word in its clause can be fixed or free, depending on the closeness or distance of the relationship. When the relationship is close, the sequence word is usually clearly an adverb. In *Thus prepared, he waited for them without anxiety, thus* makes some reference to a preceding clause—a non-syntactical reference; but within its own unit it functions clearly as an adverb of manner modifying *prepared.* In *Thus, he had no alternative, thus* means something like *for this reason* and is much less plainly an adverb. Sequence words therefore form a special class of function words not to be identified closely with the form class of adverbs. What is more significant than their classification is the semantic parallel that exists between them and certain subordinating conjunctions—and, furthermore, with certain coordinating conjunctions. The parallels can illuminate contrasting structures for the expression of semantic relationships. A concessive clause, for instance, expresses an idea that is in some way opposed to the idea of the clause to which it is subordinate. It is a kind of adversative, but of an unbalanced kind since the force of the idea in the superior clause is supposedly greater than that in the concessive clause: *Although I love him, I will not marry him.* The coordinating conjunction *but* is also an adversative, but since it connects ideas that are on the same level, they supposedly have equal force. When we express ourselves in the medium of linguistic forms, we do not, however, utilize such delicate scales for discrimination, and we make little distinction between the meaning of *Although I love him, I will not marry him* and that of *I love him, but I will not marry him.* A third way of finding a linguistic form for the same idea is to link the two clauses with a sequence word: *I love him; I will not, however, marry him.*

These parallels are more common than we may think. Since in nature cause precedes effect, the cause-and-effect relationship between clauses can be expressed by the coordinating conjunction *and* provided that the cause clause is given first and the effect or result clause second: *He hasn't arrived on time, and I'm leaving.* Two sequence orders are possible with the concessive clauses, depending on shading of meaning: *Although I love him, I will not marry him. Although I will not marry him, I love him. I love him, but I will not marry him. I will not marry him, but I love him. I love him; however, I will not marry him. I will not marry him; however, I love him.* In the causal sequence, only with the subordinating conjunction do we have two possible orders, and there the meaning in no way changes. *I'm leaving and he hasn't arrived on time* is not possible; nor is *I'm leaving; therefore, he hasn't arrived on time,* although *He hasn't arrived on time; therefore, I'm leaving* is possible. If, however, the result concept is expressed rather than the cause or reason concept, the order of the version using the dependent clause is necessarily reversed: *He hasn't arrived on time, so (that) I'm leaving.*

Conditional subordinating conjunctions (*if, unless*), like the coordinating conjunction *or* and the sequence word *otherwise,* imply alternatives. Therefore, another parallel set can be created among these:

If you cross this line, there will be a fight.
There will be a fight if you cross this line.
Don't cross this line or there will be a fight.
Don't cross this line; otherwise there will be a fight.

A negative imperative in the first clause becomes a necessary part of the structure when *or* or *otherwise* expresses a conditional relationship. When *unless* (a subordinating conjunction of negative condition) is used in place of *if,* the principal clause also must be negated, and even then the meaning is not quite the same: *Unless you cross this line there will be no fight.* If *in that case* is used as a sequence phrase, the negation is not called for: *Go ahead and cross this line; in that case there will be a fight.* *In case (that)* functions as a subordinating conjunction of condition: *In case you cross this line there will be a fight.*

Since past time in nature precedes present time, time connections expressed by the subordinating conjunctions *when, before, after, as,* and *while* can be alternatively expressed by the coordinating conjunction *and* (with some ambiguity or lack of specification).

When the sun came out during the rain, there was a rainbow.
The sun came out during the rain and there was a rainbow.
After the sun came out, the hay began to dry.
The sun came out and the hay began to dry.

Before the rains began, the ground was parched.
The rains had not yet begun and the ground was parched.
While (or as) the rains continued, the small animals kept to their
burrows.
The rains continued and the small animals kept to their burrows.

These time connections can also be expressed by sequence words
or phrases, alone or supporting coordinating conjunctions:

The sun came out during the rain; there was then a rainbow.
The sun came out during the rain and there was then a rainbow.
The sun came out and afterwards the hay began to dry.
The rains had not yet begun; at that time the ground was parched.
The rains continued; during that time the small animals kept to
their burrows.

We can see from these sentences the lexical pliability or expand-
ability of the corpus of sequence words. Some occur with great
frequency and function abstractly within the limits of their significances, and so are true function words. Others are word combinations that express uniquely the relationship between clauses
and so can be as numerous as there are relationships.

In the written language, failure to discriminate among these
contrasting structures is common, and much time is spent in the
schools in teaching the standard modes of punctuation for the
three kinds of structures. If the contrasts between patterns were
emphasized more, perhaps the amount of time spent in this way
could be reduced appreciably. But awareness of the contrasts is
of more value to the rhetorician than to the grammarian, since it
is by choice among competing structures that one style is created
and not another. So by calling attention to these competing structures the grammarian can be of real use to the rhetorician.

Style, and grammar too for that matter, is less a matter of absolute logical choices than it is one of the strategic disposing of
forces in terms of the ideational contours of the moment, conditioned surely by the habits that the strategist has formed. In a
situation, for instance, involving a causal chain of more than two
predications, the speaker or writer does not on principle commit
himself ahead of time to any one or another of these three ways
we have been discussing for giving form to causal relationships.
Take the sentence:

The quarry that has supplied the city with building stone for the
past century is now exhausted, and from now on building mate-

*rials will be imported at a higher price, and the cost of erecting
stone structures will rise.*

This string of *ands* is not good, rhetorically. In a sense, the exhaustion of the quarry is the cause of the importing of building materials and the subsequent rise in prices of them, and in turn of the increase in cost of erecting stone structures. Another way of stating this is: A is the cause of B, B is the cause of C, and C is the cause of D. Rhetorically, however, it may be good to ignore the internal causations and present as parallel items those that are actually parallel only because they both are links in the causal chain, as in:

> *Since the quarry that has supplied the city with building stone for
> the past century is now exhausted, and from now on building
> materials will be imported at a higher price, the cost of erecting
> stone structures will rise.*

Other parallelings here are also possible. This is the kind of problem speakers and writers face constantly in the disposing of their materials. The grammarian can describe the structures that are available for the disposing.

NOUN CLAUSES

Noun clauses differ from relative clauses and the so-called adverbial clauses in that they complicate a basic sentence pattern not by a simple addition of one clause to another or by the expansion that comes from an interruptive insertion of one clause between items in another, but by the supplanting of a noun or pronoun by a clause. In some instances, as when the noun supplanted is part of an outlying structure, this distinction is not an important one; but in connection with the expansion of basic sentence patterns it is. Young children are likely to form habits of using noun clauses as direct objects at an early stage. Other uses of them they master only after they have achieved a degree of sophistication in using language.

The mechanisms for transforming an independent formal finite predication into a noun clause of the usual declarative pattern are few and relatively simple: the particle *that* is added before the clause (sometimes even this is deleted when the noun clause serves as direct object—*I think he will go; I know Jones wants to*), and the verb is simplified to a kind of subjunctive form if the situation is one calling for certain modal auxiliaries in its independent form. Usage in connection with this use of subjunctive forms varies and is unstable. Often what is involved is a redistribution of modality from the independent to the dependent clause: *He must go > It is imperative that he go* (here we have a dummy *it; imperative,* the predicate adjective of the principal clause, makes lexically explicit an idea of modality; what we have in the verb of the noun clause is perhaps less a subjunctive than a retreat into simplicity from modality; thus, we can have *It is nice that you could go* in which the modality is expressed in the noun clause, and *It is important that you go* in which it is not expressed unless by simplification of the verb form. If we have true subjunctive forms, they are usually found in dependent noun or adverbial clauses of condition—*I wish that he were here, If I were king, I would . . .*). Only after extensive analysis could we indicate when these so-called subjunctive forms are found and when modal auxiliaries are used.

Noun clauses can be derived from questions as well as from declarative clauses. The form of a question is already a transformation, as we have seen in the chapter on First-Level Transformations. The interrogative noun clause begins with the question word, as does the independent question, unless the question word is the object of a preposition or functions adjectivally modifying the object of a preposition, in which case the preposition may precede it or may be detached from its object and be left at the end of the clause (*whose dog you are afraid of*). In the question transformation, subject and verb are inverted with *be* and with *be, have,* and modals as auxiliaries, or *do* is introduced as a function auxiliary before the subject. In the process of further transformation in becoming an interrogative noun clause, the verb-subject order of the question with *be, have,* and modal auxiliaries reverts to the declarative subject-verb order, and with other verbs the *do* disappears again. (*Why did you complain? > why you complained*). Because the order reverts to normal, questions taking "yes" or "no" answers are not distinct from declarative sentences in noun clause transformations. As with the parent questions, a preposition does not usually precede *what* as question word in interrogative noun clauses but is left at the end (*what you are afraid of*). The full range of question words appears in interrogative noun clauses: *who, whom, whose, which, what, how, when, where, why, whoever, whomever,* etc.

Exclamatory noun clauses, now rarer than they once were, superficially resemble interrogative noun clauses (*How green was my valley!* > *how green my valley was; What a liar he is! What a liar he is* or *how big a liar he is.*

It is to be expected that noun clauses can function almost anywhere that a noun can function. In actuality this is not entirely true, if for no other reason than that a whole clause is cumbersome in some positions. The "dummy" *it* functions to offset the cumbersomeness of the clause used as subject, or as object before an objective complement. Since only rarely do words denoting abstract entities function as indirect objects, noun clauses as indirect objects are rare. The noun clause used as subject (without "dummy" *it*) is more common in formal writing than in colloquial speech. The speaker or writer who is trying to climb to the level of fully developed expression should no doubt encourage himself to use noun clauses directly as subjects even if the habit has not been formed in the practice of his childhood. The most common use—and the one most based in elementary practice—is as the direct object after verbs denoting mental activity of some kind (*think, say, feel, believe, ask, demand, trust,* etc.—the list is rather long). Noun clauses can readily function as predicate nouns in copula predications when the subjects are nouns denoting mental activity (*His argument was that the Congress should adjourn*). Since such copula predications can be reduced to infinitive phrases, or, further, to the construction we call object-objective complement, noun clauses can function as the predicate part of reduced copula predications if the subject-part is a noun or pronoun denoting mental activity, but in this case the infinitive *to be* is rarely deleted (*I think his argument to be that the Congress should adjourn.*) The construction that occurs when the noun clause is in so-called close apposition is not so easily explained (*His argument that the Congress should adjourn surprised no one*) even though it should be obvious that the chief structural difference between close and non-restrictive apposition in this case is the use of commas to set off the non-restrictive appositive unit in writing or the corresponding pauses and shift of pitch contour in speaking. Actually, for the transformational grammarian, the difference is greater than this, for the noun clause in close apposition can be more readily construed as the direct object of the verb activity still resident in the noun derived from a verb of mental activity. This is to say that the total noun phrase *his argument that the Congress should adjourn* is more directly an organic transformation of the formal predication *He argued that the Congress should adjourn* than it is of the copula version *His argument was that the Congress should adjourn,* since the latter is in effect a transformation of the former and there is no reason to imply the reality of the intermediate transformation. In common usage a gerund can take a direct object without transformation no matter what the structure of the object may be (*his desiring an apple, his intending to go home, his arguing that the Congress should adjourn*). When a verb is transformed into an abstract noun, its object must assume the form of an objective genitive or periphrastically be the object of the preposition *of* (*his painting, Picasso's depiction of him*), except when that object is itself a reduced or formal predication—that is, when it is an infinitive phrase, a "for" construction, or a noun clause, in which case the object-predication will not undergo change (*his intention to go home, the wish for him to come, his argument that Congress should adjourn*). Consequently, in these circumstances, the deletion of the copula does not have to be imputed, since the transformation can be explained more simply. Thus, a noun clause can be said to function as the retained direct object of a verb that has been transformed into an abstract noun, if the verb denotes mental activity. This may be true even if the noun denoting mental activity does not have a corresponding verb form in English (*his idea that the Congress should adjourn, his notion that the Congress should adjourn*), although in these instances the imputation of a deleted copula would be simpler.

Noun clauses (particularly interrogative noun clauses) can also function as objects of prepositions (*after what you have said, from where he sat, in response to why he came,* etc.). Noun clauses can obviously not enter easily into the structures of compounds nor serve as pre-positional noun adjuncts. Instead of attempting to explain why time and place adverbial clauses can modify nouns of time and place (and so tempt us to call them adjective clauses if we are obsessed by the need for a static logic of terminology), we might do better to treat the clauses as interrogative noun clauses used adjunctively in post-position (*the town where I was born—Where was I born? the year when I lived there —the when-I-lived-there year < When did I live there?*) But since we can lose ourselves in the argument of whether or not a noun adjunct functions as an adjective, this further distinction that rests on the base of an unanswerable question is futile.

These three kinds of dependent clauses—relative clauses, the so-called adverbial clauses, and noun clauses—are the units that most obviously illustrate the inclusion of one predication within a larger structure. As clauses they retain the form of full predications; they formally remain predications; but by transformations that are sometimes subtle (sometimes very simple: *I know you are here*) they become dependent parts of larger predications— and even sometimes dependent upon very lowly parts of those larger predications. "Larger" here means "on a higher linguistic level," not "number of words" or "physical length of statement." "Linguistic level" is a term that applies to "steps of dependency," not to "steps of transformation." Thus, a noun clause that takes the place of a noun in a basic sentence pattern remains on the top linguistic level, since predicational nuclei in basic sentence patterns are on the same linguistic level. In semi-predicational structures this is not true. In the sentence *Hunting in the woods, I met a bear*, two predications are given expression: *I was hunting in the woods* and *I met a bear*. One of these is transformed into the semi-predicative unit *hunting in the woods*, which presents us with only the predicate-part of the predication. A semi-predication like this is a dependent unit, on the next-lower linguistic level than the word, phrase, or clause with which it makes syntactic connection. We have pondered the possibility of allowing adverbs to function as adverbial complements in basic sentence patterns. If we can do this, we may also be able to think that some adverbial clauses can exist on the top linguistic level (*I put it where I wanted it*). This interpretation cannot clearly be supported. What is obvious is that most adverbial clauses exist on a lower level, as do relative clauses, since adjectives exist in basic sentence patterns only in the predicate position and relative clauses cannot supplant them there.

MATERIALS FOR EXERCISE AND FURTHER STUDY

Here is raw material that may be useful to you in creating your own grammar of dependent clauses. Since you can almost certainly find relevant instances in whatever pieces of writing lie at hand (but more in sophisticated writing than in writing intended for children), you do not need to have this collection to work with, except insofar as it may be useful to a group of students to have a common body of material in front of them. Study these. Group the evidence according to some workable scheme, keeping in mind the transformational processes by which the dependent clauses come to be included in the result sentences.

1. Such a correlation, at least, appears to be in Addison's mind when he asserts that satire must discriminate between those who are and are not its proper object, and a parallel between ridiculing natural infirmities and attacking human nature in a lump is made explicitly by Fielding.—BERTRAND A. GOLDGAR (*PMLA*)

2. Other critics, taking a somewhat different tack, argue that satire on man is useless because it fails aesthetically; it is so overgeneralized that it does not ring true.—BERTRAND A. GOLDGAR

3. Young, in the Preface to *Love of Fame* (1728), makes the same point: "Such writers encourage vice and folly, which they pretend to combat, by setting them on an equal foot with better things." Elsewhere in the same preface Young says historians may be considered severe satirists, since "such are most human actions, that to *relate*, is to *expose* them." But his pessimism does not extend to approval of those satirists who "are for lessening the true dignity of mankind," satirists whom he condemns as irresponsible and cynical descendents of Lucian. A more temperate view, finally, is expressed by William Melmoth, for whom the dignity of man is by no means to be taken for granted. Melmoth recognizes the ease with which observation of the world about us may lead us to a low estimate of human nature, but he feels we must struggle against this "ungenerous disposition," since it will kill the seeds of benevolence in our hearts.—BERTRAND A. GOLDGAR (*PMLA*)

4. Secretary of State Rusk has put a grim doctrine before the people of this country. He was a responsive and forthright witness before the Senate Foreign Relations Committee and it is important that we understand what he thinks our duties and responsibilities are in the world.

First, in Vietnam, we are to commit to the battle whatever is necessary to end the aggression and bring about the freedom and security of South Vietnam.

What this means, he conceded, depends primarily on what the enemy commits (the Chinese committed 1,000,000 men to the battle in Korea). He would not say there was no limit to the men and material the United States would send to Vietnam, but he stuck to his proposition that he would maintain military superiority there no matter how long it took to stop the fighting.—JAMES RESTON, *New York Times*, Feb. 20, 1966

5. The deep faith that Americans have in science and technology produces the complacent conviction that these intellectual disciplines

can master all the problems they help to create. This conviction is not wholly warranted. Since this country has no reason to believe itself exempt from the tragic fate that has overcome proud, reckless societies in the past, a measure of humility is in order. But even within the framework of traditional optimism, too few realize that man still lacks much of the scientific knowledge needed to make wise decisions about the use of land, water, and air.—Editorial, *New York Times,* Feb. 20, 1966

6. He stayed to gaze over the level fields of the hill-top, at the village which strewed the bare upland as if it had been tumbled off the passing wagons of industry, and been forsaken.—D. H. LAWRENCE

7. And from under the twig-purple of the bushes swam the shadowed blue, as if the flowers lay in flood water over the woodland.— D. H. LAWRENCE

8. My father, I am afraid, carried a natural incompetence in practical affairs to an exceptionally high level. He combined practical incompetence, practical enterprise and a thoroughly sanguine temperament, in a manner that I have never seen paralleled in any human being. He was always trying to do new things in the briskest manner, under the suggestion of books or papers or his own spontaneous imagination, and as he had never been trained to do anything whatever in his life properly, his futilities were extensive and thorough. At one time he nearly gave up his classes for intensive culture, so enamoured was he of its possibilities; the peculiar pungency of the manure he got, in pursuit of a chemical theory of his own, has scarred my olfactory memories for a lifetime.—H. G. WELLS

9. They walked into Benno's, which was half-empty tonight, and sat, in a rather abrupt and mysterious silence, at one of the tables in the back. This silence was produced by the fact that each of them had more on their minds than they could easily say.—JAMES BALDWIN

10. The manager asked repeatedly did no one know who the injured man was or where had his friends gone. The door of the bar opened and an immense constable entered. A crowd which had followed him down the laneway collected outside the door, struggling to look in through the glass panels.—JAMES JOYCE

11. There wasn't another soul in the place who didn't know the story—the whole story of the Halling Investment Trust and the proceedings for extradition. Any man doing dusty business in any of the wooden booths of the town is better fitted by long observation to tell Mr. Calloway's tale than I am, except that I was in—literally—at the finish.—GRAHAM GREENE

12. During the reign of parties for about forty years past, it is a melancholy consideration to observe how philology has been neg-

lected, which was before the darling employment of the greatest authors, from the restoration of learning in Europe. Neither do I remember it to have been cultivated, since the Revolution, by any one person, with great success, except our illustrious modern star, doctor Richard Bentley, with whom the republic of learning must expire, as mathematics did with sir Isaac Newton. My ambition has been gradually attempting, from my early youth, to be the holder of a rush-light before that great luminary; which, at least, might be of some little use during those short intervals while he was snuffing the candle, or peeping with it under a bushel.—JONATHAN SWIFT

13. He was now feeling so much better that he conceived the bold project of reserving the biscuits for later in the afternoon. He would finish the tea, then have as much free milk and sugar as he could lay his hands on, then walk carefully to the Cockpit and there eat the biscuits. Someone in Oxford Street might offer him a position of the highest trust. He settled down to plan how exactly he could get from where he was to Tottenham Court Road, what cutting reply he would make to the magnate and in what order he would eat the biscuits when the time came. He had proceeded no further than the British Museum and was recruiting himself in the Archaic Room before the Harpy Tomb, when a sharp surface thrust against his nose caused him to open his eyes.—SAMUEL BECKETT

14. Little fish have to keep moving all the time. The big ones never stop picking on them.

Avis knows all about the problems of little fish.

We're only No. 2 in rent a cars. We'd be swallowed up if we didn't try harder. There's no rest for us.

We're always emptying ashtrays. Making sure gas tanks are full before we rent our cars. Seeing that the batteries are full of life. Checking our windshield wipers.

And the cars we rent out can't be anything less than spanking new Plymouths.

And since we're not the big fish, you won't feel like a sardine when you come to our counter.

We're not jammed with customers.—Advertisement, Avis Rent a Car System, Inc.

15. The future attracted him less. Lying there for a week he reflected on what he could do next. He had just come up from the South Seas with John La Farge, who had reluctantly crawled away towards New York to resume the grinding routine of studio-work at an age when life runs low. Adams would rather, as choice, have gone back to the east, if it were only to sleep forever in the trade-winds under the southern stars, wandering over the dark purple ocean, with its purple sense of solitude and void.—HENRY ADAMS

9

SEMI-PREDICATIVE STRUCTURES

THE NATURE OF MODIFICATION

Two obvious kinds of semi-predicative structures are appositive phrases and participial phrases. These units are called semi-predicative because, although they are derived from full predications, they are, in their transformed condition, not formally complete predications in themselves. When the two sentences *Jonas often visits me* and *Jonas is a man of my acquaintance* are put together to yield *Jonas, a man of my acquaintance, often visits me*, the appositive phrase *a man of my acquaintance* in the result sentence is only half of a predication now because its original subject part is to be found in the matrix sentence into which the appositive unit is inserted. Thus, semi-predicative structures, which are included structures, contain only one of the two essential parts of a formal predication—the predicate-part. They can come into being by a process of transformation when the subject-part is present in the matrix sentence. The subject-part of the included predication that is completed by the semi-predicative unit thus exists upon a higher linguistic level than does the predicate-part. In traditional grammatical analysis, it is customary to say that the headword in a semi-predicative unit "modifies" its subject-part. It is necessary that we understand here in what ways this traditional interpretation applies. In the traditional sense, an appositive is said to "modify" the word with which it is in apposition. Thus, in *Zuglu, a man from Mars, came to our house for dinner, man*, which is the headword in the appositive phrase *a man from Mars,* is said to "modify" *Zuglu.* In the predication *Zuglu is a man from Mars, Zuglu* is the subject-part and *is a man from Mars* is the predicate-part. We cannot say that one nucleus of a formal predication modifies another nucleus, even though in some reduced transforms of predications A may become grammatically dependent on B and in others B upon A. Thus, when the predication *Zuglu is a man from Mars* is truncated to a semi-predicative by the deletion of *Zuglu* and *is* and is inserted into the matrix predication *Zuglu came to our house for dinner,* its syntactical point of attachment is its missing subject-part *Zuglu,* which functions as the subject-part of the matrix predication. Firmly implied here is the notion that a matrix predication ends up on a higher linguistic level than that of an inserted predication. This notion must be modified to make exception for any kind of transformation by which a predication merely supplants a nuclear item in a matrix sentence—as in the case of noun clauses or sometimes the nominal forms of reduced predication. In these instances the change is in one of the essential segments of a basic sentence pattern, and since these segments are "basic," they are not dependent upon other segments. Redistributions may be merely re-arrangements of basic segments or casting the "ideal content" of one basic sentence pattern into the form of a different one. Other kinds of transformations, however, demand the creation of "dependencies"—the incorporation of structures on lower linguistic levels. Semi-predicatives are structures of this latter kind. We can describe them as "modifying" something only if we can define modification as something's "being grammatically dependent upon" something. This does not mean that anything that modifies a noun must therefore be an adjective, unless by circular definition "adjective" is then defined as anything syntactically dependent upon a noun—a definition by function solely, and by only one function, so that other functions of "adjective," such as the predicative function, are not included in the definition. Since, however, the concept of "modification" is deeply rooted in our thinking, we may need to continue to use the term, provided that we make it mean only "syntactical dependence." Only in this sense is a semi-predicative structure a modifier of the subject-part of the predication that it completes and in so doing is "included" in the matrix sentence. The traditionalist who calls a noun appositive a "modifier" is not necessarily insisting that it is an adjective. He does not, however, usually recognize the parallel between appositive nouns and appositive adjectives as semi-predicative structures—and hence as "modifiers."

This definition of "modification" we have already wrestled with in connection with the use of the term for pre-positional adjectives. Pre-positional adjectives were excluded from basic sentence patterns on the ground that they are transforms of predicate adjectives added to basic sentence patterns in first-level transformations or that they are derivations from nouns or verbs that are given adjectival suffixes and that occupy this common position for adjectives even though the relationships existing between them and their headword nouns are ones not within the range of those that can be expressed by a predicate adjective in relation to its subject. This point may be a fine one: if we redistribute the terms in *G. B. Shaw was tolerant* and come up with a nominal phrase in which *Shaw* is made into an adjective and *tolerant* is changed to the headword noun *tolerance* (*Shavian tolerance*), can we therefore assume that the way station to this final form is *tolerance is Shavian?* I assume that we cannot since *tolerant* is an abstract attribute that can be applied to many particulars, whereas Shaw is a particular man and *Shaw* is the subject of which *tolerance* is predicated. *Shavian* must become a class term to function as predicative adjective, but *Shaw* in the original sentence was subject of a finite predication and this finiteness of predication cannot be expressed in a structure that makes *Shavian* a class term. We can say *This kind of wit is Shavian* and then transform the structure to *the Shavian kind of wit* or *Shavian wit*, but *Shavian* is a class term in these circumstances.

This is going a long way around when the point at hand concerns the difficulty of distinguishing between semi-predicative appositive adjectives as transforms of predicate adjectives and pre-positional adjectives as also transforms of predicate adjectives. For the sake of clarity, we must first exclude from the distinction those pre-positional adjectives (like *Shavian* in the non-class sense) that are not transforms of predicate adjectives but usurpers of the structure. The attempt has been made (p. 107) to distinguish between these kinds of structures on the basis of the "priority" of transformation of the pre-positional adjective. The adjective *dry* in *Dry grass burns quickly* is an essential restrictive constituent of the noun phrase *dry grass*. The statement is framed as a generality. A post-positional relative clause, *which is dry,* could serve equally well in constituting the class of things about which something is to be asserted. To have access to the implied predication in *dry grass* we have to get out of generality and project our minds back to particulars: *this grass is dry, that grass is not dry, some grass is dry,* and so on. Then we select as subject for the general statement *the grass* with the attribute of *dryness.* Thus, in terms of immediacy or presentness of predication there is a key difference between *The dry grass burned quickly* (provided the meaning is that all the grass burned quickly because it was dry, not that the green grass did not burn, for the construction is ambiguous) and *Dry grass burns quickly.* *Dry* in the latter statement is a "prior" transformation in contrast to *dry* in the former. Both are prior transformations in contrast to *dry* in *The grass, dry from the weeks without rain, burned quickly,* for now we have a semi-predicative form that structurally (as present construction) inserts a new predication into the sentence. We can, if we wish, use other terms in order to make these distinctions clear. *Dry* in *The dry grass burned quickly* presents us with a "hidden" predication, or we can say that this predication is more compressed or is a further reduction of predication than is *dry* in *The grass, dry from the weeks without rain, burned quickly.* Or we can make the distinction between restrictive and non-restrictive modifiers—except that these terms apply better to adjectival semi-predicative constructions than to semi-predicatives that are not adjectival. Paul Roberts has adopted a transformational procedure by which all semi-predicative constructions are treated as reductions of relative clauses. This adds what is often an unnecessary step to the transformational procedure but has the advantage of making all these constructions pass through a stage that can be called adjectival (but only because relative clauses have traditionally been called adjective clauses). But initial appositives and participial phrases, which Roberts calls sentence modifiers, evade his rationalization.

Participial phrases and appositive phrases are the chief kinds of semi-predicative constructions. An appositive phrase represents the truncation of the predicate of a copula predication by the deletion of *be,* leaving the predicate word or phrase as predicator. A participial phrase (to be kept distinct from pre-positional participles, participles used in the formation of verb phrases of progressive aspect, participles used as objective complements, and participles used as predicators in such reduced predicational constructions as absolutes and "with" constructions) similarly represents a truncation of a basic sentence pattern, by the transformation of any verb that is not a copula (i.e., any transitive or intransitive verb) to one of its participial forms (active, past, passive), leaving unchanged any direct object, indirect object, or any dependent unit in the predicate part of the transformed predication. With both appositive phrases and participial phrases the subject-part of the reduced predication is to be found in the predication on which these semi-predicatives are dependent, and the syntactical nexus of dependency is with the subject-part. Since some infinitives in infinitive phrases have agents or subjects that likewise appear on a higher linguistic level, some infinitive phrases can also be called semi-predicative constructions. These will be discussed in the separate chapter on Infinitives and Infinitive Phrases.

APPOSITIVE PHRASES

One of the crucial failures of the static methodology of traditional grammar has been its inability to give a satisfactory account of the nature of apposition. In the usual schoolbook of the past only apposed nouns have been called appositives. Appositives of other kinds went nameless or were ignored completely. Appositives were nouns that somehow or other were "put alongside" other nouns. Thus there was no way of dealing with them when they were not "alongside." They were vaguely called modifiers without any understanding of the nature of the modification that they effected. They were said "to provide added information" about the substantive with which they were in apposition. But many other kinds of units could be said to provide added information; how then were appositives different from other constructions? Some grammarians of our own day have confused apposition with restatement and reiteration or have made restatement the central concept in the definition of apposition (Lloyd and Warfel in particular). The traditionalist, in saying that an appositive "provided added information," came close to indicating the semi-predicative nature of the construction, but, since he lacked interest in the transformation of predicational structures, he had no framework that would give meaning to his description. Even now the traditionalist will fight bitterly against accepting the definition of an appositive as a truncated copula predication. One difficulty is that he begins his inquiry with what is called "close apposition" and then moves to appositives that are not "close." He thus starts with phrases like *my brother John, Charles the Fat, fellow Americans, Aunt Sally, Lake Michigan, Lawyer Brown, President Johnson, Winnie the Pooh,* and then moves to constructions that seem to be extensions of these such as *John, my favorite brother, arrived; Charles, the fattest king France ever had, lost . . . ; Americans all, my fellows in this enterprise, join me . . . ; Brown, our ablest lawyer, conducted the trial,* and so on. Actually, close apposition is hard to explain because there are many kinds of it. Explanations that apply to titles and proper names do not necessarily apply to other instances. In general, however, when nouns are found in close apposition, they should be classed as noun adjuncts, and so treated as part of the compositional system in English syntax. The indeclinable *fellow* in *fellow Americans* (noun adjuncts are indeclinable) is a case in point (*you Americans are my fellows*). Appositives used as noun adjuncts should be considered as further compressions or transformations of loose appositives, or, to go further back toward basic sentence patterns, of predicate nouns but functioning in the compositional system. Noun adjuncts are of many kinds and the distinctions of the relationships possible between them and their headwords are never explicitly signaled. Only indistinctly can we define a class of noun adjuncts to be called appositive noun adjuncts (that *fool* man, the *lumberjack* kid: that man is a *fool,* the kid is a *lumberjack;* as over against *the Nevada kid—the kid comes from Nevada,* or *woman hater—he hates women*). The former can be called appositives only because they have been derived from appositives, or from predicate nouns just as appositives have been. When adjectives are found in close apposition in titles or in proper names (*Charles the Fat*), we may suspect a lingering French influence, as in *court-martial* or *heir apparent,* or an ellipsis that is alien to modern English (*Charles, the fat king of that name*). The French, who are still dominated by seventeenth-century rhetorical concepts, and have stoutly resisted the expansion of the area of usage of noun adjuncts that has characterized American English in recent years, put noun adjuncts after their headwords when they do use them. A short time ago, readers of Parisian newspapers could protest the reference to a woman taxicab driver as *la femme taxi*. This to them was a barbarism and a sign of the deadly Americanization of Europe. What would strike the American reader of the same newspaper item is the position of the noun adjunct after the headword; his first thought would be of a "female taxi." The usual French writer is more likely to remain faithful to the analytic system and prefer *femme de taxi*, or to add a derivational suffix and create *femme taxienne*. Our conversion of *Shaw* to *Shavian* has a French ring to it. In most of the languages of Western Europe a proper name is more readily converted to an adjective by derivational suffix (without capitalization) than in English (*la tendenza erasmiana* instead of *the tendency of Erasmus*.) With some of these variants we are not prepared to cope in our description of the chief structures of English. For one reason or another, adjectives or nouns existing in what we call close apposition should be treated in English as transformations prior (i.e., further than) to appositive transformations. Our account of the appositive construction should be based on the loose, or non-restrictive, appositive.

> *His vote against the plan, a rejection of us that I deplore, was motivated solely by greed* (his vote was a rejection).
> *A newcomer to the local political scene, Charles was not acute enough to recognize Dean's stratagem* (Charles was newcomer).
> *He was born in southern Arkansas, the great-grandson of an early governor of that state* (he was great-grandson).

These examples show us only nouns as appositives. In each instance the appositive phrase contains dependent elements as well as the noun that is the headword in the construction. These dependent elements are not, however, always of the kind that can easily be construed as modifiers of nouns. Syntactically, the deleted copula must often be implied to account for the relation of the dependent item. In *His acceptance, clearly a consequence of Jake's maneuvering, was a surprise, clearly* can best be accounted for by the absent *was*. But in a copula predication the *be* is merely a formal signal of predication, and the predicate complement actually becomes the predicator so far as specific lexical content is concerned. Consequently, our minds are not confused when they find no predicating element to attach an adverb to since they recognize that only the formal signal of predication has been deleted in the reduction of the predication. These examples are, however, at the extreme end of the gamut of the kinds of appositive phrases. In the first of the three illustrative sentences, we have an instance of the kind of complex redistribution that we can call the copula redistribution since the basic copula sentence pattern is used to link together two nominal transforms: *when he voted against the plan, he rejected us.* To these two predications to be found at the source can be added the other predications *I deplore the rejection* and *His vote was motivated solely by greed.* When ideas to be expressed move up a semantic ladder toward abstraction, the copula *be* comes into play more and more often. The grammarian concocting illustrations too often confines himself to the structures of concretion (*John Jones, a handsome boy who lives in the next block, took me to the dance on Saturday*). We can also see from the illustrative sentences that the position of an appositive phrase in a sentence is not rigidly fixed, even though our expectations are that it will follow immediately after the noun or pronoun constituting its missing subject-part, on which it is syntactically dependent. When an appositive unit precedes its subject-part, as in the second example, it often but not always signals a causal relation (*Since he was a newcomer to the local political scene, he was not . . .*). The structure can be a signal of causality only because it is frequently used in that way, since no connector makes the relation explicit.

Any kind of unit that can function as a complement in a copula predication can function as the headword or functional center of an appositive phrase, although sometimes the union between an appositive and the unit on which it is dependent will be so close that calling the construction an appositive will seem gratuitous. Often the structural significance of the appositive as a device for the inclusion of subordinate predications within a basic sentence pattern will depend upon the capability of the kind of appositive in question to have dependencies in turn. We can say, in a basic copula pattern, *I am in a hurry.* Since the prepositional phrase *in a hurry* acts as complement of the copula predication, it should be capable of functioning as an appositive. We can say, *In a hurry, he did not comprehend what she was doing,* in which the fronted appositive signals causality: *Since he was in a hurry, he did not . . . .* This is an addition of some importance to the sentence, but when some item in *in a hurry* becomes the headword of other dependent elements, the importance increases, as in: *In a hurry to get to the business district where he had several press-*

ing matters to attend to, he did not . . . . Whether certain other prepositional phrases that can conceivably function as complements after copulas can in fact become appositives by transformation will depend somewhat on the normality of the use of the prepositional phrase as complement. Some such prepositional phrases are too idiomatic to undergo the transformation well. We can say *She is after my own heart* but may look askance at *She, after my own heart, came to see me.* Since it has been shown that pre-positional adjectives represent transformations that are prior to appositive adjective transformations, we may well ask again if post-positional prepositional phrases of place and time following nouns of place and time meaning should not be considered close appositives rather than adverbs modifying nouns, as Fries called them: *the man in the next room, the day before yesterday, the lull after the storm, the meeting behind the barn,* etc. All of these can be expanded (or re-transformed) to relative clauses with copulas: *the man who is in the next room, the day which was (came?) before yesterday, the lull that is (comes?) after the storm, the meeting that was behind the barn.* (Copulas are semantically often simplified variants of certain intransitive verbs, like *come, take place,* or *occur;* this represents an indeterminacy between grammar and semantics.) Base adverbs and adverbial nouns can likewise function both as complements after copulas and as post-positional close appositives by transformation; they can therefore also serve as loose appositives: *I was home all afternoon, home is the sailor, the voyage home, the way home; the sailor, home at last from his long voyage, met* . . . ; *Home for the summer from the year at school, I started* . . . ; *My work was nights (at night); My work nights was tedious; My work, nights, was tedious; the work was there, the work there, The work, there where I did not want to be, tired me.* We should realize that usage here depends somewhat upon both the nature of the substantive that must be the subject-part of an appositive predication and of the adverbial form that must serve as predicate complement. It seems impossible to determine why we can say *The jump was ten feet (He jumped ten feet),* in which *ten feet* is an adverbial noun unit of measure, and we can use this adverbial noun as a loose appositive (*his jump, ten feet according to the measurement of the judges, climaxed* . . .), but not as a close appositive—*his jump ten feet;* in the system of compounds we can use *ten feet* as a pre-positional adverbial noun adjunct (indeclinable): *his ten-foot jump. Jump* is a noun that has undergone functional shift from a verb, and so can be the headword in a nominal transformation of a predication, with *his* as its subject-part. When we say *his jumping ten feet* we are creating a nominal transformation using a gerund as headword noun, and a gerund can take an adverbial-noun object without alteration. When we say *his jump of ten feet* we reveal the fact that in a nominal transformation the adverbial-noun object is treated like a direct object—taking the phrasing of a periphrastic objective genitive. From analyzing these distinctions we can conclude that a general rule for the creation of adverbial close appositives must take into consideration such things as whether the noun to which the appositive attaches is concrete or abstract, whether it has undergone functional shift from a verb, or whether it is some other kind of noun. We are in no position to make such fine discriminations and so must not attempt to define the limits of appositives of these kinds. That they can exist under some circumstances is obvious.

Although prepositional phrases and adverbial nouns can function as predicate complements of copula predications, and can therefore be transformed into appositive phrases, predicate complements are most often either nouns or adjectives (*I am a man; I am sick*). Since the structure of the noun appositive was well recognized by traditional grammarians even though their description of the construction was a distortion, it was in their failure to deal adequately with the adjective appositive that the traditional grammarians were most remiss. And here we come face to face with the distinction between the pre-positional adjective as a prior transform and the appositive adjective as an immediate or "present" transform. The pre-positional adjective is analogous to the close appositive. According to the concept of "priority of transformation" some distinction needs to be made between a restrictive pre-positional adjective (which is the true example of prior transformation) and the descriptive or non-restrictive pre-positional adjective (which may come to its position ahead of the noun from some other source than the predicate adjective source and so represent a different kind of transformation, or it may actually have a predicate adjective as its source but not truly represent a prior transformation—in which case we can say that it appears to be a prior transform but that in reality, taking the vagaries of the composing of sentences into consideration, it may not be). These distinctions may seem to be more finely drawn than necessary, especially when we remember that derivational adjectives can express almost any semantic relationship with their headwords and that, if we chose to include as adjectivals all such forms as pre-determiners, determiners, nouns in the genitive, intensifiers, noun adjuncts, and adjectives, we could arrange these in the order in which they are likely to appear before a noun and confuse distinctions of this kind completely.

The central problem in distinguishing between appositive adjectives and adjectives modifying nouns by prior transformation is that not all adjectives of this second class are pre-positional. There are at least three reasons why some are not. (1) In many phrases that are relics of Norman-French, that are borrowings from French or similar languages, or that are constructed in imitation of French structure, an adjective that normally would be pre-positional in English is post-positional (as in *court-martial* and *heir apparent, cordon bleu, idée fixe, the man ideal,* etc.). (2) Often adjectives that would normally be pre-positional become post-positional when they have attracted units dependent upon them (contrast *units dependent upon them* with *dependent units*) that make their position before the noun untenable (a box *large enough to hold all these things,* a strength *so great that he could bend a horseshoe*). In some constructions involving near-nouns or adjectives of comparative degree the attracted modifier may follow the noun and the adjective remain pre-positional (*such a great man that* . . . , *so great a man that* . . . , *a greater man than* . . .), but these are notable exceptions and can be separately explained. (3) Just as there is a no-man's-land between the concept of restriction and that of non-restriction, so some appositives that represent reduced relative clauses that are in that borderland between restriction and non-restriction are indistinguishable except by position from pre-positional adjectives; usually, however, there is some stylistic reason for making them post-positional. In *Men healthy, young, and prosperous make ideal husbands*, the adjectives are post-positional because they form a series, although a series can appear just as well before a noun. Sometimes when a writer has to use a string of descriptive adjectives he will arbitrarily cast some pre-positionally and some post-positionally: *This big, slap-happy, frustrated Jack-of-all-trades, ugly, unreflective, and even-tempered, came once too often to Joel's tavern.* In this case, the post-positional trio are by intonation and punctuation appositive adjectives, even though the writer may have cast them into that construction merely because he wanted to break up his long series. In describing the transformational steps by which predicate adjectives become prepositional adjectives, Paul Roberts posits an intermediate step of a relative clause in which the predicate adjective remains just that: *fat men < men who are fat < (some) men are fat.* Were we to follow this procedure, we would be tempted to say that all predicative adjectives in non-restrictive relative clauses become appositive adjectives when by the next transformational step the relative pronoun and the copula are deleted (*men who are fat > men, fat,*), and that all predicate adjectives in restrictive relative clauses must then go through the further transformation of shifting position before the noun. But some pre-positional adjectives are descriptive (non-restrictive) and for special reasons some restrictive adjectives do not remain pre-positional. Furthermore, we have to account for those appositive adjectives that appear, not after the nouns, but preceding the subjects of the predications to which they are attached. If we could limit the relations expressed by initial appositive adjectives (or initial appositives of any kind), we could perhaps trace out a different series of transformational steps for them. Suppose, for instance, that all initial appositives express causality; we could then show these steps: *The man was angry. The man insulted his hostess > Because the man was angry, he insulted his hostess > Angry, the man insulted his hostess.* Here the step of the relative clause is not implied. In fact, if a relative clause were to express this idea of causality, we would have to transform the initial appositive by a further step into a relative clause: *Angry, the man insulted his hostess > The man, who was angry, insulted his hostess.* And, no doubt, if we were to reduce this relative clause to an appositive adjective, still carrying the idea of causality, we would have to transform the clause back into an appositive, still compelled to follow this series of steps in order to arrive at the given result: *The man, who was angry, insulted his hostess > The man, angry, insulted his hostess.* There are two further difficulties. We cannot be sure that even restrictive adjectives cannot express causality: *Angry men insult their hostesses.* Initial appositive phrases do not always express causality. Some are in effect coordinate. Although a slight increase of stress on *angry* helps to indicate the causality when the relative clause *who was angry* is made to perform that function (and this means that our fast-moving minds anticipate the possibility of making the causal connection by means of the stress), it is highly unlikely that our minds actually move along these divergent paths unless a time distinction must be made between the action of the superior predication and that of the included one. But further modifiers can often convey a time distinction as well as a finite verb can with tense signals. To change *Jones, who was a janitor, is now president of the bank* to *Jones, a janitor, is now president of the bank* is confusing since Jones seems to be janitor and president at one and the same time. But when the time distinction is specified by a modifier (as in *Jones, once a janitor, is now president . . .*) the disability of the appositive transform vanishes. In our actual rhetorical practice, we behave as if an appositive can form a syntactical nexus with a whole clause better than a relative pronoun can: *Mozart was already composing music at the age of five, an astounding instance of the powers of a child's imagination* in contrast to *. . . , which is an astounding instance . . . .* The range of appositives is limited to the reduction of copula predications, but since by functional shift almost any part of speech can be made to function as a predicate complement, this limitation is less serious than it might appear to be (*something demonstrates something* becomes by functional change *something is a demonstration of something*—this is possible of course only when a noun exists that corresponds in meaning to the verb, and these shifts are more possible with abstractions than with concretions). Inquiry into the functional range of appositives has been hampered by the tendency of grammarians to consider only nouns as appositives, rather than to ask what happens in transformations to any kind of unit that can function as a predicate complement. Noun clauses and infinitive phrases can function as predicate complements and, consequently, as appositives.

PARTICIPIAL PHRASES

Participial phrases, the other main kind of semi-predicative constructions, function much as appositives do. Most of what has been said about appositives applies to them too. If we go back to our basic sentence patterns, we can see that a participial phrase represents the same kind of reduction of predications with transitive or intransitive verbs that an appositive represents with copula predications, since in both the source predication is truncated and the subject-part is found in the superior unit upon which appositive or participial phrase depends. One difference is that in the creation of an appositive the *be* of the copula predication is deleted, but in the creation of a participial phrase the transitive or intransitive verb undergoes morphological change from finite form to *-ing*, or *-en* form (*-en* representing here all of the varieties of the suffix of the second participle).

Participial phrases can be transforms of either active or passive sentences; therefore, it is necessary to suppose that passive participial phrases are the result first of a transformation of an active basic sentence to its passive equivalent and then the reduction of the passive sentence by the deletion of the auxiliary *be* that has functioned in the formation of the passive verb (together with the act of truncation by which the subject of the verb is located on a higher linguistic level). In this respect, the formation of a passive participial phrase would seem to parallel exactly the formation of an appositive unit, since *be* is deleted in each case, even though the deleted *be* does not function in the same way in the two instances.

In fact, some grammarians prefer, in describing the mechanics of the transformation of an active verb to the *-ing* form, to interpose a stage in which the verb phrase is first converted to its copula equivalent (*he goes > he is going*), and then to follow the usual procedure of deleting the copula, so that appositive, active participle, and passive participle share a last stage of the transformation. Perhaps it is unimportant that *be* has three separate functions in *I am a man* (pure copula), *I was compelled* (auxiliary effecting a passive form), and *I was going* (auxiliary effecting a verb form of progressive aspect). If all of these can travel the same transformational road together without traffic mishaps, their difference need not bother us. But a semantic confusion occurs when we assume that *he goes* is equivalent to *he is going* in the same way that *he observes* may be considered equivalent to *he is observant*. Furthermore, distinctions of progressive and perfect aspect, as well as of passive voice, can find expression in special participial forms. (We note that in the transformation of copula predications of progressive or perfect aspect the result is not appositive phrases but participial phrases: *he was being rude > being rude; he had been rude > having been rude; he shall have been rude > having been rude; he has been* *rude > having been rude,* etc.). Pure copulas do not undergo passive transformation, but progressive passive participles can be derived from transitive verbs: *I was being sent > being sent; I am being sent > being sent.*

Considering these difficulties, we should keep distinct the mechanics of transformation for appositive phrases and participial phrases, just as, to be precise, we must describe separate procedures of transformation for each of these kinds of participles. For the same reason, as well as for the reasons already given for not accepting the necessity of the intermediate transformation for appositives, we need not suppose that basic sentence patterns must be transformed into relative clauses before they can be transformed into participial phrases. As with appositives, many but not all participial phrases that come at the beginning of resulting sentences function as equivalents of causal clauses: *Having disobeyed his parents, Jonas could expect the worst < Since he had disobeyed his parents, Jonas . . .* (the participles in these causal participial phrases are often perfect participles).

Again, some are logically, but not formally, coordinate with the principal clauses, or at least stand in the relationship of attendant circumstance. The predications in the following three sentences are presumably coordinate, although we may be able to find vague causal connections among them, as there are in most juxtaposed predications that bear any resemblance to one another: *The miners no longer wanted a company union. They rented a hall as a meeting place. They started a drive among themselves to bring in a C.I.O. organier.* These can be coordinated by an easy transformation (so easy that we have ignored it in this study of transformations): *The miners no longer wanted a company union and they rented a hall as a meeting place and they started a drive among themselves to bring in a C.I.O. organizer.* In order to reduce the number of formal clauses in this series, a stylist will feel that he has the option of reducing any one of them to a participial phrase, thus making predications that are coordinate logically not coordinate formally. There are several possible combinations and rearrangements of position. To show them all would require too much space; one illustration will have to suffice: *No longer wanting a company union and starting a drive among themselves to bring in a C.I.O. organizer, the miners rented a hall as a meeting place.* Rhetoricians may feel that some of the possible combinations are better than others, since better or worse may depend upon congruence of form and the emphasis desired. Thus, a stylist may prefer *Slamming the door, he startled his mother* to *He slammed the door, startling his mother* on the grounds that in idea *He slammed the door* is subordinate to *He startled his mother* (so that the second version shows false subordination). He may believe that sentences are better built when subordinate material appears at the beginning or in the middle of a sentence. These discriminations are chiefly rhetorical and not grammatical, although there are distinct limits to the functions that a dependent unit can grammatically signal. A rough correspondence exists between grammaticality and logicality. However, when either one of two coordinate predications can optionally be made the dependent of the other, we need to be wary of defining modification too strictly. And we cannot expect that any easy formulas will describe all the transformations that are possible in the creation of participial phrases.

Acting as headword in a participial phrase is only one of the many functions of the *-ing* and *-en* forms. All participles retain through their transformation from finite verbs their abilities to be modified by adverbs and to take direct and indirect objects, double objects, and adverbial complements. Having so many syntactic capabilities, they can function in a very wide range. Participial phrases have been traditionally thought of as a kind of adjective modifier, since their syntactic nexus is with nominals. We have already seen that this connection is a formal accommodation only and that the logical functions of participles can be quite other than adjectival. As with appositives, which by the same token of the nominal nexus have been considered adjectival modifiers, participial phrases are not limited to positions directly following their noun headwords (their subject-parts), provided that the connection between the participle and its subject-part is not accidentally lost in the construction of the sentence. In *He told me the story of his glorious adventures in the far corners of the globe, reminding me that I too could someday become a hero*, the participle *reminding* is separated by five nominals and various other words from the subject-part *he* on which it is syntactically dependent, and yet there is no doubt about its nexus.

Most of the so-called "dangling" participles, which occur when the nexus is lost, come at the beginning of their sentences. The expectation is that the subject of the main clause that will immediately follow the participial phrase will complete the nexus and be the missing subject-part of the semi-predication expressed by the participial phrase. When for some reason the nexus-point does not appear when it should, it is felt that the participle is left "dangling." The reasons for the loss of connection are usually not hard to find. The subject-part of the participle may be lost because the main clause has been cast in passive form: *Rowing around in a rowboat, a fish was caught by me.* The subject-part is stated in the sentence but not where we expect to find it. Or the subject-part is subject of an included clause, not of the main clause: *Coming in on the 5:15, I thought he would find me easily* (Who is coming in on the 5:15, *I* or *he?*). Worse constructions occur when the nexus is not present at all. Grammarians will sometimes argue that the question of the dangling participle is one for the rhetoricians, not for them; but since the question concerns the signals sent out by the participial structure, it would seem to be properly grammatical. Signals are signals whether or not any given speaker or writer has forgotten them or is inattentive to them. Failure to heed them can lead to failure to communicate.

We must exclude from consideration here the functions of participles in reduced predications with two nuclei, such as "absolute" and "with" constructions (see the following chapter), for these constructions are not semi-predicative, inasmuch as both subject-part and predicate-part of the transformed basic sentence are present *within* the dependent unit and neither part is dependent upon the other. Also excluded here are -*ing* and -*en* forms that appear as the predicate parts of reduced predications used as objects (see Infinitives and Infinitive Phrases): *I saw him leaving, I found him sleeping in the park.* We have already dealt with these when they can be considered redistributions (p. 119). Nominal -*ing* forms, often called "gerunds" in order to distinguish between their nominal and other functions, may be either abstract, agentless nominals while still controlling objects and adverbial modifiers, or transforms of the verbs of basic sentences in one kind of nominal transformation: *I don't approve of his giving you the money now.* Here again we are not dealing with semi-predicatives. Whether participles cease to be participles when they function as gerunds is the kind of enigma we would do well to eschew. Since we speak of participles as functioning in absolute constructions, we apparently use the term for the form in any of its functionings; a "gerund" then becomes a participle in one of its functionings as a noun.

A participial phrase is thus to be defined arbitrarily as one of the participial forms together with its complements and modifiers when it functions semi-predicatively—that is, when it functions appositively. Just as we were able only with difficulty to distinguish among appositive adjectives, pre-positional adjectives, and restrictive post-positional adjectives, we shall have much the same difficulty with the same varieties of participial phrases and the same need to make the distinctions. The parallel is close—so close, in fact, that grammarians of the old tradition have treated pre-positional participles simply as adjectives. There are no compelling reasons for not treating them as adjectives since, unlike other participles, they cannot in that position take their complements and modifiers, or rather can be modified only by what are in turn pre-positional modifiers and can take complements only in the compositional system—*high-flying birds, clean-washed windows, war-hating generals, student recreation facilities providing committee* (a far-fetched example!).

A distinction can be made, by means both of the differences of stress pattern and of the analytic periphrases that can be made of them, between pre-positional participles functioning much as adjectives function and the similar forms functioning nominally as noun adjuncts that we can call gerunds. The difference in stress pattern is that between *móving óbjects* (adjectival) and *móving vàn* (nominal adjunct). Other examples are: *dáncing gîrl* and *dáncing gìrl, éarth-mòving equîpment* and *wôrld-shàking evénts* (*equipment for moving earth* contrasting with *events that shake the world*), *the wârming sún* (the sun warms) or *the wârming pán* (the pan is warming up) and *the wárming pàn* (a pan for warming things up). Since in our present polysystemic approach to grammatical description noun adjuncts are described in terms of the compositional system and adjectival participles in terms of the analytic and derivational systems, the distinction ultimately pertains more to system than to part-of-speech or to stress pattern.

Just as adjectives appear post-positionally when they are modified by cumbersome items, a restrictive participial phrase (containing complements and modifiers as well as the participle) likewise appears post-positionally: *any man coming home that late at night, Workers watching the clock all the time never get ahead* (compare *Clock-watching workers never get ahead. Your eternal clock-watching workers never get ahead*). It is possible to consider these restrictive participial phrases as further reductions of restrictive relative clauses (*any man who comes home . . . > any man coming home,* etc.), but again there is no compelling reason for adding the extra step in the transformational process. The class of pre-positional participles breaks down into the same sub-groups as that of pre-positional adjectives and they too can be described as the result of prior transformations even if as non-restrictive units they are rhetorically equivalent to non-restrictive post-positional participial phrases—that is, even if a speaker or writer, at a given stage in the composing of a sentence, has the option of putting the participle either before or after the nominal on which it depends. The speaker or writer has to determine how much compression of predication he wishes to use. This is a rhetorical matter. The concept of priority applies literally to restrictive modifiers; the non-restrictive pre-positional modifier "usurps" the structure. The broadest generalization that we can arrive at is that all pre-positional adjectives (except those not derived from predicate adjectives), all appositive adjectives, all post-positional adjectives, all pre-positional participles (excluding gerunds used as noun adjuncts), and all participial phrases (as we have defined them) can be classed together as semi-predicative structures derived from verbs or predicate adjectives, represent included predications, and can all be called appositives, along with appositive nouns, and adverbial nouns and prepositional phrases derived from predicate complements of copula predications. The difference between pre-position and post-position is largely one of "priority" of transformation.

RESTATEMENT AND REITERATION

To clarify the whole picture, we still need a distinction between apposition, on one hand, and "restatement" and "reiteration" on the other. "Series," a structure of coordination, differs from both. Restatement is a rhetorical device that does not really affect the grammar. When we say *Our yearning for fame, our lust after reputation, our questing for ego-expansion, is our downfall,* we use a singular verb after a subject-part that seems to contain three items. This is not a coordinate series of the kind found in *Red, white, and blue are my favorite colors.* Items 2 and 3 in the subject-part are not appositives in relation to *our yearning for fame* since these are not semi-predicative—that is, we are not saying *our yearning is our lust* or *our yearning is our questing.* To the contrary, each of the three items is equally the subject of *is.* The writer or speaker has simply gone back to the beginning and restated his idea. He is exerting himself rhetorically. At times, to be sure, we cannot sensibly distinguish between restatement and apposition, since a construction may sometimes be interpreted either way. But at other times the two kinds are quite distinct. Words of form classes that cannot function as appositives can be the headwords of restatements (verbs, for instance: *I loathe, despise, have no use for him; He jumped my frame, cleaned my clock, altered my status*). Restatements are synonymous expressions, substitutes in the same slot. The intention is not to say different things but to say the same thing in more than one way. Perhaps none of the alternatives quite hits the nail on the head. A poet may use the device to enclose an area within which his meaning lies and aim at depicting the whole all the time that he seems to spend it distinguishing its parts. When Lincoln spoke of *government of the people, by the people, and for the people,* he was not restating but setting up a series of modifiers, coordinate with one another. We do not use *and* between the penultimate and ultimate items in restatement; we may do so in a series.

Reiteration is also a rhetorical device, and also may use any part of speech as its key word, but it does affect the grammar, if only by interfering with it and cutting across it. Should a writer write *The revolutionaries had nothing but contempt for the whole complex of beliefs that had buoyed up their forebears for centuries—a contempt that lay open for all to sense in everything that they did or said,* the repeated word *contempt* could, by a stretch of the imagination, be considered in apposition with its first appearance—*a contempt is a contempt,* but the reiterated word may be an adverb or a verb as well as a noun or adjective, may be a participle or infinitive, or may even be a preposition, particularly if it is a noticeable one like *toward* or *despite.* By means of the repeated word, the sequence of ideas may take a quite different tack. The shift of direction of idea would seem to be, actually, the chief rhetorical reason for the use of the construction. All of this evades the tight, internal syntactic signaling that we expect from a construction like an appositive. Reiteration is likely to be an ellipsis on a grand scale. The ramifications and variations of it as a grammatical principle are so extensive that a grammarian who wished to be useful to highly sophisticated writers should perhaps spend much time in working out its precise features and limitations. But we must content ourselves with distinguishing between such constructions and apposition.

A semi-predicative structure (to summarize) is a transform of a predication in which the subject-part does not appear in the constituent itself but is the constituent upon which the semi-predicative structure now depends. In other kinds of reduced predication, subject-parts and predicate-parts of included predications are both on the same linguistic level. Varieties of these will be described in the following chapters.

MATERIALS FOR EXERCISE AND FURTHER STUDY

I. These sentences illustrating appositives present an incomplete sampling of the range and variety of these constructions, and so are to be taken as only a beginning toward an adequate assemblage of a corpus upon which definitive descriptions can be based. The student of language soon discovers that he can look endlessly in certain kinds of writing for examples of the structures he is looking for, and in other kinds can find them in great plenty. One conclusion he can draw is that the job at hand dictates to a considerable degree the linguistic structures that a writer uses. Usage levels are determined by the needs of certain professional or occupational situations as well as by social class structures, geographical dialects, age groups, or literary fashions. Study these sentences and add to them from your own searching. Re-create the source sentences from which the appositive units have been transformed.

1. We parted that night hostile.—EMILY BRONTË
2. The eighth annual tour to Puerto Rico and the Virgin Islands to study the culture of those islands has attracted an enrollment of 30, the largest since 1959.—*Ithaca Journal*
3. Rosen connected against the Yanks' rookie left-hander, Steve Kraly.—*New York Times*
4. . . . gave Frazier a four-to-one advantage over his nearest rival, Frank Torney, infielder of the Dallas Eagles.—*New York Times*
5. Cherry, 3 down at the halfway mark, squared the match on the twenty-ninth . . . .—*New York Times*

6. Ribald and poetic, lyrical and turbulent, it is the essence of Shakespeare recovered . . . .—*New York Times*
7. Cherry, brilliant under pressure, scored a birdie 2 on the 165-yard thirty-fifth.—*New York Times*
8. Dubious little damsel as you thought her, she had kept a firm hold on that [her respectability] . . . .—HENRY JAMES
9. Highbury, the large and populous village almost amounting to a town, to which Hartfield, in spite of its separate lawn and shrubberies, and name, did really belong, afforded her no equals.—JANE AUSTEN
10. A bold, tensely good-natured fellow, Lester always looked to Annie as though he expected everybody to make him walk the gangplank.—LILLIAN ROSS
11. The impressionist is Marcel Carné, a director and scriptwriter who has been making fine movies in France (among them "Port of Shadows" and "Children of Paradise") for many years.
12. He plays the president of Concordia, a country so unimportant that when he rises in the U. N. General Assembly to abstain from voting, even the presiding officer has no idea who he is.
13. A doctor who fought against epidemics, against the disease of poverty, he was also an enlightened thinker and despised . . . .
14. This machine can total 200 figures a minute, an astonishing feat when you think of it.
15. Phlebas the Phoenician, a fortnight dead,/Forgot the cry of gulls . . . .—T. S. ELIOT
16. After the torchlight red on sweaty faces . . . .—T. S. ELIOT
17. Navy, in complete charge, used its first team for twenty minutes . . . .
18. Peyton Farquhar was a well-to-do planter, of an old and highly respected Alabama family.—AMBROSE BIERCE
19. It was experiencing a spasm of virtuous reaction, quite as lawless and ungovernable as any of the acts that had provoked it.—BRET HARTE
20. The road to Sandy Flat—a camp that, not having as yet experienced the regenerating influences of Poker Flat, consequently seemed to offer some invitation to the emigrants—lay over a steep mountain range.—BRET HARTE
21. Embosomed amongst a family of lofty mountains, there was a valley so spacious that it contained many thousand inhabitants.—NATHANIEL HAWTHORNE
22. Religion is the opium of the people. He believed that, that dyspeptic little joint-keeper.—ERNEST HEMINGWAY
23. Although some prefer the radio, another opium of the people, a cheap one he had just been using.—ERNEST HEMINGWAY
24. By the time the boy had got to the house the walking man was

only halfway down the road, a lean man, very straight in the shoulders.—JOHN STEINBECK

25. Over his shoulder he carried a gunny sack, lumpy and full.— JOHN STEINBECK

26. Jody stood overwhelmed by the thing in Gitano's hand.—JOHN STEINBECK

27. Pa'd come home from the courthouse drunk as a wheelbarrow, and she'd just pick up an' go sit on the front step facin' the hill an' sing.—EUDORA WELTY

28. Mr. Gene, the proprietor, a white-haired man with little dark freckles all over his face and hands, looked up and shoved out his arm at the same time.—EUDORA WELTY

29. His big hands, rough with frost and swollen with rheumatism, were awkward but gentle at their task.—WALTER VAN TILBURG CLARK

30. His mind, more just alert than cunning or speculative, roamed widely over the universe.

31. A spectral voice, flat but with subtle overtones of menace, blurted a warning over the loudspeaker.

32. . . . he sank into a chair, weak in the knees, and clasped his head in his hands.—WILLA CATHER

33. There he was already standing in front of his store, ready to do business with all comers.

34. Resentful as he may be on this elbowing, it is unlikely that President Ho Chi Minh will react violently, as did Premier Fidel Castro of Cuba, and denounce the Chinese Communists.—SEYMOUR TOPPING, *New York Times*

35. Jealous of the recent expansion of the Soviet presence in Hanoi, the Peking leadership is pressuring the North Vietnamese to line up on its side in the ideological dispute against the Soviet Communist party.—SEYMOUR TOPPING, *New York Times*

36. My belief in teachers' unlimited wisdom and power rested not so much on what I saw in them—how important most of them looked, how wary—but on our abysmal humility, at least in those of us who were "good" boys, who proved by our ready compliance and "manners" that we wanted to get on.—ALFRED KAZIN

37. If, angry at always being put down as lazy or stupid, I did get up to speak, the black wooden floor would roll away under my feet, the teacher would frown at me in amazement, and in unbearable loneliness I would hear behind me the groans and laughter: *tuh-tuh-tuh-tuh.*—ALFRED KAZIN

38. Like so many men in positions of authority in Jesuit education, McCoska is young, handsome and deft, with a well-developed sense of humor.—MARTIN MAYER

39. Where the state university must accept all applicants with high-school diplomas—a condition that prevails in nearly half the states—even the college bound child need take only seven to ten units of *academic* work during his "four years" of high school.—MARTIN MAYER

40. In 1897, at the age of thirty-eight, John Dewey published a stirring and prophetic work entitled *My Pedagogic Creed.*—JEROME S. BRUNER

41. But to have spent one's youth at college, in contact with the choice and rare and precious, and yet still be a blind prig or vulgarian, unable to scent out human excellence or to divine it amid its accidents, to know it only when ticketed and labelled and forced on us by others, this indeed should be accounted the very calamity and shipwreck of a higher education.—WILLIAM JAMES

42. It is a disquieting fact that Rousseau, the man whose influence is everywhere in the new education, was remarkable for nothing so much as his inability to distinguish between nature and human nature.—IRVING BABBITT

43. The tourist on the trail of "Historic Massachusetts," doing his best to excuse the bedragglement of post-historic Boston, is quite likely to approach Harvard along the Storrow Drive—the highway that hugs the right bank of the Charles River.—MARCUS CUNLIFFE

44. Toiling through the sticky heat of the midsummer tourist season, the visitor will no doubt inspect the other obligatory sights, such as the bare and beautiful churches of the Colonial period which lie near the Cambridge Common, at peace among the abominable traffic.—MARCUS CUNLIFFE

45. The influence of Ruskin—art medievalist, devout student of clouds, mountains, trees—is pervasive in Hopkins' sketches (five of which are reproduced in the *Note-Books*) and in his journalizing, his meticulously technical descriptions of church architecture (often neo-Gothic) and scenery.—AUSTIN WARREN

46. Newman, much the more complex and psychologically subtle, could feel his way into other men's minds as Hopkins could not.—AUSTIN WARREN

47. Scotus, the Franciscan critic of the Dominican Aquinas, was centrally dear to Hopkins as undertaking the philosophical validation of the individual.—AUSTIN WARREN

48. A Saturn 1B, most powerful rocket ever built by the United States, was to have boosted the Apollo into space today.—(AP)

49. First firemen on the scene removed the victims and watered down the remains of the wooden building—one of four at the plant located 10 miles northeast of Uniontown.—(AP)

50. The claimed enemy toll rose to 1,357 killed, the second highest toll of the year, and 132 captured last week.—(AP)
51. The leader of the extremist wing is Maj. Gen. Salah Jedid, former chief of staff of the army who was ousted from power last year.—(AP)
52. It had been assumed that on the vast polar plateau, level as the Western plains and hundreds of miles from any visible mountains, there would be no danger from crevasses.—WALTER SULLIVAN, *New York Times*
53. The Dutch, once the hated masters of Indonesia, have been coming back very quietly.—SETH KING, *New York Times*

II. We have defined "restatement" and "reiteration" as structures that have more rhetorical than grammatical importance. On the other hand, their range can be very great. The following few illustrations are offered merely as a test of their difference from appositive structures. Tell which are "restatements" and which are "reiterations."

1. . . . that made his mystery, his charm.—W. D. HOWELLS
2. But now, it flashed upon her, if he could do something worthy to have won her—be a hero, *her* hero—it would be even better than if he had done it before asking her; it would be grander.— W. D. HOWELLS
3. . . . but she felt a sort of noble distinction in the abstraction, the almost unconsciousness, with which they parted.—W. D. HOWELLS
4. Revolution is a catharsis; an ecstasy which can only be prolonged by tyranny.—ERNEST HEMINGWAY
5. He was thinking well, a little too well.—ERNEST HEMINGWAY
6. A sensation of torment, of two-sided, unpredictable nature, arose from the stillness of the earth air beneath the violence of the upper air.—WALTER VAN TILBURG CLARK
7. We had to prove that we were really alert, ready for anything, always in the race. That white thinly ruled record book figured in my mind as the judgment seat; the very thinness and remote blue lightness of its lines instantly showed its cold authority over me; so much space had been left on each page, columns and columns in which to note down everything about us, implacably and forever.—ALFRED KAZIN
8. The school transmits some of the knowledge and some of the intellectual skills and attitudes on which the tradition of Western civility depends—depends more precariously than ever.— EDGAR Z. FRIEDENBERG
9. We are told that the psychological definition of education is barren and formal—that it gives us only the idea of a develop-

ment of all the mental powers without giving us any idea of the use to which these powers are put.—JOHN DEWEY

10. Dewey was writing with an eye to the sterility and rigidity of school instruction in the 1890s—particularly its failure to appreciate the nature of the child.—JEROME S. BRUNER

11. The feeling for a good human job anywhere, the admiration of the really admirable, the disesteem of what is cheap and trashy and impermanent—this is what we call the critical sense, the sense for ideal values.—WILLIAM JAMES

12. In this minimal integrity, the particular has to counterbalance a heavy bulk of statement—statement which, except in the first stanza, is weighed down with bureaucratic jargon.—SIGURD BURKHARDT

13. Rhyme, meter, richness of image and sound—all the devices which, being external and immediately perceptible emblems of order and splendor (however fleeting), affirm an ordered and in some sense splendid world outside of the poet's created act, a world within which he can act because he shares it with his audience—all these are no longer available.—SIGURD BURKHARDT

III. What is the range of uses of participles? By what transformational procedures do they permit the reduction and inclusion of source predications within matrix sentences? The sentences appended here show a variety of the uses of participles, but hardly all of them. If participles represent reduced predicate-parts, as semi-predicatives, determine the subject-part for each of these participles. Solve if you can also the problem of word order. Ignore pre-positional participles here and participles that represent the predicate-parts of two-nuclei reduced predications (as in *with his whole body shaking*). Two-nuclei dependent units are the subject of the next chapter.

1. She had decided that she could not let him stay, when she saw him at the end of the still leafless avenue, making slowly up towards the house, with his head down and his figure relaxed.— W. D. HOWELLS

2. Gearson came again next afternoon, looking pale and rather sick, but quite himself, even to his languid irony.—W. D. HOWELLS

3. Two or three men, conversing earnestly together, ceased as he approached, and exchanged significant glances.—BRET HARTE

4. A wooded amphitheater, surrounded on three sides by precipitous cliffs of naked granite, sloped gently toward the crest of another precipice that overlooked the valley.—BRET HARTE

5. The Indians considered them the abode of spirits, who influenced the weather, spreading sunshine or clouds over the

landscape, and sending good or bad hunting seasons.—WASH-
INGTON IRVING

6. They were ruled by an old squaw spirit, said to be their mother.—WASHINGTON IRVING

7. If displeased, however, she would brew up clouds black as ink, sitting in the middle of them like a bottle-bellied spider in the midst of its web; and when these clouds broke, woe betide the valleys.—WASHINGTON IRVING

8. Five horses came down and drank, and then stood about, nibbling at the dirt or rubbing their sides against the polished wood of the fence.—JOHN STEINBECK

9. The meadowlarks sank like water, and the wild doves, concealed among the bursting leaves of the oaks, made a sound of restrained grieving.—JOHN STEINBECK

10. And the recurring sight of hitch-hikers waiting against the sky gave him the flash of a sensation he had known as a child: standing still, with nothing to touch him, feeling tall and having the world come all at once into its round shape underfoot and rush and turn through space and make his stand very precarious and lonely.—EUDORA WELTY

11. Walking over to the party, so as not to use his car, making the only sounds in the dark wet street, and only partly aware of the indeterminate shapes of houses with their soft-shining fanlights marking them off, there with the rain falling mist-like through the trees, he almost forgot what town he was in and which house he was bound for.—EUDORA WELTY

12. He walked into the day as alertly as might be, making a definite noise with his heels, perceiving with his eyes the superficial truth of streets and structures, the trivial truth of reality.—WILLIAM SAROYAN

13. In the gutter he saw a coin which proved to be a penny dated 1923, and placing it in the palm of his hand he examined it closely, remembering that year and thinking of Lincoln whose profile was stamped upon the coin.—WILLIAM SAROYAN

14. Lonnie felt himself being swept forward, and he stumbled over the rough ground trying to keep from being knocked down and trampled upon.—ERSKINE CALDWELL

15. Consider the men and women in TV advertisements, demonstrating the product and singing the jingle.—PAUL GOODMAN

16. This is evident from the usual kind of vocational guidance, which consists of measuring the boy and finding some place in the economy where he can be fitted; chopping him down to make him fit; or neglecting him if they can't find his slot.—PAUL GOODMAN

17. Although I read walking in the street, to and from the Chil-

dren's Library on Stone Avenue; on the fire escape and the roof; at every meal when they would let me; read even when I dressed in the morning, propping my book up against the drawers of the bureau as I pulled on my long black stockings—I could never seem to get the easiest words out with the right dispatch, and would often miserably signal from my desk that I did not know the answer rather than get up to stumble and fall and crash on every word.—ALFRED KAZIN

18. Looking across the great rows of empty seats to those pebbles lining the windowsills, I could still smell summer from some long veranda surrounded by trees.—ALFRED KAZIN

19. The 175 eventually selected came from 100 different feeder schools, scattered all over the New York metropolitan area.—MARTIN MAYER

20. The class is in English, at the sophomore level, and the teacher, Mr. Gallen, is a young "scholar," doing the three years of teaching which are part of the training of all Jesuit priests.—MARTIN MAYER

21. In France, the universities recently refused to recognize the *Baccalauréat*, which is administered by the secondary department, as a matriculation examination, forcing French kids to spend yet another year in school preparing for yet another set of examinations.—MARTIN MAYER

22. It is the arena in which social forces interact, employing students, teachers, and administrative officers in roles with which they have become familiar but into which they have not developed much insight.—EDGAR Z. FRIEDENBERG

23. But this does not erase the connection, established in our minds by a hardy tradition of our culture, between education and a large measure of responsibility, detachment, and discipline.—EDGAR Z. FRIEDENBERG

24. Let us then re-examine the terms, guided by what we know today of the world and of human nature.—JEROME S. BRUNER

25. To be whole, he must create his own version of the world, using that part of his cultural heritage he has made his own through education.—JEROME S. BRUNER

26. What the colleges—teaching humanities by examples which may be special, but which must be typical and pregnant—should at least try to give us, is a general sense of what, under various disguises, *superiority* has always signified and may still signify.—WILLIAM JAMES

27. Having been the chief speaker, both dramatist and analyst, I was exalted by the lofty ideas floated up into the air around me.—HERBERT GOLD

28. Other governments of Southeast Asia, more removed from the

shadow of Communist China, have been less tolerant of Peking's heavy handed diplomacy.—SEYMOUR TOPPING, *New York Times*

29. In other parliamentary democracies it would have been taken for granted that Dr. Erhard, having led the party to victory last September, would remain in undisputed control until the election in 1969, as a minimum.—THOMAS J. HAMILTON, *New York Times*

30. He denied himself all pleasure in life, constantly saving money which would enable him to achieve this desire.

31. Mickey Mantle, making his second appearance since suffering a knee injury on Aug. 8, started and finished.—*New York Times*

32. But a week or so ago they came triumphantly home, toting twelve hundred pounds of gear and Amahuaca artifacts, and showing no signs of having been stewed, or even braised.

33. The portable burglar alarm, taken along to scare away acquisitive Indians, never went off . . . .

34. . . . it's the oldest race in North America, from the standpoint of continuity, having been run every year since 1860.

35. On the turn into the stretch, Blue Light, who had never been far behind, made his bid, bearing down on Just Don't Shove as the latter began to shorten stride.

(For how many of these participial phrases is it possible to say, as some transformational grammarians have been saying, that participial phrases represent cut-down relative clauses—that is, that in the transformational process they have passed through the step of being relative clauses?)

10

REDUCED PREDICATIONS

We have used the term "reduced predication" to apply to any grammatical structure to which a formal predication of any of the basic sentence types can be transformed so that it is no longer a formal predication and so that it can be added to, included in, or made a part of another formal predication. A formal predication we have defined as a clause containing a subject-part and a finite verb together with any other complements and modifiers it may possess. Both independent and dependent clauses are thus formal predications, since the requirements for formal predications are the "forms" of subject and finite verb. We have just seen that one large class of reduced predications is comprised of semi-predicatives, in which constructions the subject-part is detached from the predicate-part, although it is present and usually adjacent on a higher linguistic level, and in which the predicator (predicate-part) is either a predicate complement of a copula predication with the copula deleted, an infinitive deriving from a finite form, or a participle deriving from a finite form. Most often, however, when we use the term "reduced predication" we refer to a dependent unit of some sort that contains both subject-part and predicate-part, neither of which it shares with any unit on a higher linguistic level, except insofar as some word or phrase may have double valence. In this chapter we will look at two kinds of reduced predication: absolute constructions and "with" constructions. Infinitive phrases of more than one sort can also contain both subject-part and predicate-part with a finite verb transformed into an infinitive; but these, like semi-predicative infinitive phrases, will be described in the following chapter on Infinitives and Infinitive Phrases. Then reduced predications in which finite verbs or other predicators are transformed into nominals will be described in Chapter 13.

ABSOLUTE CONSTRUCTIONS

In traditional grammatical terminology, an "absolute" is a kind of "outlaw" construction that has no formal syntactic linkage with the sentence in which it appears. Certain set phrases useful in making transitions, like *granted* or *considering all this*, are sometimes called absolutes. Also, another kind of construction used frequently by Caesar and other writers in antiquity, in which a predication with a verb in the pluperfect was reduced by juxtaposing the subject-part (with an ablative inflection) and a past participle representing the verb (also with an ablative inflection), has been called by Latin grammarians an "ablative absolute," for no tie exists between the reduced construction and the rest of the sentence. A dative absolute can be found sometimes in Old English literary remains, and the corresponding Greek construction used genitive endings for subject-part and predicate-part. Kinds of reduced predications called absolutes other than those using perfect passive participles in their predicate-parts (*the battle having been won, the bridge having been built, the Belgae having been conquered*—as we translate Caesar) are also to be found in Latin, but Caesar's kind is the kind made familiar to many generations of schoolboys.

The cognate construction in English has traditionally been called the "nominative" absolute, since if a personal pronoun is used as its subject-part, it has been considered correct to use the nominative form (*I having been captured, he having been forewarned*). What the traditional grammarian has not done, usually, is to look at the English constructions as they exist, and as they most often exist, and to give any kind of balanced account of the varieties to be encountered in contemporary prose.

During the seventeenth and eighteenth centuries, when Latin syntax exerted a considerable influence upon English syntax, writers of treatises and other formal stylists frequently used a kind of absolute in which the participle *being* represented in the reduced predication the finite form of *be* that would have been used in a formal predication as predicator, or else *having* appeared in any of its functions. The opening sentence of George Washington's "Farewell Address" will serve as a typical example:

The period for a new election of a citizen to administer the executive government of the United States being not far distant, and the time actually arrived when your thoughts must be employed in designating the person who is to be clothed with that important trust, it appears to me proper, especially as it may conduce to a more distinct expression of the public voice, that I should now apprise you of the resolution I have formed, to decline being considered among the number of those out of whom a choice is to be made.

Here we have reductions of *period is not distant* and *time is actually arrived.* Neither one of these absolute constructions is built exactly in the modern manner.

What we should be aware of is, not that absolute constructions should be frowned on in modern prose, as some superficial rhetoricians have argued, but that writers in the modern world have created their own varieties that can commonly be encountered in certain kinds of writing. In the most frequent kind participles in *-ing* or *-en* represent the predicate-part; these are not usually forms expressing perfect aspect. However, the predicate-parts of absolutes cover a range strikingly similar to that of semi-predicative constructions. Two main kinds can be described: (1) those using participles in the predicate-part, representing the transformation of finite transitive or intransitive verbs, and (2) those in which the predicator is anything that can function as the predicate complement of a copula predication—predicate noun, predicate adjective, prepositional phrase, adverbial noun, adverbial complement, or noun clause or infinitive phrase. In this second class, the copula is either omitted or, particularly if progressive or perfect aspect must be expressed, is converted to *being* or *having been.* We observe that there are no participial forms for most modal auxiliaries except by periphrastic expressions (*can* > *being able to; must* or *ought* > *having to; will* > *being about to*).

Some examples of the variety of predicators to be found in absolute constructions follow:

The mountains stood out clear and cold against the western sky and, *the wind having died down,* everything was still.—perfect participle in the predicate part (*since the wind had died down*). The girls lay beside the swimming pool, *their arms dangling limply into the water.*—active participle as predicator (*The girls lay beside the swimming pool. Their arms dangled limply into the water*); in this kind of sentence, in which the absolute construction is notionally coordinate with the clause upon which it depends, the subject of the absolute is likely to represent some kind of partition of the referent of the subject of the superior unit; thus, the two subject-parts represent a cutting down of scope of reference from *girls* to *their arms;* it is by cutting down of scope that we can identify a unit of attendant circumstance, which is a coordinate except for the smaller scope of reference; however, if we should seek to replace one of the coordinates by a dependent clause, either could become the dependency, according to the emphasis desired: *As the girls lay beside the swimming pool, their arms dangled limply into the water* or *The girls lay beside the swimming pool, while their arms dangled limply . . .* (strangely enough, the first version seems to be the more natural, even though it makes the predication with the broader reference dependent).

The sailors came charging down the waterfront, *their leader a burly fellow in flaming red pantaloons.*—with predicate noun as predicator, copula deleted; again we have partition of the subject of the superior clause as the scope of reference to *sailors* is reduced to *their leader;* but this reduction in scope is the only excuse here for thinking the one predication dependent notionally on the other.

The palms stand in the palm court, *their leaves gray and dead, the stems wound with old coco-matting.*—Ludwig Bemelmans (In the first of two absolutes, the predicators are the predicate adjectives *gray* and *dead* with the copula deleted—*Their leaves were gray and dead;* in the second, *wound* is a passive participle.)

He was always absent-minded, and on this occasion he stood in a daze, *his thoughts on far-away places.*—prepositional phrase as predicator, copula deleted: *his thoughts were on far-away places.*

Their friends home now from their European trip, they no longer needed to stand guard.—adverbial noun as predicator, copula deleted.

His adversary there, the duel began.—adverbial complement as predicator, copula deleted.

Each of them argued for a different cause, *his that the prisoners be released and the Lieutenant's that all be shot.*—noun clauses as predicators; the genitives imply ellipsis of *cause,* but the copula is deleted; it is quite possible that a single absolute of this kind would seem strained, for the two together create an over-all structure supporting the parts.

The inherited money finally came through, *each of them to get a substantial sum.*—infinitive phrase as predicator, copula deleted.

The boys being good, we must reward them.—We cannot determine from the presence of *being* that the source clause had a copula of progressive aspect (*are being good*) and not a simple present tense (*are good*); however, the progressive transform demands *being*.

Their mittens having been lost, the kittens did not dare return home.—perfect passive participle of a transitive verb as predicator.

The kittens having been attentive, their mother rewarded them.— perfect participle of *be* as predicator.

In the light of the process by which these absolute structures are generated and the close parallel that exists between semi-predicatives and the varieties of predicate-parts to be found in them, it would seem that their subject-parts could consist of anything that could act as subject of any predication. Actually, as we have already seen, this is not entirely true. Some word or phrase in the absolute usually has a semantic connection with the structure on which it depends, and in the recognition of the syntax we rely more on this semantic connection than on signaling that is purely structural. Absolutes are rarely, if ever, restrictive—unlike appositive and participial phrases in this respect —and only by going out of our way can we show how they can be derived from relative clauses, since a relative pronoun cannot very well act as their subject-part, inasmuch as by definition the absolute must have its own subject-part. In the parallel constructing of

Butterflies gathered in droves at this marshy spot, predominant among them tiger swallowtails and fritillaries and
Butterflies gathered in droves at this marshy spot, predominant among which were tiger swallowtails and fritillaries

the absolute can be derived from the basic sentence pattern as easily as from the relative clause. We note the inversion of subject-part and predicate adjective in both constructions. As non-restrictive units, absolutes end with a 3–2 or 3–1 pitch contour, are set off by distinct juncture, and, as two-nuclei constructions, usually contain two stresses that are either primary or secondary—even more often in fact than the formal predications from which they may be reduced. Thus we find *I'm a béast* with only one strong stress, but the corresponding absolute *I' a béast* shows two, with a glide between. Sometimes only by supra-segmental signals can we catch the distinction between an absolute construction and the construction of an appositive modified by a restrictive participle: *Dúke, the búsiness manager còming from Chicàgo, arrived fírst* (meaning Duke who is the business manager who is coming from Chicago) in contrast with *Dúke, the búsiness manager còming from Chicágo, arrived fírst* (the business manager is now not the same person as Duke, or if Duke is the business manager only a hidden predication exists between manager and Duke, and the absolute is derived from *since the business manager came from Chicago*).

In fact, a kind of absolute construction can exist for which we must arbitrarily decide which of two participles is the predicate-part of the absolute construction and which of them is dependent upon the subject-part of the absolute construction: *the house standing upon the hill blocking our path.* Should this be read as *the house that stood upon the hill blocked our path* or *the house that blocked our path stood upon the hill?* Only by intonation contour can the distinction be signaled; yet the two participial phrases cannot exist in parallel construction, on the same linguistic level. A similar ambiguity can exist in a formal predication in which *be* can be variously interpreted as copula or as auxiliary signifying progressive aspect. Thus, *They were standing among us* can be read as *They were among us, standing* (in which the prepositional phrase is the primary predicator after the copula) or as "They *were standing* among us" (in which *among us* is a prepositional phrase of place modifying the progressive verb form *were standing*). This ambiguity is a necessary consequence of the possibility of creating a copula predication with a prepositional phrase as predicator.

In our sentences illustrating varieties of predicate-parts in absolute constructions, we have seen that the semantic connection between absolute construction and superior unit is often made by a reduction of scope of reference. This reduction is often made by the use of near-nouns (pre-determiners—or what the traditionalists have called numerical pronouns) as subject-parts: *the men, few of them wearing Klan regalia, marched; the boys, several of them without swimming suits, dived; the cowpunchers, both of them angry, pulled; the debutantes, one prettier than the other, arrived; the diplomats, each trying to be clever, talked,* etc.

It sometimes happens, in literary description, that absolutes are treated as if they can be parallel (coordinate) to participial phrases (but are rarely indiscriminately intermingled with them);

this can happen because the semantic reduction of scope of reference gives the illusion that the same subject operates for both, even though grammatically the two are separate items. A sentence by Hanson W. Baldwin illustrates this paralleling:

> And it was then, in all its white-green majesty, that the Titanic's survivors saw the iceberg, *tinted with the sunrise, floating idly, pack-ice jammed about its base, other bergs heaving slowly nearby on the blue breast of the sea.*

In this case, the semantic relation is, in the first instance, carried by the personal pronoun *its* which is not a member of the subject-part at all, and, in the second instance, the relating phrase is *other bergs* which can hardly limit the scope of reference, but makes use of *other,* a near-noun.

Zandvoort indicates (*A Handbook of English Grammar,* pp. 35–36) that absolute constructions can express relations of time, cause, condition, and attendant circumstance, or be semantically coordinate with the superior predication. All of these have been exemplified in the illustrative sentences, with the exception of condition. Examples of the conditional relationship are: *Weather permitting,* we shall go (*If the weather permits, we shall go*); *This removed,* the whole will collapse (*If this is removed, the whole will collapse*); There will be roughnecks in the crowd, but, *Jonas being present,* no one will dare to start a fight (*If Jonas is present, no one . . .*). As with the so-called adverbial clauses, there is much overlapping among relations of time, condition, cause, and attendant circumstance. The implication is that absolute constructions are most commonly reduced adverbial clauses. This is true only to the extent that absolutes are not semantically coordinates.

"WITH" CONSTRUCTIONS

The kind of reduced predication that uses the particle *with* as a connector of dependent to superior units is somewhat more complex in its varieties and operations than absolute constructions, perhaps because of the complexity of functioning of the particle *with.* *With* is often a preposition expressing means, instrument, manner, and accompaniment: *I outfoxed him with a sacrifice bunt; He hit Grandpa with an ax; He bowed with a flourish; He came with me.* We have indicated (p. 42) that a

prepositional phrase of accompaniment can be considered periphrastic of coordination: *He came with me = He and I came.*
The concept of "accompaniment" is important to the interpretation of many of the reduced predications introduced by *with,*
since it can be said that in those instances predication accompanies predication, rather than nominal accompanies nominal.
We move to harder problems when we encounter instances in
which *with* is an analytic particle that seems to have the functional attributes of the verb *have. Have* is a peculiar function
verb of more logical than descriptive content. We have indicated that it partakes of the relational concept of "possession" (p.
40). If we compare *of* an as analytic particle denoting possession
with *with* as a similar particle denoting possession, we note that a
reversal of headwords is found. The synthetic *man's hat* is not
directly equivalent to *man with the hat* as *the hat of the man* is.
We cannot say *hat's man.* But we can more directly equate *the
man with a hat* and *the man who has a hat* (or *the man having
a hat*) than we can equate *the man's hat* and *the man has a hat.*

A functional ambiguity often exists, in those constructions
using *with* as a connector, between an interpretation according
to which *with* functions as an analytic substitute for *have* and an
interpretation according to which *with* introduces a two-nuclei
reduced predication functioning in the area of "accompaniment"
and not in that of "possession." A "with" construction with two
nuclei resembles an absolute construction in internal structure and
process of reduction from a basic sentence pattern except for the
addition of *with* at the beginning as a connector. Having the connector, the "with" construction can function in a somewhat larger
range than an absolute construction can—at least the ranges of
the two are not precisely the same. The *with* connector usually
seems out-of-place when the subject-part of the reduced predication represents an aspect of, or a reduction of scope of reference
of, the item in the superior clause to which the dependent predication semantically relates. Thus absolutes appear more frequently under those conditions; but somewhat looser semantic
references usually are present in the "with" construction.

The ambiguity between the two kinds of "with" constructions
is most evident when a prepositional phrase occurs in the predicate-part that could be construed as predicator in a reduced
copula predication or, on the other hand, as an adverbial modifier
of *have.* Thus, in the phrase *with his hand on the throttle,* the

two source sentences from which the construction can be derived are *His hand was on the throttle* (to which *with* must be
added as a connector in the process of transformation, and the
copula deleted), and *He had his hand on the throttle* (in which
on the throttle is a "place" modifier of *had,* and what was the
subject-part of the copula predication is now the direct object of
had). In our discussion of basic sentence patterns, we hinted
that it might be necessary to constitute a class of adverbial complements functioning not unlike objective complements—result
adjuncts in particular. *He had his hand* is semantically an incomplete predication. A full paraphrase of the basic sentence may
well be *he had his hand so that it was on the throttle,* in which
we find both the *have* predication and the copula predication. In
a sentence like *He had his hand on the throttle,* the notion of
"possession" in *had* has given way completely to *had* as a function verb effecting a redistribution.

The urgency of making some of these fine distinctions may be
apparent when we see the problems we encounter in certain sentences. We shall present illustrations and commentary:

> *The situation was just as we remembered it, the young girls with
> sunbonnets pulled tight over their long curls, the boys in knee-
> length boots called "high-tops," with "beanies" perched jauntily
> on their heads.*

The first thing we notice here is that the two principal constructions after the first comma are absolute constructions, with
girls as the headword in the subject-part of one and *boys* as the
subject-part of the other. In the first—*the young girls with sunbonnets pulled tight over their long curls*—the particle *with* functions either as an analytic particle substituting for the finite verb
form *had* in the reduction of predication, or as connector and in-
troducer of a two-nuclei "with" construction which, as a reduced predication itself, functions as the predicate-part of the
absolute construction—also a reduced predication. In neither case
is *with* a preposition. Few if any grammars have as yet faced
up to the functionings of analytic particles. The particle *as* is
used in a wide range of constructions as a replacement of *to be*
or of a finite copula form in transforms. The structure *with "girls"
as the headword in the subject-part of one* to be found in the
first sentence of this comment is an example. This "with" construction has been reduced from the relative clause *in which*

"girls" is the headword in the subject part of one—*with* replacing *in which* and *as* replacing *is*. *As* can function as the substitute for a copula in an absolute construction: *each as the counterpart of the other, the male as the bully and the female as the oppressed.* The use of these particles as verb-replacements may be hard to understand since it seems to defy the logic of our parts-of-speech grammars. The functioning goes back to a logic beyond parts-of-speech distinctions. *With* like *as* in these functionings is purely a function word with no lexical content. If our reading is *girls had sunbonnets pulled tight over curls,* we are faced with a re-distribution in which both the passive participle *pulled* and the result adjective *tight* represent layers of compressed predication. If we treat the construction as a two-nuclei "with" construction, *pulled* is a passive participle predicator and *tight* is a result adjunct. In the second of these "with" constructions—*the boys in knee-length boots*—we have a simpler case in which only the interpretation *the boys were in knee-length boots* is possible, an absolute with prepositional phrase in the predicate-part. The construction in which a "with" construction acts as predicate-part of an absolute is frequently encountered, however difficult it may be to explain. When *with* is treated as an analytic equivalent of *have,* the meaning of *have* can shade from "possession" to a function in a redistribution with no lexical content at all.

> *With his treatment of his subjects forgotten, the exiled king was in a position to return to the throne.*

Here the "with" construction, at the beginning of a sentence where we might expect to find a time or causal clause, is solely a two-nuclei reduction of a predication. The *have* interpretation is impossible.

> *The bedrooms they showed us to early were timber-ceilinged and timber-walled, with a balcony on the front of each facing Mont Blanc across the abyss of dark. And all night in the starlit cold, with the implacable white of the mountains like the face of death on the valley's other side, we seemed to be . . .* —KAY BOYLE

The problems here also are complex but not unlike those we have already encountered. Ambiguities of structure of two kinds are found in *with a balcony on the front of each facing Mont Blanc across the abyss of dark.* (1) Is *with* to be read as a substitute for *having* so that *on the front* is a "place" prepositional phrase, or as a connector introducing a reduced predication that is a transform of *a balcony was on the front of each,* in which the prepositional phrase is the predicator when *was* is deleted? We note the possibility of recasting the whole to create an absolute construction with *each* as the subject-part and with the "with" construction as the predicate-part: *each with a balcony on the front.* That this recasting is possible makes clear the great range of possibilities in grammatical redistribution still for the most part unexplored, rather than the chaotic dubieties of grammatical structure. (2) Granting that *with* is a connector, which of two possible predicate-parts of the "with" construction is on the same linguistic level as the subject-part *balcony* and which of the two is a semi-predicative construction—*on the front of each* or *facing Mont Blanc across the abyss of dark?* We have already encountered this ambiguity in assigning direct predicators in connection with absolute constructions. Paraphrases will reveal the difference: *A balcony facing Mont Blanc across the abyss of dark was on the front of each* in contrast to *A balcony that was on the front of each faced Mont Blanc across the abyss of dark.* The question is unanswerable. Since the same structures can function as predicators in both semi-predicatives and reduced predications with two nuclei—transformation of finite verb to participle or deletion of the copula leaving the predicate complement as predicator —we are at liberty to assign levels arbitrarily when the two kinds appear together so long as we realize that the assigning of different levels is imposed upon us by the overall structure. The intonation contours of the contrasting syntactic interpretations differ. If we return to the interpretation by which *with* is an analytic particle substituting for *having,* we can perhaps avoid assigning different linguistic levels to *on the front of each* and *facing Mont Blanc* since we are accustomed to the notion that unlike adverbial complements can be strung out on the same level—*I went home quickly yesterday*—but we can see all the more clearly that *having* is merely a function word rather than a verb of lexical content and that it allows a redistribution of items to a structure in which the assigning of levels is unimportant, and that the idea of "possession" in *having* has all but disappeared, particularly in relation to *facing Mont Blanc.*

The "with" construction in the second sentence of the illustration—*with the implacable white of the mountains like the face of death on the valley's other side*—contains fewer structural ambiguities since the *having* interpretation is harder to maintain, though not impossible, and two prepositional phrases, one of place and one of manner or comparison, are the alternative predicators: *the white was like the face of death* or *the white was on the valley's other side.* We cannot clearly exclude a sentence like *The white was like the face of death on the valley's other side* from the basic sentence pattern of subject-copula-complement, except that we have two complements and consequently a first-level transformation by which two predications are fused into one.

In the vast corpus of modern prose we encounter frequently a kind of "with" construction that has been further transformed from a two-nuclei structure to a one-nucleus structure. *With his nose burnt* is changed to *with his burnt nose.* This transformation is not markedly different from that by which any semi-predicative adjective or participle becomes pre-positional; but in the "with" phrase the sense of priority of transformation or "deadness" of included predication is often lacking. In a sentence such as *With his torn ligament, the second baseman may not be able to return to the game until after Labor Day,* the sense of included predication is strong—*Since his ligament is torn, the second baseman . . . .* The transformation and compression of predication can be described as: *since his ligament has been torn* > *with his ligament torn* > *with his torn ligament.* We must think of the transformation of the unit as a whole. The semantic question is how much *with* remains a connector, particularly if the "with" phrase is non-restrictive, and does not function simply as a preposition, now that it is followed by a noun and a pre-positional adjective or participle. It is significant to note the functioning of *their* in the following sentences:

> *The Brown children, with their dirty faces, must stay outside; the Green children, with their clean faces, may come in.*
> *Children with dirty faces must stay outside; children with clean faces may come in.*

The difference here is largely that of restriction and non-restriction, but the stress patterns are different and perhaps the presence of the genitive reference *their* accounts for the difference. There are more than one equivalent structures for both kinds (*because their faces are dirty, having their faces dirty, who have dirty faces, whose faces are dirty*); in the non-restrictive unit, particularly, we have evidence of redistribution. In a transformational grammar, the process of generating structures is more important than superficial resemblances among structures generated by different processes. Here we keep our eye on the "with" construction as a whole (a reduced predication) and trace the reduction through further change rather than content ourselves with identifying the result as a prepositional phrase in which a pre-positional adjective modifies the object of the preposition.

Another curious example of compression of predication along with redistribution is found in *It will be cloudy with early snow tomorrow.* Semantically, *snow* and *clouds* are coordinates here: *that it will be cloudy* and *that it will snow early.* According to the concept of "accompaniment," noun accompanies noun or predication accompanies predication. This construction seems to mix the two.

With must be regarded as a function word of great range and adaptability in English. In reduced predication the usages that are significant are those in which it acts as connector between predications and those in which it replaces the verb *have* either when the sense of *have* is possession or when *have* is purely a function word in redistributions. Some of the resulting constructions are among the most complex in the language.

MATERIALS FOR EXERCISE AND FURTHER STUDY

I. Of particular importance to the grammarian in the structure of absolute constructions are (1) the kind of unit that functions as the second nucleus, the predicate part, and (2) the relation between the absolute and the structure upon which it is dependent. Attempt to make these discriminations about the absolute constructions in the following sentences:

1. Before her reasoning went her emotioning; her nature pulling upon his nature, her womanhood upon his manhood, without her knowing the means she was using to the end she was willing.—W. D. HOWELLS
2. With blood streaming from his broken head, he was slumped down upon the guitar, his legs bowed around it, his arms at either side, his whole body limp in a posture of a bareback rider.—EUDORA WELTY
3. The girl across the table from him turned away from the band and faced him, her hands, knuckles white, clenched, apparently in anger, and a sour smile flitting across her lips.

4. The old man in the doorway, shirt open to the evening breezes, called out a greeting to Pablo.

5. The men had already begun to creep forward, guns raised as if stalking a deer.—ERSKINE CALDWELL

6. Soon a car came riding down the road, its headlights lighting up the whole place, hog pen and all.—ERSKINE CALDWELL

7. There is an hypothesis that an important predisposition to juvenile delinquency is the combination of low verbal intelligence with high manual intelligence, delinquency giving a way of self-expression where other avenues are blocked by lack of schooling.—PAUL GOODMAN

8. . . . by bringing little gifts at Christmas, on their birthdays, and at the end of the term—the well-known significance of these gifts being that they came not from us, but from our parents, whose eagerness in this matter showed a high level of social consideration, and thus raised our standard in turn.—ALFRED KAZIN

9. A very few cities—among them Columbus—maintain "occupational" schools below the vocational program.—MARTIN MAYER

10. Education being a social process, the school is simply that form of community life in which all those agencies are concentrated that will be most effective in bringing the child to share in the inherited resources of the race, and to use his own powers for social ends.—JOHN DEWEY

11. Who else could have made them fight: could have struck them so aghast with fear and dread as to turn shoulder to shoulder and face one way and even stop talking for a while and after two years of it keep them still so wrung with terror that some among them would seriously propose moving their very capital into a foreign country lest it be ravaged and pillaged by a people whose entire white male population would have little more than filled any one of their larger cities: except Jackson in the Valley and three separate armies trying to catch him and none of them ever knowing whether they were just retreating from a battle or just running into one and Stuart riding his whole command entirely around the biggest single armed force this continent ever saw in order to see what it looked like from behind and Morgan leading a cavalry charge against a stranded man-of-war.—WILLIAM FAULKNER

12. . . . and even the tragic and miscast Percival Brownlee, who couldn't keep books and couldn't farm either, found his true niche at last, reappeared in 1862 during the boy's father's absence and had apparently been living on the plantation for at least a month before his uncle found out about it, conducting impromptu revival meetings among negroes, preaching and

leading the singing also in his high sweet true soprano voice and disappeared again on foot and at top speed, not behind but ahead of a body of raiding Federal horse and reappeared for the third and last time in the entourage of a travelling Army paymaster, the two of them passing through Jefferson in a surrey at the exact moment when the boy's father (it was 1866) also happened to be crossing the Square, the surrey and its occupants traversing rapidly that quiet and bucolic scene and even in that fleeting moment and to others beside the boy's father giving an illusion of flight and illicit holiday . . . .
—WILLIAM FAULKNER

13. When he had gone halfway he turned around and stared at the scene—his wife and Catherine scolding and consoling as they stumbled here and there among the crowded furniture with articles of aid, and the despairing figure on the couch, bleeding fluently, and trying to spread a copy of *Town Tattle* over the tapestry scenes of Versailles.—F. SCOTT FITZGERALD

14. Sure enough, in five minutes there was a boy in the corner squatted Indian-style on the floor, the back of his frayed polo shirt to the others.—PHILIP ROTH

15. Sabinsky walked on, his body bent to the insistence of the April wind.—BARRY SPACKS

16. We don't see his face, for he is turned towards the blackboard, one hand on the chalk-well clutching a long piece of chalk.—HARRIS DOWNEY

17. She has not seen the sudden gesture at the door—hands lifting and opening in wonder, shoulders shrugged, head tilting, and blue eyes gazing in mock bewilderment.—HARRIS DOWNEY

18. He could hear them talking downstairs, his sister's voice louder than his mother's or father's.—OAKLEY HALL

19. This afternoon turns half transparent to reveal a fixed progression of scenes, none of them utterly opaque and therefore perhaps not real, of summer afternoons I spent at my grandfather's place when I was a child.—R. V. CASSILL

20. She stepped outside and watched the shredded sky clear; birds moved inland again along the broadening flyway; back along the ridges she could see goats stepping down to watering places, their polished horns making a circuit of many suns around them.—LEONARD CASPER

21. The smelt run having begun to diminish, the lights began to wink out along the creek and the spring water to gurgle its way in darkness.

22. He was standing by the door, his hand on the latch.

23. The three shepherds had drifted to the barnyard, each with his crook in his hand.

24. They were lined up by the wall, each five feet from the other.
25. The lumber not having been cut to the right specifications, the pieces would not fit together properly.

II. Reconstruct the source predications for the "with" constructions to be found in the sentences collected here. Describe the subject-parts and predicate-parts of these two-nuclei constructions. What relations do they express with the units on which they are dependent?

1. . . . when she came back with two tall glasses of clouded liquid on a tray, and the ice clucking in them, he still sat as she had left him.—W. D. HOWELLS
2. Near the foot of it is a small lake, the haunt of the solitary bittern, with water snakes basking in the sun on the leaves of the pond lilies which lie on the surface.—WASHINGTON IRVING
3. They had but to lift their eyes, and there it was plainly to be seen, though miles away, with the sunshine brightening all its features.—NATHANIEL HAWTHORNE
4. . . . and the farther he withdrew from them, the more like a human face, with all its original divinity intact, did they appear; until, as it grew dim in the distance, with the clouds and glorified vapor of the mountain clustering about it, the Great Stone Face seemed positively to be alive.—NATHANIEL HAWTHORNE
5. From the other window, if the bed was turned, you could see the town, with a little smoke above it, and the Dawson mountains looking like real mountains with the winter snow on them. —ERNEST HEMINGWAY
6. With hoofs battering the ground the stallion appeared and charged down the hill trailing a broken halter rope.—JOHN STEINBECK
7. Harris was aware of the other face not a yard away: the man the guitar player had called Sobby was standing on the curb, with two men unnecessarily holding him.—EUDORA WELTY
8. With the constable scuttling along after and then riding on the running board, glasses held tenderly in one fist, the handcuffed Sobby dragged along by the other, with a long line of little boys in flowered shirts accompanying him on bicycles, riding in and out of the headlight beam, with the rain falling in front of him and with Mr. Gene shouting in a sort of plea from the hotel behind and Mike beginning to echo the barking of the rest of the dogs, Harris drove in all carefulness down the long tree-dark street, with his wet hand pressed on the horn.—EUDORA WELTY
9. The red sunset, with narrow, black cloud strips like threats

across it, lay on the curved horizon of the prairie.—WALTER VAN TILBURG CLARK

10. With its standard New York public-school brown brick courtyard shut in on three sides of the square and the pretentious battlements overlooking that cockpit in which I can still smell the fiery sheen of the rubber ball, it looks like a factory over which has been imposed the façade of a castle.—ALFRED KAZIN

11. With the Communists shattered and the threat of a leftist takeover ended, they have appeared to slow down in their domestic actions and to be relying once more on the old Sukarno cabinet with men like third Deputy Prime Minister Chaerul Saleh still calling the economic turns and first Deputy Prime Minister and Foreign Minister Dr. Subandrio, the architect of the Peking-Jakarta axis, still speaking on foreign matters.—SETH KING, *New York Times*

12. Since then, the dispute between Peking and Moscow has worsened with the Chinese Communists referring to the Russians as "pimps of U.S. imperialism" and accusing them of joining with the United States in an encirclement of China.—SEYMOUR TOPPING, *New York Times*

13. Mr. McKee was asleep on a chair with his fists clenched in his lap, like a photograph of a man of action.—F. SCOTT FITZGERALD

14. I supposed there'd be a curious crowd around there all day with little boys searching for dark spots in the dust, and some garrulous man telling over and over what had happened, until it became less and less real even to him and he could tell it no longer, and Myrtle Wilson's tragic achievement was forgotten. —F. SCOTT FITZGERALD

15. They repeated it here on July 21, 22 and 23, with the three hurlers working in the same order.—*New York Times*

16. A week ago, in the Grand Union Hotel Stakes, Artismo took the money with six lengths to spare, with his rider easing him through the final seventy yards.—*New York Times*

17. With Red Schoendienst, Monty Irvin and Jackie Robinson all on the shelf, Ashburn is the lone healthy player among the National League's top four hitters.—*New York Times*

18. The Dodgers are ten and a half games in front of the second-place Braves, with eleven in the loss column and twenty-six left to play.—*New York Times*

19. Last month, with Photographer Joe Clark on hand to picture the results, she took dead aim at some eggs.—*Life*

20. The 1961–62 television season, with 34 new programs making their debuts on the three major networks, is experimenting with early curtains this year.—(AP)

21. Newman . . . took a place at the end of the table with the bril-

liant girl on his left and the dingy old man on the other side.—
Henry James

22. For good measure, this year's renewal was as thrilling as this
year's Kentucky Derby or Preakness, with Blue Light, a 20–1
chance, getting up in the very last stride to beat Just Don't
Shove, one of the favorites, by inches.—*New York Times*

23. It reached storm intensity during the night, with highest winds
40 to 50 miles per hour in squalls extending out 100 miles from
the center.—(AP)

24. . . . all shelves are of solid aluminum with individual freezing
coils fastened directly to them.—Advertisement, *Life*

25. Crisp new form with defatted wheat germ added . . . .—Advertisement, *Life*

III. The two-nuclei constructions of Exercise II should be kept distinct from the one-nucleus constructions using *with* or *without* as connectors carrying the predicational sense of *have* or *does not have* or showing the reduced predicate-part of the two-nuclei construction moved to pre-position, as when *with their faces dirty* is further reduced to *with their dirty faces*. The following instances can be used as the beginning of an assemblage of relevant materials for an inductive study of these constructions. Attempt to add to them and reduce the resulting evidence to order.

1. With life insurance, a man can guarantee that there will be
money to pay . . . .

2. And remember—with L & M's modern filter, only pure white
touches your lips.—Advertisement

3. And with Ford's I-beam front axle, front tires track true . . . .
—Advertisement

4. a tall man with a slender face

5. . . . on an inclement morning, with sleep and snowflakes in our
eyes, we made our way . . . .

6. Present day university students, with scholarships to aid them
and a whole series of museums to serve them, will hardly be
able to imagine . . . .

7. Among those of rayon-and-Arnel crêpe are overblouses (they
can pass as jackets) with round, collarless necks and short
sleeves, button-in-back overblouses without collars and sleeves,
cap-sleeved blouses with boat necks and elasticized waists, and
slim knife-pleated skirts.

8. The wedding over, and the bride people gone, her father and
herself were left to dine together, with no prospect of a third
to cheer a long evening.—Jane Austen

9. . . . and with all her advantages, natural and domestic, she

was now in great danger of suffering from intellectual solitude.
—JANE AUSTEN

10. with a hardly suppressed grimace
11. . . . people can have many cousins and of all sorts, Miss Cathy, without being any the worse for it . . . .—EMILY BRONTË
12. . . . she arrived without adventure to the gate of the farm-house . . . .—EMILY BRONTË
13. I knew that you could not keep up an acquaintance with your cousin, without being brought into contact with him . . . . —EMILY BRONTË
14. Their performances are the product of a repertory theatre with continuity and a community of interests.—*New York Times*
15. You can do that without risk of discovery.

11

INFINITIVES AND INFINITIVE PHRASES

DEFINING INFINITIVES

It is customary in dictionaries to list verbs by their infinitive forms. The implication is, somehow, that an infinitive presents a verb in all its "verb-ness," that if we are assigning words to various form classes we must define verbs in such a way that infinitives will be called verbs and not nouns, adjectives, or adverbs. If, however, we are defining parts of speech by function and not by form, we are tempted to call infinitives nouns, adjectives, or adverbs, depending upon their function in particular situations, since they can perform the functions and fill the positions of all of these, but without auxiliaries they can never function as finite verbs. If in some constructions of reduced predication they take the place of verbs, without clear indication of functional shift (as in *I don't know whether to go or not* < *I don't know whether I should go or not*), the traditionalists have tended to define the part of speech by giving to the infinitive the function of the whole reduced predication rather than to give the infinitive standing as a verb-substitute that is not by form a finite verb. In English the problem of classification becomes particularly acute since morphologically infinitives of most verbs are indistinguishable from some of their finite forms when the so-called *to*-sign of the infinitive is not present. The more hide-bound of the structuralist grammarians of the recent past, who have refused to believe in the existence of anything without tangible proof of it, have described forms that look alike as if they were alike. Thus, the easy description of such structures as *they can go, I made him go, I demanded that they go,* and *will you go?* is that the "common form" of the verb is used in these instances. Grammarians who have been unwilling to call certain function words analytic particles have believed that *to* in historical origin was a preposition when it came before an infinitive, so that by rights infinitives should be classed as nouns when the *to*-sign is present since they are "objects of prepositions." By this distinction the *go* forms function differently in *I made him go* and *I forced him to go.* All of this confusion comes from taking parts-of-speech classifications too seriously and not thinking enough about the actual dynamics of predications.

Infinitives, like participles, derive from verbs but are not verbs, since both formally and functionally only finite forms are verbs. That the infinitive forms are the same as many of the finite forms is immaterial. They are abstractions from finite forms uncommitted to any part-of-speech classification; they are unspecialized forms that are freed from the class limitations of specialized forms. In spite of all this, their force is primarily verbal. They continue to have verb properties. They can combine with auxiliaries to form analytic verb phrases; they can take direct and indirect objects without periphrasis; adverbs can be dependent upon them; they can express aspect and voice, but not person, tense, or number. They can be agentless or subjectless in some constructions and have agents or subjects in others. Since the grammar we are concerned with is the grammar of predications, we shall be particularly concerned with what happens to subjects and agents in infinitive phrases.

There are four principal kinds of constructions in which infinitives play a part: (1) verb phrases in which the infinitive joins with modal auxiliaries, or with the auxiliaries *shall* and *will* to express future tense analytically (whether our periphrastic future is modal or not is beside the question; *should* and *would* are without question modal auxiliaries), or is part of an unclassifiable periphrastic verb phrase; like *am about to go* or *is to go;* (2) abstract infinitive phrases without explicit subjects or agents, used nominally as abstract nouns or as modifiers of abstract nouns; here the agents or subjects are completely generalized (*anyone, anything, everything, someone, something*) in implication but even the generalized forms are not made explicit; (3) structures in which no agent appears in the infinitive phrase itself but is explicitly found in the context; (4) infinitive phrases in which the infinitive has its own subject within the limits of the phrase, either exclusively or in double valence. The structures of the third kind can loosely be compared to semi-predicative structures; those of the fourth kind to full reduced predications.

About the uses of infinitives in verb phrases we need say little more, since the problems in this category are mainly morphological. Some disagreement exists concerning when a verb phrase is a verb phrase and when an infinitive is not part of a verb phrase but the direct object of the verb phrase. Is *dare* an auxiliary in *I dare go* but not in *He didn't dare to go?* Highly particularized idioms like *he made do with* or *let go* are outside the question either way. Are the infinitives without question direct objects in *want to go, wish to go, like to go, hope to go, mean to go?* Since noun clauses can be substituted for the infinitives in these instances without total loss of the same meaning (*I want that I go,* etc.) the belief is tenable that these are direct objects, but who is to say that direct objects are necessarily excluded from analytic verb phrases? These are cases in which the subject of the verb is also agent or subject of the direct object infinitive, so that verb and infinitive are in line to form a single verb phrase. The infinitive in *I am to go* can perhaps be construed as a predicate complement, but this fact does not prohibit our calling *am to go* a verb phrase. The descriptive grammar of an analytic system must differ from that of a synthetic system.

AGENTS AND SUBJECTS OF INFINITIVES

Finite verbs always have subjects, no matter how abstract the concept is that they express, but they do not always have agents. There are two main kinds of agentless verbs: (1) passive forms, in predications in which direct or indirect objects have been transformed to subjects, so that the agent-subject of the active base-form is expressed obliquely—usually as the object of a preposition—or not at all; and (2) active forms in which there is a discrepancy between form and content—i.e., those verb forms that actively predicate something about the subject without implying that the subject is the agent (*Peace obtains, The bread toasts well,* even *I saw the movie* although the passive transformation is possible). Copula predications are by nature agentless. When we are dealing with finite verbs we can readily look for subjects—a formal matter—rather than for agents—a semantic matter, since we expect agreement between subjects and verbs. When finite predicational structures are reduced to non-finite structures we are encouraged to look for agents rather than for subjects since reduced predications can be described more clearly when agents and subjects coincide; but we must remember that we are looking for subjects, not agents, and that we look for agents only as an aid in the process. In a completely abstract infinitive phrase neither subject nor agent is given formal expression. Verbs are in their base-form finite; nouns are in their base-form non-finite. The philosophical implication is that we cannot have a noun *cat* without having encountered more than one cat—more than one object with similar attributes. A thing encountered only once is nameless. In fact, an experience that bears no resemblance to any other experience cannot be said to exist, or exists only to the degree that we sense some shadow of resemblance. Abstractions can be made from finite assertions. We can move from *he runs, we run, we ran, the colors run* (?), *the candidates have run,* and *everyone has run* (all finite assertions) to *running is dangerous* or *to run is to court danger* in which the abstraction is made from the finite instances and the finite verbs have become nominal. We note, however, that the change of state is not measured either by degree of abstraction or by the presence or absence of expressed agents. Finite assertions can be extremely general or extremely concrete semantically (from *All things pass* to *I am biting my thumb hard at this moment*), but the whole range can be transformed from verb-ness to noun-ness (*the passing of all things* and *my biting my thumb hard at this moment*), just as a play requiring actors of both sexes can be presented either at an all-boys school or at all-girls school. It is as if the human mind in its striving for expression is willing to betray whenever it can its most cherished distinction—that between the finite and the non-finite. When we say *Running is dangerous* we have no indication of who is doing the running, but the form of the assertion remains the same when we proceed to qualify the assertion: *Running is dangerous for little boys like you who can't control their energy,* but the form changes when we say *You should not run so fast, since little boys like you cannot control their energy.* In setting up basic sentence patterns, we had to ignore (or to try to ignore) the range of forms that could serve as components in the patterns, even though the whole concept of redistribution is founded on the borrowing of basic patterns to express relations not most native to them. Yet, strictly speaking, we can identify basic patterns more easily than we can distinguish between simple and non-simple (native and alien) uses of the patterns. We can argue that *For us to praise God is good* is a transform since one predication is substituted for one of the component parts of another predication, and that, to the contrary, *Jimmy is good* is an instance of a basic sentence pattern without qualification, even though the basic sentence pattern is the same in the two instances. These difficulties of distinction we will have to learn to live with.

Abstract infinitives may or may not be given agents or subjects by inference; formally their existence in no way depends upon them. In *I want to court disaster*, the presence of the infinitive as direct object of a transitive verb may well depend upon the fact that the subject-agent of *want* also functions as subject-agent of *to court*. We have said that abstract infinitives without agents implied a function as abstract nouns or as modifiers of abstract nouns. Thus, we can say *To court disaster is fatal* and *The desire to court disaster is fatal* without expression of agent or subject for either *to court* or *desire*. Whether *to court* in *the desire to court disaster* is a modifier of *desire* or the direct object of verb potencies remaining in the noun that has been shifted from a verb is immaterial to the question at hand; a purpose infinitive may also carry over into a nominal phrase (*going to the store to buy milk is less costly* . . .). In summary, we can conclude that the distinction among infinitives with their own subjects, those with implied or shared subjects, and subjectless ones is a matter of contingencies only, except that the range of functioning may depend upon the kind.

Abstract infinitive phrases may, however, be included predications as well as other kinds since an abstraction always implies the possibility of being manifested in the concrete. *Cat* can always be made manifest as *this cat*. *To buy apples* can be made manifest as *for him to buy these apples*. A predication without an expressed subject within its own unit we have called a semi-predicative construction, but we have left no room for semi-predicatives used nominally as subjects since we have said that the subject-part of a semi-predicative construction must exist in the structure upon which the semi-predicative is dependent. In the process of transformation therefore, abstraction as well as inclusion is necessary if a predication is to become an abstract infinitive phrase as subject or predicate nominal in another predication. Rhetorically, a shift up or down on the abstraction ladder is a way of synecdochizing, of creating one kind of figure of speech. If instead of saying *You should buy milk at the store instead of having the milkman deliver it; it's cheaper that way*, someone says *To buy milk at the store is cheaper than to have the milkman deliver it*, he means the same thing but has cast his assertions into an abstract, agentless, impersonal mold. Indefinite or impersonal agents and subjects are often no more than empty shells of form. They are obligatory in active formal predications since finite verbs must have subjects present. To the contrary, nominals, which are basically abstractions, acquire subjects or agents outside of our minimal expectations. The formal presence of an indefinite agent or subject is not imperative. In most real-life situations a speaker who uses an abstract infinitive is aiming his remarks at somebody or something that can be the subject. The construction in which a "dummy" *it* delays the appearance of an abstract infinitive is very common in our everyday life: *It's not a good idea to come in right now; It doesn't help much to disengage the clutch.* Note, however, the oblique relation between agent and infinitive in *It did not take him long to find the answer.* A different kind of redistribution is found in the use of *to have: It gave him the willies to have Jane drive the car. To have* here is an empty formality. The meaning is not that *he has Jane drive the car* (that is, that he makes, forces, allows, or permits Jane to drive the car).

Infinitives can also function as nominals in the direct object position. Even in this function they are theoretically abstract; actually, however, the subject of the verb is also the "subject" of the infinitive in almost all cases. We cannot say the "agent" of the verb is also the "agent" of the infinitive since one may be active and the other passive (*He has been told to stay away, I think he wants to be hurt by life;* compare with *I think he wants life to hurt him, We told him to stay away;* in these last sentences the infinitive phrases have their own subjects). When both verb and infinitive are passive, the agents are not the same but the subjects are: *He was expected to be beaten by Dempsey* (this is a strained and often ambiguous construction—*expected by Dempsey* or *beaten by Dempsey?*). When the verb is passive—whether or not the infinitive is passive—the sentence has undergone the "passive" transformation and the subject-part of a reduced predication functioning as direct object has become the subject of the superior predication. Consequently, when we try to understand how basic sentences can be combined with others or included within them by means of infinitives, we can see that the transformational process is somewhat different when the verb that is followed by an infinitive is active from when the verb is passive.

ONE-NUCLEUS REDUCTIONS

When the subject of the verb "controls" or "acts as subject of" a direct object infinitive, the infinitive phrase is in most cases a reduction of a noun clause to a construction that is semi-predicative to the extent that it presents only the predicate part of the included predication, but since subject and direct object exist on the same linguistic level the direct object infinitive phrase is not dependent upon its subject. The modality of the verb in the noun clause that is reduced is usually not made explicit in the infinitive phrase. Some examples of the reduction are:

He decided that he ought to go home > He decided to go home.
He did not want that he should be seen in those old clothes > He did not want to be seen in those old clothes.
They arranged that they would meet in Verona > They arranged to meet in Verona.
I would hate that I should lose this medal > I would hate to lose this medal.

Even from these few examples we can see how strained and "over-expressed" the noun clause versions seem to be. Flexibility in a grammar depends much on its ability to dispense with making expressed distinctions oversubtle. But in compensation, the infinitive substitute makes us rely more heavily upon cliché phrasings.

Interrogative noun clauses in the direct object position retain the interrogative word in their reduction to infinitive phrases:

I couldn't decide what I should wear > I couldn't decide what to wear.
I didn't know how I should do it > I didn't know how to do it.
He couldn't tell which door he should choose > He couldn't tell which door to choose.
I can't decide who I will be at the costume ball > I can't decide who to be at the costume ball.

The same principle may even carry over to the construction in which a "dummy" *it* replaces an infinitive used as a subject-part of a reduced predication functioning as direct object after a factitive verb, the infinitive phrase being a reduction of an interrogative noun clause; but this can usually happen only if the subject does not change:

> *He did not make it clear what end I should pursue* > *He did not make it clear to me what end to pursue* (note the oblique expression of the subject of the infinitive).

It has already been indicated that direct object infinitives carry over without change in transformations of clauses to nominal phrases, particularly when a subjective genitive (or its analytic equivalent, an *of* prepositional phrase) still expresses the subject-part of the source predication:

> *in his determination to free you from your worries* < *when he determines to free you from your worries* < *when he determines that he will free you from your worries*

The control of the subject of the superior clause can even extend to infinitives used as objects of participles, gerunds, *-ing* forms in reduced adverbial clauses, and other infinitives, when the range of functioning of these is in turn controlled by their syntactic relation with a subject-part in a superior predication:

> *Seeing how to do it at last, he unbolted the housing.*
> *Pretending to know how to do everything is my chief vice* (but these infinitives are syntactically subjectless and abstract unless we indulge in extensive paraphrase: *I have a chief vice which is that I pretend that I know how I should do everything.* Gerund and infinitives become completely abstract in *Pretending to know how to do everything is a vice*).
> *Since learning how to drive a car, I have had no accidents.*
> *To learn how to drive a car* (a "purpose" or "goal" phrase), *you need lessons.*
> *his desire to learn how to drive a car to ease his transportation problems*

The kind of infinitive phrase that follows a predicate adjective and seems to modify it constitutes a construction that is very hard to square (notice *is very hard to square*) with our usual concepts of syntactic arrangements. The reason for the difficulty presumably is that in structures of this kind we are dealing either with a special kind of periphrastic or with a redistribution. We can, if we wish, fall back upon the catch-all syntactic relationship of "respect" in interpreting the construction, but to do so would be to supplant one vague answer with another. In phrasings such as *I shall be glad to make the arrangements, Jonas was quick to end the affair,* or *They were all too ready to point out my faults,* redistributions will turn the infinitives into verbs and the predicate adjectives into adverbs: *I shall gladly make the arrangements, Jonas quickly ended the affair,* and *They all too readily pointed out my faults.* In copula predications the predicate complements are normally the predicators of lexical content. We can test our redistributions here against other kinds of predicate complements: *They were in a hurry to close the deal* (this is not quite the same as *They hurriedly closed the deal* since the idea of "goal" or "respect" or "to what end?" is involved); *They were after me to close the deal* (again the idea of "to what end?" is involved and the redistribution is impossible); *He was a hero to stick his finger in the hole in the dike* (*He was a hero when he stuck* . . . rather than *He heroically stuck* . . .). While redistributions are not impossible with these other kinds of predicate complements, they are not frequent or exact. The redistribution of verb + adverb to copula + predicate adjective + infinitive should be considered periphrasis of a verb phrase, but not all infinitives after predicate complements come into being by way of this redistribution.

Our recent illustrations have given indication of two other varieties of reductions accomplished by these infinitives after predicate complements: (1) a construction in which the infinitive functions approximately in the area of the relationships of "respect," "goal," or "manner"; and (2) a construction in which the infinitive phrase represents a reduction of a time or conditional clause and a redistribution.

1. *We are not free to divulge that information.*
   The gang was anxious to begin the job.
   They were ready to protect themselves.
   He seemed to be a fool to have expected a real reform.

(Since these relationships are at best approximate, we need not be surprised that constructions of these kinds overlap and blend into one another.)

2. *He will become excited to find that he has been betrayed.*
   He will be a nincompoop to enter the room unarmed. (The

infinitive as equivalent of a conditional clause often follows
will.)
To make that move he will have to be desperate.
*He was greedy to have done that (He was greedy when he did
that).*

Degree clauses can likewise be reduced to infinitive phrases
under some circumstances, particularly when they modify predicate adjectives and the degree word is a degree adverb: *He is too
proud to do anything like that; He is too much a fool to solve his
own problems.*

Other infinitives in this position can best be explained by recourse to the concept of double valence. Thus in *That is good to
know, to know* has two possible syntactic attachments—(1) *good
in respect to knowing*, and (2) *to know that is good.* Similar ambivalences can be found with *difficult to answer, hard to manage.*
The ambivalence is, of course, superficially resolved when the
subject of the sentence is plural, so that the copula is likewise
plural: *A good man is hard to find* can be recast as *To find a good
man is hard,* but *Good men are hard to find* cannot be recast as
To find good men are hard without changing *are* to *is.* It can be
argued, however, that number in the verb in such a situation is
contingent on the "fall-out" of the subject and does not actually
obviate the double valence.

One of the commonest kinds of infinitive phrases, in order of
frequency, is the "purpose" or "result" phrase, representing usually
the reduction of a purpose or result clause when the subject of the
dependent clause and the subject of the unit upon which it is dependent are aligned—that is, when they are the same. Notionally,
the terms "purpose" and "result" are approximate names for a
group of closely allied relations that could also be subsumed under
"goal" or "to what end?" According to the plan of reduction we
are describing here, *I went there so that I could see what was going on* can be reduced to *I went there to see what was going on* because *I* is subject in both clauses. Infinitive phrases of purpose
are introduced more or less optionally by *to* or *in order to.* Often
they are attached at the end of a matrix unit but can also appear
preceding it or inserted within it. Some examples are:

He has arrived here to make our acquaintance.
You have taken a lot of trouble to do that for us.
*He arrived at the top of the hill only to see another range of hills
beyond it.*

I'm waiting for your letter to arrive to answer your questions. (We shall discuss the "for" construction in a short time. The juxtaposing of the two infinitive phrases here suggests a reduction of two adverbial clauses: *I am waiting until your letter arrives before I answer your questions.* The subjects of the dependent clauses are different, but the second infinitive phrase has the same subject as the main clause.)

He came to town one sultry morning last week to look things over in the local offices of the union and to make a speech at a dinner in honor of the mayor.

Passive infinitives are like active infinitives in these functions and positions in requiring the same subjects as the superior units:

The groups joined together to be subjected to a heavy barrage of questions.

In order to be free from parental domination, they kept away from home.

When, however, the agent-subject of an active superior clause disappears as a result of a passive transformation, a purpose infinitive may be left without a subject to control it, except that the lost subject can usually be inferred from the passive construction:

No purchase is required to win a prize. (This is the exception in which the infinitive is abstracted as a result of a general redistribution: *You are not required to purchase anything in order that you win a prize* < *We do not require that you purchase anything in order that you may become eligible to win a prize.* This is loose paraphrasing, but it should suggest the complexity of the redistribution.)

The meeting was arranged to clear the air.

This was done to let you in on the secret.

The gusher was capped to bring it under control.

This system was designed to improve the efficiency of delivery. (This sentence is ambiguous since we cannot be sure what is doing the *improving—this system* or an implied agent such as *our engineers.*)

This construction of passive verb followed by purpose infinite must be kept distinct from the construction of passive verb followed by a retained infinitive as predicate-part of a reduced predication used as object of an active sentence:

He was required to walk a tightrope < *They required him to walk a tightrope* < *They required that he walk a tightrope.*

in contrast to

A *tightrope was required to enter the contest.*

The extreme adaptability of infinitives to many kinds of reductions and redistributions is fully revealed in the nominal forms of reduced predications. Purpose infinitives as well as infinitives of other kinds become dependencies in such phrasings. The traditionalist grammarian has long identified certain uses of infinitives as adjectival. If whatever is a dependency of a headword noun is adjectival, we can follow the same nomenclature. Our attention has been focused on the manipulation of predications, and the process of transformation has been more important for us than a static nomenclature. We need to distinguish among kinds of infinitives that are syntactically dependent upon headword nominals. We have seen that *his desire to go* is a transformation of *He desired to go,* in which *to go* is the direct object of *desired* and a reduction of *that he go*—a possibility since the subjects of *desired* and *go* are the same. We have said that in the transformation *to go* still functions as the direct object of *his desire;* in traditionalist nomenclature it has an adjectival function since it modifies a noun. These interpretations are not necessarily inconsistent; they merely emphasize different aspects of the situation. In *his trip to town to buy a hat* we find a purpose infinitive phrase functioning as a dependency in a nominal phrase that represents a transformation and reduction of *He took a trip* (or *He tripped . . .*) *to town so that he could buy a hat.* The subjective genitive *his* is present as a specified subject. The finiteness of the predication can, however, be removed by abstraction: *trips to town to buy hats.* The relation of the purpose infinitive to *trip* is disturbed only by the pluralizing of *hats.*

Some infinitives are dependent upon nouns that hardly seem to represent transformations from verbs. In some of these cases the infinitives can be construed as reduced relative clauses. Thus, the infinitive phrase in *features and sizes to fit the needs of everyone in the family* is the reduction of *that will fit the needs . . . .* This functioning is truly semi-predicative. Some other examples are:

songs to remember me by
It has only one job to do—to collect refuse.
new goals to aim at
the best way to put a frosting on this kind of cake (sometimes the

relative pronoun is not deleted in the reduction: *the best way by which to get the better of such people is* . . . , *the best town in which to buy hats is* . . .)
legends to enhance the image of Washington

A special kind of infinitive as reduction of a relative clause is found in *a house to rent, a sight to see, suppers to take out;* in these the voice of the infinitive is ambiguous (*a sight for you to see* or *a sight to be seen by you*).

TWO-NUCLEI REDUCTIONS

All of these many infinitive constructions represent reductions in which the actions are abstracted to leave the infinitives without specified subjects or in which the subjects are to be found in the context, usually as subjects of the superior predication. Infinitive structures are not markedly different when the infinitive has its own subject, although these are reductions of full predications—with both subject and predicate parts. There are two principal sub-classes of these infinitive phrases representing reductions of full predications: those functioning as reduced noun clause direct objects, with or without double valence in the subject-parts of the reduced phrases, and "for" constructions—those infinitive phrases introduced by the particle *for*, performing a variety of functions.

In excluding from our list of basic sentence patterns the kind of sentence in which a direct object has two nuclei (and therefore represents a reduction of a predication with both subject-part and predicate-part present), we have prepared the way for description of that kind of infinitive phrase that functions as direct object and that has its own subject. In this classification, the double-object construction (object + objective complement) is treated as a further-reduced infinitive phrase (with the deletion of the infinitive *to be*). The obliquities that occur because the subject-part may have double valence (that is, serve both as object of the superior verb and as subject-part of the infinitive phrase) or because the predicate-part may also function as something like a result adjunct in relation to the superior unit need not destroy the fundamental simplicity of this classification. We now find on the same linguistic level subject-parts and predicate-parts in the same range of kinds that we found in semi-predicative constructions, except that in general infinitives correspond to participles when the clause to be reduced contains a verb that is not a copula. When a copula exists between subject and predicator (predicate complement), we generally have a choice of substituting *to be* for the finite form of the copula or of deleting the copula. Thus, *him a hero* in *We considered him a hero* is to be classed as an infinitive phrase further reduced through the deletion of the copula *to be*. The transformational process is: *He was a hero. We considered this. > We considered that he was a hero. > We considered him to be a hero. > We considered him a hero.* The amount of obliquity that becomes hidden in this process of reduction depends in large measure upon the lexical content of the superior verb. It is obvious that only certain kinds of transitive verbs can be followed by clause objects. Usually these are verbs denoting mental activity of some kind or are factitive verbs (denoting "forcing," "causing," "compelling," or "bringing about"). Sometimes the semantic range of verbs is extended so that they partly fit within these categories. Thus lexically *called* is different in *He called me to supper* and *He called me a liar.* Both are presumably extensions from the intransitive *He called* (made a noise). We cannot be sure that *He called to me* differs from *He called me* except that *to me* is an analytic expression and *me* is a synthetic one. If *me* means *to me* after *called,* it is in what we call an oblique relation to *called.* In dealing with inflected languages we customarily call all cases except the nominative oblique cases. In distinguishing between direct and indirect objects in English we treat the one as not oblique and the other as oblique while at the same time extending the area of the direct object to include within it many obliquities. These are revealed when we look closely at the variation in range of direct objects that are reduced predications. Much depends upon the relation of the object to the verb. Double valence occurs most often when a single-word direct object shows some obliquity in its relation to the verb, as with *call, ask, tell, charge, demand, request,* etc. The full paraphrase of *He called me a liar* is *He called (in reference to) me that I am a liar;* the word signifying *me* must be duplicated in the full paraphrase to show its double functioning. We cannot so readily say *He called that I am a liar* as *He asked that I be here,* but some degree of obliquity is found in the relation between *asked* and *me* in *He asked me here.* (*Here* is a predicator in relation to *me,* not an adverb modifying *asked.*) Suppose we interpret *He called me a liar* as *He called in reference to me "liar";* *liar* is then a direct object in direct discourse. In structures such as these, fine relational distinctions are compressed so tightly that accurate description of sub-types becomes almost an impossibility. When reversion of infinitive phrase to source clause is difficult, we should look first for signs of double valence. Some examples are:

> *He told me to go* < *He told me that I should go.*
> *He commanded me to stay on guard* < *He commanded me that I stay on guard.*
> *He requested me not to fail him* < *He requested of me that I not fail him.*

Compare: *He demanded me to pay him,* and *He demanded of me a payment.* Difficulty of reversion to source clause does not, however, imply double valence in *I would like you to go home* < *I would like that you go home.* Usage varies with *hate.* In the author's dialect *for* is needed as an introductory particle, but many speakers of English find it natural to say *I hate George to have to do that.* Probably neither group would say *I hate that George has to do that.* Observe the more usual but redundant *I hate it that George has to do that.* The slavery of grammatical types to usage is nowhere more apparent than in these object infinitive phrases.

A fuller range of constructions is found with factitive verbs or verbs denoting mental activity. With these the further compression of copula infinitive phrases by the deletion of the copula is common. Anything can function as the predicate-part of such a further reduced phrase that can function as predicate complement in a formal copula predication. Some examples of reductions with factitive verbs are:

> *He made me go.*
> *He forced me to go* (usage varies with the verb on the use of the *to*-marker).
> *He let me go.*
> *He allowed me to go.*
> *He permitted me to go.*
> *He made me a hero.*
> *He made it clear that I was no hero.*
> *You make me nervous.*
> *This makes a new approach necessary.*

Some examples of reductions with verbs of mental activity are:

> *You can't expect an old man to thank you for depriving him of his support.*

I thought him (to be) a good catch.
I found the book very interesting. (This is different from *I found the book in the corner.* The meaning of *found* is different, and the place relation of the prepositional phrase *in the corner* applies to the one meaning and not to the other. It is true that the predication *The book was in the corner* is implied by the phrase but not by syntactic signals.)
God found his newly created earth (to be) good.
They consider this one (to be) theirs.
We have found no necessity to shut off the water supply. (Can this be construed as *To shut off the water supply is no necessity?* or that *there is no necessity to shut off the water supply?*)
He believed it to be a fact.
He considered Jonas's arguments to the point.
He found the resulting product (to be) of high quality.
He thought her (to be) home.
He estimated the log to be ten feet.
We showed the cause to be found in the shifting of earth.
Imagine a superhuman being to be looking down on us right now.
We felt him to be lacking in the proper qualities.
I could hear their voices (to be) rising in anger.
The Zeros watched us come closer.
I beg you to think of me.
She got me hopping mad.
They had us running all over town.

All of these constructions are approximately alike—as similar in fact as we can expect instances of a reduced structure to be when the structures depend somewhat on the lexical content of the verbs of which they are objects. We have already seen, in the description of the passive transformation, that when a sentence containing one of these infinitive phrase direct objects is made passive the subject-part of the reduced clause becomes the subject of the passive verb and the infinitive (or objective complement when a copula is deleted) is stranded as a retained object. This comprises a complex redistribution.

Modern grammarians have been sufficiently aware of the similarities between the construction of these reduced-clause objects and constructions involving result adjuncts that they have on occasion refused to distinguish between them, if only because they have been able to handle them similarly in describing transformations. Notice the similar handling of the following sentences:

He painted the barn red > He painted red the barn.

I found him sober > I found sober him.
I made him go > I made go him.
We keep them in the cupboard > We keep in the cupboard them.

According to this transformational procedure, result adjuncts as well as predicate parts of reduced clauses are treated as if they are integral parts of the verb phrase of the superior unit. This treatment is rarely theoretically satisfactory even though it may cause no trouble operationally most of the time.

A result adjunct often can be construed as the predicate-part of an included predication. The sentence *We painted the barn red* can conceivably be factored out as *We painted the barn* and *The barn is (now) red.* In the reduction both *barn* and *red* have double valence—*barn* as object of *painted* and subject-part for the predicator *red; red* as an adverb in relation to *painted* and as predicate adjective in relation to *barn.* The double valences involve us in obliquities. Even prepositional phrases expressing the place relation—that we are tempted to consider as an adverbial function—can be shown to have double valence. Let us consider a progressive series of constructions:

> *Milk remains cold in our refrigerator < If milk is in our refrigerator it remains cold* or *Milk that is in our refrigerator remains cold* or *If milk remains in our refrigerator it is cold* or *Milk that remains in our refrigerator is cold.*

(Two predications so nearly coincide as to be interchangeable, because *remains* adds only the idea of continuity to the pure copula and *milk* can both *remain cold* and *remain in our refrigerator* but it can also *be cold* and *be in our refrigerator.* But it cannot logically *remain where* and *be what* in the same predicational frame. We are dealing with structural ambivalence. This is not to condemn structural ambivalence but to be aware of its existence.)

> *Milk keeps cold in our refrigerator < Milk that is in our refrigerator keeps cold* or *If milk is (kept) in our refrigerator it keeps cold* (the meanings of *keep* are distinct here) but not *Milk that keeps cold is in our refrigerator* or *Milk that is cold keeps in our refrigerator* (another shift of meaning in *keeps*).

(We are faced here with semantic as well as structural ambivalence. When *keeps* is a variant of the copula, we can consider *in our refrigerator* as an adverbial modifier only by treating *keeps cold* as the verb phrase, just as we have said that in pure copula predication it is the predicate complement that is the predicator with lexical content.)

> *Our refrigerator keeps milk cold < In our refrigerator milk is kept cold or Our refrigerator makes milk keep cold.*

(A semantic shift has taken place in the word *keeps*. The simplest explanation is that the factitive function has been incorporated within the morpheme. Thus there is a partial parallel between *The moon brightens the landscape < The moon makes the landscape (become) bright* and *Our refrigerator keeps milk cold < Our refrigerator makes milk (keep) cold*. The parallel is partial only because we would have *Our refrigerator cold (en)s milk* if it were complete. But the parallel is close enough to show the obliquity of predication wrapped up in the "result adjunct" *cold*. This kind of internal complication from semantic and morphemic shifting cannot be handled very neatly by the grammarian, transformationalist or otherwise, since the precise nature of the obliquity is likely to change with each case.)

We can define a kind of post-positional adjunct that obliquely represents a predicate-part of an included predication (usually a copula predication) to be seen in such sentences as:

> Our refrigerator keeps milk *cold* (the phrase *in our refrigerator* is
> then a predicate appositive in *Milk remains cold in our refrig-*
> *erator*).
> We washed the windows *clean*.
> They cut their visit *short*.
> The battalion was kept *intact* (with passive transformation).
> The party was kept *in a dither*.

It is, however, less easy to tell what the outer limits are of such constructions. When the form of the adjunct is clearly adjectival there may be little confusion. Since nouns function as predicate nouns we might expect to find them as oblique predicate parts in this kind of construction, as in *He was kept a hero by their constant praise*. With nouns we usually find the analytic particle *as* brought into play, as in *I want this as a memento of our togetherness*. The distinction between prepositional phrases used adverbially and prepositional phrases used as predicative adjuncts, or between adverbial particles used as separable parts of a verb phrase and the same particles used as predicative adjuncts presents a much thornier problem—a problem to which a clear answer will not be forthcoming. Do we have a distinction only of optional word orders in *He held the book up* and *He held up the book,* or does *up* become an oblique adjunct in *He held the book up* (*He held the book so that it is now up*)? Syntactic principles coincide; no meaningful answer can be given. Some particles cannot be end-shifted and some that can be end-shifted are not subject to interpretation as adjuncts (*I put him off, I turned his proposal down*). These are not free morphemes. Only particles that are not "bound" in the creation of special phrase meanings can conceivably function as oblique predicators.

It may seem strange that we are dealing with the whole question of oblique predicators as part of the problem of further reductions of infinitive phrases when infinitive phrases have their own subjects, or at least a share in subjects in constructions with double valence. With some strain upon our sense of grammaticality, we can impute the deletion of *to be* before predicative adjuncts: *We kept the battalion* (*to be*) *intact, He held it* (*to be*) *up, We washed the windows* (*to be*) *clean.* It may seem equally strange to deal with the analytic particle *as* under the rubric of infinitive phrases. However, the copulative functioning of *as* was recognized long before the advent of transformationalist grammars, particularly as a signal of predication between object and objective complement—in that structure which we have described as a further reduced infinitive phrase. Thus in many instances we have an option of using one of three phrasings:

> *I consider him a bore.*
> *I consider him to be a bore.*
> *I consider him as a bore.*

This is the simplest use of *as* as signaler of a copula relation. Even within these confines its range is extensive and deserves thorough study, but the evidence here is readily accessible, and we need to conserve space in order to deal with the greater range. *As* often secures semi-predicative connections and the connections often add obliquity to the pure copula. In certain constructions that make full use of analytic devices for showing relationships, *as* will work in conjunction with other particles in the reduction of predications. Thus: *I thought of him as a bore* in contrast to *I thought him a bore.* Examples of other uses are:

> *He listed his taxes for two years as $35,000 (Taxes were $35,000).*
> *He joined the company as sales-manager in 1950 (He was sales manager when he joined the company . . .).*

The concert will begin at 8:30 with Jonas as first violinist (Jonas will be first violinist when . . .).

The project was regarded as a liability (Someone regarded the project to be a liability) (double valence in direct object).

The project was written off as a liability (The project was a liability. The project was written off > The project was written off because it was a liability > The project was written off as a liability—a good case of the rendering of an obliquity).

His own description of the mechanism as the rationalization of such a subjective analysis we have already quoted in Chapter II (As he describes it, the mechanism is the rationalization of an analysis).

Jonas was picked today as "player of the year."

Jonas received the citation from the local chapter commander today "as an outstanding practitioner of his profession."

related to the development of word order as a grammatical device This was thought of as encroaching upon their territory.

He regarded this as taking too much for granted.

Since the skeleton structure of *I think of you as a monster* can be depicted as I think concerning _____ in this manner (how), the traditionalist might protest that treating *as* as an analytic expresser of a copula relation is unreal. What is real depends upon the system upon which the reality is based.

When an infinitive phrase having its own subject is used in other than a direct object or adjunctive function, the particle *for* is generally used in front of it as a connector (in a few phrasings *of* is used instead of *for: It was good of you to come*). The resulting reduction of a predication can perform a variety of functions, particularly as a substitute for noun clauses, adverbial clauses, and relative clauses. We have already seen that the distribution of the components of this construction would be different in an inflected language like Latin (see p. 125).

The "for" infinitive phrase is usually used with a "dummy" *it* when it functions as subject: *It is necessary for you to telephone home right away, It is easier for a camel to go through the eye of a needle than for a rich man to enter the kingdom of God. It* can likewise be a proxy for the "for" construction functioning as subject-part of a direct-object reduced predication: *We find it important for you to be here.* In some dialects the construction even functions as direct object: *I want for you to come.* In the nominal phrase forms of reduced predication, a noun clause functioning as direct object of the verb of the source predication undergoes no change when the verb is converted to the noun headword of the reduction (*I wish that you would come home > my wish that you would come home*); also in this transformation no change is required in an infinitive phrase without its own subject (*I wish to go home > my wish to go home*). However, *I wish you to go home* becomes *my wish for you to go home*. The "for" construction is also used nominally as predicate complement: *My wish is for you to go home. The fashion at present is for boys to look like girls and girls like boys.*

When "for" constructions function in lieu of relative clauses, the noun or pronoun on which the construction is dependent and which would have been supplanted by the relative pronoun in the clause must function notionally as the object of the infinitive or of a terminal preposition: *the map that you should use > the map for you to use; a star that you can steer by > a star for you to steer by.*

"For" constructions can function in lieu of the so-called adverbial clauses in a variety of relationships, prominent among which are time, condition, purpose, and degree.

> *We waited for him to get out of the way. < We waited until (while) he got out of the way.* (time, or conceivably, purpose)
> *For him to reach us, the roadblock will have to be removed. < If he is to reach us, the roadblock . . . .* (condition)
> *It was dunked in hot water for its wrapper to melt. < It was dunked in hot water so that its wrapper would melt.* (purpose or, with slight change or none, result)
> *There are enough cars on the market for everyone to have one. < There are enough cars on the market so that everyone could have one.* (degree)

The functioning of infinitives and infinitive phrases, we can thus see, is exceedingly complex. Its description can consume hundreds of pages in exhaustive descriptive grammars, for of all grammatical forms the infinitive is the most truly "universal"; it can be all things to all contexts. In addition to all the functions we have found for it, a stylist may even choose to use it in situations in which it is notionally coordinate with the verb on which it is grammatically dependent. An illustration or two must suffice:

> *Jonas replaced Smith on the pitcher's mound to go the rest of the way and to post his sixth triumph in seven starts.*
> *Jonas rallied to win the championship.*

The reverse of this pseudo-subordination is found in the familiar *try and do it*. Much of the history of the transformation of predications can be written in terms of the manipulation of infinitives. On many occasions infinitives are interchangeable with the other derivatives from verbs, gerunds and participles, but the functional range of infinitives is wider than that of the other two, even if they cannot undergo the pre-positional adjectival transformation as participles can.

MATERIALS FOR EXERCISE AND FURTHER STUDY

I. Collected here are (1) fifty items taken from the news pages of the *New York Times* for February 27, 1966, and (2) fifty items taken from advertisements appearing in the February 26, 1966, issue of *The New Yorker*. They can serve not only to illustrate the range in which infinitives function but also to tell us something about the way in which specialized kinds of prose adapt the potentialities of constructions like infinitives to their purposes. The differences are not, of course, complete. Can you ascertain what the differences of usage are? The first task is to determine the transformational process to account for the infinitives in each of the items, and then keep score of frequencies. Or set up a project of your own by collecting instances from a philosophical treatise, comic books, a novel.

A. *New York Times*

1. . . . it would introduce legislation to revamp the Board of Education . . .
2. A giant rocket that almost never got off the ground hurled the nation's Apollo spacecraft on a successful unmanned test flight today to open a new era in space exploration.
3. . . . called the flight a "successful first step" in the nation's Apollo program to land men on the moon.
4. Mr. Johnson . . . clearly intended to suggest that . . .
5. . . . he has no reason to be worried about . . .
6. I don't want to be critical of . . .
7. The members of Congress are going to follow the course that . . . [Don't forget that infinitives can be part of verb phrases.]
8. . . . on the ground that it had tried to undermine his authority . . .
9. Tomorrow he is expected to address a rally . . .
10. . . . refused today to join open battle . . .
11. I have never . . . been willing to predict my own defeat . . .
12. . . . would be the first Negro to serve on the board . . .
13. I am not going to predict any defeats . . .

14. . . . was named by President Johnson to fill a vacancy . . .
15. Mr. Brimmer is to replace C. Canby Balderston
16. Dr. Bowker has threatened to resign if . . .
17. . . . that is to carry three astronauts toward a landing on the moon . . .
18. . . . so that the City University would not have to reduce the number of new students . . .
19. . . . it would have to raise admissions requirements to reduce the number of students it accepts . . .
20. The Regents sought to dispel fears that the state wanted to take over the City University and merge it with the State University.
21. . . . he could not make a decision on whether to support a city personal income tax . . .
22. . . . it would tend to stop the flight of business from New York . . .
23. I oppose any gambling measure that is enacted solely to provide taxes.
24. . . . he was careful to check with me first . . .
25. He reiterated his intention to consider and approve promptly all requests . . .
26. Thousands have marched through the streets and attempted to storm the presidential palace . . .
27. . . . by replacing those considered to be involved in the abortive Communist-led coup Oct. 1.
28. . . . the leaders . . . seemed to be chicken-hearted . . .
29. The students . . . had called upon the armed forces chief to follow the example of military leaders in Ghana . . .
30. . . . was asking workers to sacrifice legitimate wage gains . . .
31. . . . they asked the Government to lift the state of emergency . . .
32. . . . if we continue to use them after the real danger has passed . . .
33. . . . in an effort to keep a concentration of power out of the hands of one leader . . .
34. . . . a special committee to write a new Constitution would be named soon . . .
35. . . . one of these steps or a combination of them "will be needed to dampen down the pressures on economic resources."
36. Algerians greeted the return with cheers and rushed to pick up copies of their favorite Paris dailies.
37. . . . was not the worst calamity to strike this hard-pressed Moslem country . . .
38. . . . the formation of a state company to handle all foreign publications . . .

39. . . . its 257 workers were told to take inventory . . .
40. . . . the foreign press serves to preserve Algeria's "intellectual impoverishment."
41. . . . a Cabinet shuffle was to take place shortly . . .
42. . . . the Government is trying to meet the challenge . . .
43. . . . making efforts to improve the press . . .
44. Dozens of well-known French journalists are being invited here to give lectures . . .
45. . . . the government's desire to control the press . . .
46. . . . for allegedly refusing to come to the aid of a policeman . . .
47. . . . it is a misdemeanor to refuse to assist . . .
48. . . . the public's unwillingness to get involved . . .
49. Traditionally, Egyptian peasants have dipped in the muddy, disease-ridden Nile, not only to irrigate crops but for drinking as well.
50. . . . built new wells to provide clean water . . .

B. Advertisements in *The New Yorker*

1. How far in Europe do you want to go?
2. Another reason to fly Sabena: the food is Belgian
3. If you need more reasons to buy a Jaguar . . .
4. He likes to be alone with it on the road
   He likes to run up the rev's and fill the air with a throaty growl.
   He likes to downshift coming into a curve
5. There is nothing in the world to compare with the Jaguar feeling and there's only one way to get it.
6. She was said to be beautiful, wise and deeply in love.
7. So he vowed to build a love memorial.
8. . . . we'd like to reassure those of you who might be reluctant to visit India
9. allows you to get a reasonable supply
10. This formula sets up a silicone barrier to repel wind and water.
11. Each assigned to combat a specific grooming problem.
12. To enlist their services, just give the word.
13. If you are going to be recorded for posterity . . .
14. If the photographer is going to shoot you . . .
15. Where customers ask us to put their extension phones—and why
16. A lovely Princess phone to bring calls to the bedside, save year-round stair climbing, create a haven of privacy
17. A nook to work in, plus a phone to work with and help you run the house, organize programs for church and charity, play your role in community affairs.
18. To order in your choice of style and color, just call the Business Office.

19. The sky is likely to be sunny, the air spring-like.
20. Brush-on eye shadows so easy to use you can't go wrong, be-
    cause each color comes in two tones—one dark and one light,
    to help you blend from dark to light . . .
21. Don't wait to inherit Spode.
22. Bold, bright, sassy—navy and white checks to zing straight
    toward spring.
23. Now the set most sought in Europe is here. To give body.
    Lights. Look. Life. And, above all, hold.
24. Hair with health. With hold. With life. With lights. To stay
    in the heat or rain or whatever.
25. More freedom to come and go as you please. More cities to
    come and go to.
26. Our new Rolls-Royce powered triple-jet Tridents, for instance,
    are about the quickest, most comfortable way there is to bring
    you and Europe's cities closer together.
27. Which makes everything run a lot smoother
28. the happiest way to go places in Europe
29. Now you don't have to stay at home to enjoy furniture by
    Drexel.
30. Save enough to stay longer, see more, enjoy more.
31. NBC News has been able to provide outstanding coverage
32. Over the past decade, ours has been the only network to expand
    its color programming . . .
33. So it was only natural for NBC, last fall, to become known as
    the Full Color Network.
34. features you don't expect to find on a car of this price
35. when you wanted to drive your car just for the fun of it
36. They have everything needed to keep you and your car happy
37. do what that tiny voice tells you to do
38. Poland Water doesn't want to get mixed up with phonies.
39. Docked there is a small fleet of boats to take you sailing across
    the turquoise sea . . .
40. Would it be proper for Ireland's finest crystal, Waterford, to
    keep company with any napkin other than fine Irish linen?
41. Air France is for gourmets who can't wait to get there.
42. From now on is the time to wear this season-skipping three-
    part costume.
43. It's just that we want to be able to.
44. We'll put our resources to work for you.
45. This purposeful weather coat is just long enough to look good;
    short enough to behave itself on the move.
46. the wine stewards as quick, if not quicker, than the thirstiest
    man had any right to expect.

47. That's quite a compliment to our Bourbon, and to the exclusive process we use to distill it.

48. *Look.* Tough magazine to ignore—if you want to keep up with today's woman and her swiftly changing world.

49. We made the Volkswagen Station Wagon big enough to hold about twice as much as a regular station wagon.

50. And enough windows to go around.

II. Here are some infinitive phrases for which a dummy-*it* substitutes. Work out the transformations for each sentence.

1. I took it upon myself to try to get him to change his mind.

2. It is my wish to have you here with me at the end of the summer. (Note the double valence of the infinitive)

3. It is not a good idea for him to go there by himself.

4. He always considered it imperative to have things go his way.

5. It is in the cards for him to get into trouble.

III. In a penetrating article, R. B. Lees has described eight types of construction in which an infinitive can follow a predicate adjective ("A Multiply Ambiguous Adjectival Construction," *Language,* XXXVI, 207–21). These eight types can be illustrated thus:

1. It's too humid to play.

2. It's tedious to stay.

3. He's free to go.

4. He's too old to send.

5. He's too tired to swim.

6. He's eligible to vote.

7. He's hard to convince.

8. He's splendid to wait.

In Exercise I of Chapter 7, Redistributions (p. 129), we listed five varieties of this ambiguous construction. Study the two lists to determine which of our five types are to be found among Lees' eight. Notice the degree adverb *too* in Lees' 1, 4, and 5. Comparable to *too* is *enough* in *He is brash enough to stare down the whole army* or *He did not have enough strength to finish the job* or *He is not enough a gentleman to deserve that honor.* Are these infinitive phrases after *too* and *enough* equivalents of degree clauses? Purpose infinitives are also possible after predicate adjectives: *This plan is attractive to achieve our ends.* With slightly different signals from pitch, stress, or juncture, a kind featuring a result infinitive may also be added to the list: *His laws were repressive, to choke off any possibility of reform.* Gather evidence of your own to test these attempts to bring order to a very complex situation. As usual, keep your eye on the predicational nexus (in this case, between the infinitive as reduced predicate-part and whatever is its subject-part, stated or implied).

IV. In what syntactic relationships do the units of *for* + subject-part + infinitive function in these sentences? Collect other instances in order to see if you can add other relationships to the range.

1. It is absurd for me to try to play that concerto when you are here to do it.
2. He held open the door for the visiting dignitary to enter.
3. It's a good time for me to thank you.
4. These three subjects are the most important ones for your child to master.
5. I dislike for all these strange people to be overrunning our town.
6. That was the season for all the connivers in the county to circulate petitions and run for public office.
7. On the board are some new problems for you to solve.
8. It is better for you to do it than to have your mother do it.
9. The car slowed down for the train to clear the crossing.
10. There will be an eternity for them to practice harp-playing all they want to.
11. The correct principle is for the right hand knobs to be fastened to the top knobs.
12. There is enough water in the sea for everyone to have a drink.
13. He gave an order for the B Squadron to proceed to Lyons.
14. The regulation for all scouts to pay particular attention to is the one about campfires.
15. We put the salt block over the fence for the deer to get at it.

V. The following materials, which are presented more or less at random, should prove useful as a corpus from which rules and guiding principles can be drawn about the reduction of clauses to two-nucleus infinitive phrases used as objects or as double objects in the predicate parts of sentences, with or without double valence for the subject-parts of the reduced predications. Since we have treated object-objective complement constructions as if they are such two-nucleus infinitive phrases with the copula infinitive deleted, such constructions are amply represented here, mixed in with sentences in which the infinitives are not deleted. Also we have seen that the analytical particle *as* can signal the relationship between subject-part and predicate-part in these reduced predications. Result adjuncts can be found in some of these sentences. If you are puzzled by them, try to determine the predicational nexus involved, for that nexus is what is important in a transformational grammar.

1. They consecrated the bishop a saint.
2. An official characterized the demands as outrageous.

3. He made the task pleasant.
4. He would suspect the noises not to mean anything.
5. The institute wanted to make the government put all agricultural products in the same category as corn.
6. The prosecution proved him negligent.
7. I find him hard to work for.
8. He wanted us to color it blue.
9. Make it all one color.
10. The critic branded the production a tawdry caricature.
11. He prefers man a beast to man a tree.
12. A research paper requires you to collect and evaluate the information.
13. She decided to ask him not to bring the subject up at the meeting.
14. . . . or that she should allow him to tell her that he loved her. —HENRY JAMES
15. Would you be interested to know that he broke the record?
16. Make your story good.
17. I will ask you once more to spell it before the class is up.
18. I am not the fool that you take me to be.
19. This medicine keeps you from getting too excited.
20. The boss stopped them from breaking all the furniture.
21. I now pronounce you man and wife.
22. We ought to consider this robbing Peter to pay Paul.
23. I call this being swindled properly.
24. Jeb's confession made solving the problem easier.
25. I want you to think about what you've just done.
26. That error made figuring out the cost difficult.
27. The Cain Hoy Stable's Irish-bred Turn-To was the one that was expected to carry the fight to the favorite.—*New York Times*
28. And we know simply using Chlorodent, our chlorophyll-plus toothpaste, won't get you married in a week . . . or make your husband shower you with orchids!—Advertisement
29. More of the same during the early stages of the race might have made this an entirely different season.—*New York Times*
30. In addition to considering the newspaper an excellent advertising medium . . . .
31. He found it right where he left it.
32. The weather compelled us to call off the picnic.
33. I know him to be a detestable man.
34. We wrote the central office to send us a new folder.
35. The jury found him not guilty.
36. Her remarks made him furious.
37. I always found his pretensions empty and vain.
38. The cow knocked him galley-west.

39. I know him to be a substantial citizen.
40. The storekeeper told the boys to reconsider their decision.
41. His girl friend gave him to understand that she wanted no more of him.
42. It pleased him to see her gentle.—EMILY BRONTË
43. As soon as she saw him vexed again . . . .—EMILY BRONTË
44. I imagined her as little likely to die as myself . . . .—EMILY BRONTË
45. Now that they saw me returned . . . .—EMILY BRONTË
46. I desired Mrs. Dean to sit down.—EMILY BRONTË
47. My pinches moved him only to draw in a breath.—EMILY BRONTË
48. . . . not as if you thought her converted into a stranger . . . . —EMILY BRONTË
49. . . . the mistress made them merry with lively talk . . . . —EMILY BRONTË
50. I . . . was pained to behold Catherine, with dry eyes and an indifferent air, commence cutting up the wing of a goose before her.—EMILY BRONTË
51. I could not have supposed her to be so selfish.—EMILY BRONTË
52. I advised her to value him the more for his affection.—EMILY BRONTË
53. I'd as soon put that little canary into the park on a winter's day as recommend you to bestow your heart on him.—EMILY BRONTË
54. It will teach me to be careful next time.
55. I'll make her howl a recantation.
56. The servants thought me gone to shake off . . . .—EMILY BRONTË
57. Curiosity and a quick intellect urged her into an apt scholar . . . .—EMILY BRONTË
58. letting him see you cheerful
59. . . . fretted over the separation he has judged it expedient to make . . . .—EMILY BRONTË
60. I had not felt it hurt until that minute.
61. Beginning with prices that are below those of other popular trucks, Ford pickups make saving money a full time job.—Advertisement
62. American officials considered the proposed committee a symbol of the trade partnership between the United States and Japan and an answer to critics who contend that military security forms the only real tie between the two nations.—(AP)
63. He hates me to have a good time.
64. He listed his taxes for the two years as $35,000.
65. They regarded the holding company as a liability.

66. Words worry him sick.
67. They considered him dead.
68. They took him for dead.
69. I had my hair long.
70. I take him for a person of good intentions.
71. They sought him as mediator.
72. He chose her for his wife.
73. He chose her as his wife.
74. They described her as peculiar.
75. We have the Joneses here often.
76. I don't allow the children in the study.
77. Atlantic keeps your car on the go.
78. There was no longer any need to worry about the American teacher as too meek.—FRED HECHINGER, *New York Times*
79. We elected him chairman.

12

NOUN-HEADED REDUCED PREDICATIONS

FINITE AND NON-FINITE NOMINAL PHRASES

An internal contradiction seems to exist in the proposition that a predication can be transformed and reduced to a phrase in which a noun or nominal is the headword and not lose its predicational force in the process. For predications are finite, no matter how large the territory is about which something is predicated or no matter how many separate actions are summarized semantically in the predicator. *Men are born, grow, and die, and pass away from the earth* is as much a finite predication as *The cat just ate the goldfish,* although the second is more concrete, closer to what is immediately sensed, referring more to particulars and less to universals. Our senses give us access to particulars only, but philosophers will often argue that particulars become real for us only when universals are "read into" them. I am watching the rain fall on the garden, the individual leaves of the canterbury bells suddenly bobbing as individual raindrops strike them, a yellowed leaf from the box elder slipping with uneven motion from branch to branch of the small hemlock, the mist below the top-level of the trees, and my spirits low, perhaps because of the humidity. All is flux. But even the flux I can identify only because I have come to identify entities in it (leaves, canterbury bells, trees, raindrops, mist, even myself as perceiver, some nebulous thing called my spirits). Entities are conceptual; they are not what I immediately perceive with my senses. I perceive individual shapes, forms, colors, motions, relations. Whether or not I can perceive without first conceiving entities is another question. I doubt that I can recognize anything unless I sense that perceptions recur, that some are the same and some different. Recognition depends upon that sense of sameness and difference, for identities are a product of that sense.

Predications are relational. Entities in themselves are not; but our concept of entity can be extended to apply to the sensing of recurring patterns of relationships. If we say that finite verbs are the only true predicators, we are speaking grammatically, not metaphysically; but only if we are simple-minded will we say that grammar and metaphysics necessarily differ. They may well differ, but only at the level on which we bring one or the other into the argument. Metaphysically, *adores* and *adoration* may be only two different ways of getting at the same thing. Predication is movement of thought, not of the things that thought is about. Since a movement of thought can in turn be thought of—if it can be treated as a recognizable entity—it as a predication can become part of another predication and still not lose its predicative force. When we accept readily enough the possibility of converting a formal predication into a noun clause merely by putting *that* in front of it, are we presuming that the small particle wipes out the *oneness* of the movement of thought and makes a concept of it, based upon the possibility of sameness and difference in recurring experience? Something like that, yes. Whether this is or is not a fiction is of little interest to the grammarian, who observes that we do in our daily practice convert finite predications into nominals without necessarily robbing them of their finiteness. We say "without necessarily robbing them" because in some sense or other the "robbing" must take place, if only in a fictitious sense. Metaphorically, we say that verbs "express action." What we mean is that thinking is active in them, so that nouns and adjectives can be converted into verbs. *Can* is a noun; the object referred to by *can* does not suddenly become active when we say *We canned the tomatoes,* nor does the thought-action suddenly cease when we say *Our canning the tomatoes took a lot of time.* We have been able to develop a transformational grammar by largely ignoring these metaphysical questions. We have let our linguistic behavior guide us toward metaphysics, not our metaphysics guide us toward linguistic behavior.

However, when a predication is transformed into a nominal phrase, it loses in the process some of its signals of finiteness. Neither gerunds nor abstract nouns derived from verb bases are capable of signaling tense and number, and tense and number signals are the chief signals of finiteness. All finite verbs have tense even if the tense is a fiction, as in the "abstract present" tense—*All men are mortal*. By having lost their signals of finiteness, the nominal forms of reduced predication are potentially ambiguous. To use a series of illustrations provided by R. B. Lees (*The Grammar of English Nominalizations*, p. 64), we can show how this loss of signals creates ambiguity:

1. In *His drawing fascinated me because he always did it lefthanded*, we can tell from *always* that we are dealing with a generalization and from *did* (a pro-verb) that *his drawing* is a reduced predication. By putting these bits of evidence from the context together, we know that *his drawing* is equivalent to something like *whenever he drew*. We cannot tell this from the construction itself.

2. In *His drawing fascinated me because I didn't know he could be persuaded so easily*, we know that he has been easily persuaded to do something, and can guess that he has been persuaded to draw. The *drawing* is then not an often repeated action but pretty much a one-shot affair. It is not a generalization. Now both "generalizations" and "one-shot affairs" can be predications, for predication is a reconciliation of the universal and the particular. Noun-ness is the general and finite-verb-ness the particular. When a predication is a generalization, the particularity is found in it only in the formality of the predication. When a predication that is a generalization is reduced to a nominal phrase, it moves (to speak figuratively) into its own nature of noun-generality. Nevertheless, distinctions between particularity and generality are highly relative (we must back away from these epistemological problems), and lexically words are abstractions whether they are nouns or verbs. Paradoxically, proper nouns are references to particulars and we do not have proper verbs (the references are generalized when *MacAdam* becomes *macadamize* or *Bowdler* becomes *bowdlerize*). Predications are particularized by the concord between subject and verb

as much as by the tense signal of the verb. This is where number comes in. When we say that subject and verb in a formal predication are on the same linguistic level, we imply that one is not a grammatical dependent of the other, but that they operate together to achieve the particularity of a predication. When *he draws* becomes *his drawing, drawing* becomes the headword in a one-nucleus phrase and *his* is dependent on it. The reverse of this situation is found in the transformation by which a predicator has become the dependent unit and the subject is the headword. The same is true when verb > participle > pre-positional participle. Since the direct objects of predications with active transitive verbs become the subjects of passive verb phrases, we can see that, at least indirectly, direct objects can function in the particularizing of a predication. *God loves little children* is presumably a more particular predication than *God loves everyone* because of the restricting of the semantic reference made by the object.

Lees distinguishes between (1) and (2) on the basis of the difference between the way of doing and the fact of doing. This distinction is an interesting one but may not get at the heart of the matter. The basic ambiguity perhaps resides instead in the inability of the structure of the noun phrase that represents a reduced predication to distinguish among levels of generality in predications that are reduced. The substitution of a fact of doing for a way of doing is a matter of obliquity of attachment of the noun phrase to the rest of the sentence, and we have no way of listing all of the possible kinds of obliquity. The important thing to realize is that verbs transformed into nouns can function in a whole gamut of constructions with more or less finiteness of predication. In both (1) and (2) of Lees's sentences, *his* represents the subject-part of the reduced predication. Both of these, consequently, carry a greater burden of finiteness than does *drawing* in *Drawing is fun.* An abstract gerund, like an abstract infinitive, can be said to imply an indefinite subject or a universal one. Can we have such a thing as a passive gerund when its possible subject is indefinite? We can say *Being hanged is no fun* and still hint at finiteness of predication in the gerund even though the subject is not specified, but *no fun* assists in the hinting since by indirection it limits the possible subject of *being hanged* to what is capable of experiencing fun. We note both the personification and the grammatical redistribution in *Being solved is no responsibility of a dilemma,* in which *dilemma* is the "ideal" subject although in the concrete manifestation of the structure *being solved* is seemingly abstract. If we go this far afield in looking for possible subjects for abstract gerunds we will end up finding very few by which some degree of finiteness is not conveyed.

3. *His drawing fascinated me because it was so large.* Lees provides this third sentence to show the semantic shift that can take place in many *-ing* words from gerunds to concrete nouns referring to objects. It has been frequently asserted in the past by historical linguists that the *-ing* suffix was originally a suffix attached to nouns, as in *schooling,* not to verbs, and that the beginning of its use in the formation of participles and gerunds came late in Middle English. *Schooling,* however, has verb force. *My schooling* we can derive semantically from *I was schooled,* which suggests an intermediate step in the semantic shifting. This shift is in the opposite direction from that by which *his drawing something* becomes *his drawing was large and well framed.*

An important difference between *His drawing was rapid* and *His drawing was well framed* is that *his* in the first is a subjective genitive representing the subject of the predication that has been transformed into a nominal phrase, while *his* in the second is a possessive genitive. This distinction may seem unimportant when we interpret the phrase containing this possessive and the noun that is modified by it as a reduction of *He has a drawing.* However, in the possessive transformation *drawing* has undergone no change, and the transformation is "prior" in relation to what we find when a subjective genitive results in the transforming process.

GERUND PHRASES AND ABSTRACT NOUN PHRASES

The two principal types of the noun forms of reduced predication are that in which the predicate-part is represented by a gerund and that in which the predicate-part is represented by an abstract noun transformed to a nominal from a predicator of some kind. The two principal kinds of abstract nouns conforming to this second type are (1) those derived from verbs (like *decision, rejection, request*) and (2) those derived from predicate adjectives (like *scarcity, serenity, supremacy, inferiority, goodness*). Since nouns also function as predicators in copula predications, a third kind is possible in which a predicate noun is converted into an abstract noun. The conversion of a noun into a noun is indescribable without an intermediate step. Therefore, if a predication such as *He is a fool* is to be transformed into a nominal phrase such as *his foolishness, fool* must first be transformed to the adjective *foolish* and then the predicate adjective can acquire a noun suffix making it an abstract noun.

Gerund forms can function either as gerunds or as abstract nouns. For many verbs no abstract noun form other than the gerund exists in the lexicon. The difference between the gerunds in their two functionings is found in the phrase structure as a whole. The whole predicate of a formal predication can become a whole predicate in a gerund nominal transformation simply by the conversion of the finite verb to the corresponding -*ing* form. This means that direct objects, indirect objects, predicate complements, adverbial complements, adverbial modifiers, and other units that exist in the predicate of a sentence [1] do not undergo change if the -*ing* form is functioning as a gerund and not as an abstract noun. When the gerund is used as an abstract noun, however, these predicate relations are expressed analytically, as they are when the headword in the nominal reduced predication is an abstract noun. The subject part of the reduced predication is the same—a subjective genitive—for both gerund as gerund and gerund as abstract noun, except (as we shall soon see) when the gerund is used as the object of a preposition in the predicate-part of the matrix sentence. The gerund can be subject-less, representing indeterminacy of subject, in both functions. In this respect there is no difference between it and the abstract noun.

When a formal predication is transformed into a reduced predication with abstract noun as headword, the subject, if it is expressed, becomes either an inflected subjective genitive or its analytic equivalent, the object of an *of* prepositional phrase. This is to say that when a predication such as *George established a new company* undergoes the nominal transformation the result, in its simplest form, is *George's establishment of a new company.*

---

[1] We can see a good reason for distinguishing between predicate appositives (see p. 117) and other appositives when we notice that a predicate appositive can function in a gerund phrase like other items that exist in the predicate part of a sentence. Thus: *He died the richest man in the state* > *His dying the richest man in the state was a surprise to everyone.* But *his arriving late* becomes *his late arrival* when the gerund is supplanted by the abstract noun, although *his arrival late* is not an impossibility, merely less common.

The finite verb has become a noun by the addition of a suffix. There are, of course, other ways in which nouns are derived from verbs (*prices rise > the rise of prices*), and finicky rules of phrasing are needed in the exact description of what forms are possible for each way. The subject *George* has become the subjective genitive *George's*. An abstract noun like *establishment* can show no distinction between active and passive voice, so that we have no good way of knowing whether the noun phrase is a rendition of an active or passive predication, except by signals given by the prepositional phrases that attach to the noun or notionally by the relation between a genitive and the noun headword. Up through Early Modern English objective genitives were in common usage. The phrase *his portrayal* is for us ambiguous. Does it mean (*Somebody*) *portrayed him* (so that *his* is an objective genitive—the structure for handling the object in the reduced predication), or does it mean *He portrayed* (*somebody*) (so that *his* is a subjective genitive since it renders the subject of the predication)? This so far is a semantic ambiguity. We find also a structural ambiguity in the phrase since it can be generated from *he portrayed* and *he was portrayed*. In order to make a distinction between a subjective and an objective genitive we must presumably presuppose an active verb in the source sentence. In the periphrastic equivalents of the inflected forms we do, however, find certain distinctions. Inflected objective genitives have all but disappeared from our structures, and objects are usually represented in nominal transformations by the periphrastic *of*-phrase, e.g., *establishment of a new company,* rather than *a new company's establishment*. However, by use of an agent phrase we can suggest generation from a passive: *a new company's establishment by George*. Furthermore, since the periphrastic *of*-phrase has been pre-empted by the objective genitive function, the option of the inflected or periphrastic forms for the subject is limited, and the second genitive becomes the object of *of* in the periphrasis. Thus, instead of saying *the establishment of a new company of George*, we can say *the establishment of a new company of George's;* but (this is a fine point) *of George's* represents a reduced predication separate from the rest (*A new company has been established. The new company is George's.*) since only by the imputation of the distinct predication can we explain the second-genitive form, which occurs usually as a predicate complement in copula predications or as objects of prepositional phrases that represent reductions of copula predications. Some noun headwords in these phrases can be made plural more easily than others without losing predicative force, depending perhaps more upon the nature of the predication in the source sentence than upon the derivational suffix used. Thus, we can say *the conquests of Caesar* and *the conquest of Caesar's* (with a plural form of the noun the attraction of the alternative relationships of partition or specification is perhaps felt more than with a singlar form—compare *the wars of Caesar*), but not *the conquest of Caesar* or *the establishments of George*. The value of pursuing all of these distinctions to their ultimate end is dubious. The most evident rule is that the synthetic genitive forms represent subjects and the analytic or periphrastic forms represent objects. If a *by* phrase occurs, the supposition is that the nominal transformation begins from a predication with a passive verb.

When an abstract noun is the headword, indirect objects in the source are rendered analytically, by a *to* or *for* phrase: *my gift of a bracelet to her, the government's allotment of a pension to them, the bringing of a piece for them* (in contrast to the gerund phrase *bringing them a piece*). Prepositional phrases already occurring in the source sentence often carry over unchanged in the transformation. The presence of prepositional phrases or other dependent units in the subject part of the source sentence may, in fact, compel the periphrastic expression of the subject, as in *The arrival of the first group of settlers ever to cross the high mountain range into this fertile valley was delayed until the Indians had been pacified.* We feel we can say *the first group's arrival* or even *the first group of settlers' arrival* (in line with *somebody else's problems* or *the man in the first row's hat*), but we can hardly go so far as *the first group of settlers ever to cross the high mountain range into this fertile valley's arrival,* even with hyphens to signal the immediate constituents in a nonce-construction. Prepositional phrases in the predicate of the source sentence, as well as other kinds of dependent units to be found there, cause even less difficulty in the transformation, except that *-ly* adverbs are converted to pre-positional adjectives:

Jonas transformed himself quickly into a little green pea > Jonas's quick transformation of himself into a little green pea . . .

They surrendered to the Tenth Division > their surrender to the Tenth Division . . .
They arrived with a sausage > their arrival with a sausage . . .
They arrived home > their arrival (at) home . . .
They refused to have anything to do with us > their refusal to have anything to do with us . . .
They decided that they did not want our help > their decision that they did not want our help . . .

(These last two illustrations show what happens in the transformation to infinitive phrases and noun clauses used as direct objects.)

Sometimes what appears as a direct object in the clause reveals an obliquity in the nominal transformation, particularly after verbs of Latin origin having a relational prefix:

We assisted him > our assistance to him.
We trusted him > our trust in him.
We revered him > our reverence for him.

As long as *-ing* forms are treated as abstract nouns their deployments are the same as those of other abstract nouns. Under normal conditions gerunds are incapable of pluralizing and are not used with determiners other than subjective genitives (from which we might argue that subjective genitives are not determiners at all in these nominal transforms). So, when we find phrasings such as *These quick ascendings and descendings of stairs can give us heart failure,* we know we are dealing with abstract nouns. The contrasting gerund phrase would be *our ascending and descending stairs quickly.* We normally act as if these two kinds of transformations are entirely separate—that is, as if their features cannot be blended. We will sometimes find, however, phrasing such as *our quick ascending and descending stairs,* in which the form and position of *quick* suggest that the *-ing* forms are abstract nouns and the appearance of the direct object *stairs* without periphrasis suggests that they are gerunds. Since gerunds can show verb voice and aspect (*His having seen the Mona Lisa was the cause of his insanity; his having been seen by his wife was the cause of his divorce.*) while abstract noun *-ing* forms cannot, their functional range is somewhat different. Most of our stylists do not, nevertheless, consider the constructions too different to forbid their being paralleled: *Our clear vision of the good life and our pursuing it ferociously occupied our next ten years.*

The fundamental difference between the noun transform with *-ing* form or noun derived from a verb as headword, and the noun transform with a noun derived from a predicate adjective as headword lies in the structural differences in the kinds of basic sentences from which they are generated, although the force of finite assertion may not be felt as strongly in the adjective-converted-to-noun construction as in the verb-converted-to-noun construction. When predicate adjective becomes noun in these formations, the source sentence is a copula predication in which there is predication without action. Not all transitive and intransitive verbs have lexical meanings implying action, but it is from those that do have the implication of action that we derive the sense of greater finiteness. The gerund forms from copula predications use *being* (or *having been*) together with the predicate complement. In these gerund forms we can find the full range of predicate complements: *his being a fool, his being foolish, his being home, his being in a hurry, its being yesterday, the trout's having been in the pool, the Stoic philosophy's being obligatory to all citizens,* etc. But *being* does not act like gerunds made from transitive verbs except to the extent that it carries lexical content, for only in the sense of "existence" does it have a behavior pattern like that of an abstract noun made from a verb, since with the pure copula meaning it is the predicate complement that becomes the abstract noun when this is possible. It is directly possible only when a predicate adjective is the predicate complement. Or—to speak more precisely—a predicate noun may already be an abstract noun from prior transformation (*This bridge is our accomplishment, The occasion was a clash between the Reds and the Greens, All this was the foolishness of Jonas:* from a verb or a predicate adjective); an adverbial noun cannot easily become an abstract noun although it may function as a predicate complement (*homing* in *the pigeon's homing* deriving from the verb *homed* rather than from the adverbial noun function—the adverbial noun function being only one function of nouns), and prepositional phrases can hardly make the shift to abstraction without becoming a nonce adjective or verb first (*underwaterishness, downhilling, Jonas's across-the-field-ing*). Variants of the copula like *become, remain, taste,* and *feel* have gerund forms only (*his becoming a man* and not *his becoming of a man; his feeling good; Caesar's remaining sane*).

An abstract noun is first of all a substantive in its grammatical bearing. To the extent that it is purely a substantive the finiteness of predication from which it derives is obscured and repressed. If in actual expressions we find the meanings of nominal phrases fluctuating subtlely between the poles of distinct finiteness of predication and entirely non-finite naming of concepts, the distinctions will be conveyed for the most part by the context. Thus, in *His health depends upon his exercising regularly* the sense of finite assertion (*that he is hale*) is the result of the meaning of *depends* and of the parallel between one assertion and another (*that he is hale depends upon that he exercises regularly*). To the contrary, in *His health is good, his* becomes more a possessive (*he has health*) than a subjective genitive to allow the subsequent copula predication (*is good*). That this distinction is in part a grammatical illusion is shown in a further compression of predication such as *His good health depends upon his regular exercise,* from which we can peel off predications like layers of an onion, only, however, by making distinction between present and prior predications and by not denying the noun-ness of an abstract noun while we are trying to show that the sense of finiteness is still present. These distinctions are not so vital that we can afford to have wars over them.

The difference between *the serene man* and *the serenity of the man* is that between making the subject of the source predication the headword in the transformation and making the predicate of the source predication the headword. Both derive from *The man is serene.* In one the predicate adjective becomes appositive and then becomes a pre-positional adjective (*the man is serene* > *the man serene* > *the serene man*). In the other the predicate adjective as predicator is transformed to an abstract noun and the subject is converted to the analytic equivalent of a subjective genitive (*of the man*). Although the synthetic genitive (*the man's serenity*) is quite possible in this transformation, we find that the periphrastic form is more common when predicate adjectives are converted to headwords of nominal reduced predications than when verbs are converted to abstract noun headwords.

THE RANGE OF NOUN-HEADED REDUCED PREDICATIONS

When we turn from this kind of theoretical analysis to actual examples of complex speech as we encounter them in our everyday lives, we can be made aware, first of all, of the extent to which this kind of phrasing in nominalizations intermingles with structures from the compositional system of syntactic relation. Consider the following sentence from an Associated Press report:

President Kennedy held the door open Tuesday for Soviet acceptance of his proposal to ban nuclear weapons testing in the atmosphere despite the Soviet Union's Monday explosion of a nuclear device, her second test in four days.

Such phrases as *Soviet acceptance* (instead of *the Soviets' acceptance* or *the acceptance by the Soviet Union*), *nuclear weapons testing* (instead of *the testing of nuclear weapons*—a direct object is involved here), and *the Soviet Union's Monday explosion of a nuclear device* (*The Soviet Union exploded a nuclear device on Monday,* the compositional ordering of *Monday* is the most unusual feature) show this intermingling of compositional, synthetic, and analytic phrasings. We cannot be certain whether *Soviet* in *Soviet acceptance* is a noun adjunct in the compositional system or an adjective in a derivational system. In either case we have a variation on the normal pattern of expressing the subject-part of this kind of reduced predication synthetically by a subjective genitive or analytically by a prepositional phrase (either *of* or *by*). At the end of the sentence we find the nominal reduction *her second test in four days* (*she has tested twice in four days*) in apposition to *the Soviet Union's Monday explosion of a nuclear device* (*The Soviet Union has tested a nuclear device for the second time in four days, since she exploded a nuclear device on Monday*). In the world of politics and social process, the realities of life are abstractions from predications more than they are concrete objects. Our school grammars, with their parade of illustrations from the world of concrete objects, do not, as we have said, confront us with the grammar that is the substance of our daily lives. A transformational grammar such as this one may seem forbidding to the beginner schooled on the traditional approach, but this initial difficulty should disappear when application is made to the sentences that the majority of our citizens are called upon to understand. Little children do not usually understand the sentences found in newspapers. We grow into grammatical understandings as well as into physical, emotional, and intellectual maturity. The health of a society such as ours depends upon linguistic maturation as well as upon maturation of other kinds, and our schools must somehow be responsible for this linguistic maturation. We will not attain it only by the study of the supra-segmental patterns of primitive sentences signaling the relations between concrete objects that little children can manipulate at an early age. One of the great shortcomings of the structuralist's approach is that it rarely gets beyond those primitive sentences.

In the sentence from the Associated Press report there are two instances of a use of nominal reductions of predications in which these reductions are coupled with prepositions to perform work that we might expect a so-called adverbial clause to do. These are (1) *for Soviet acceptance of his proposal to ban nuclear weapons testing in the atmosphere* (*President Kennedy held the door open so that the Soviets could accept his proposal that the testing of nuclear weapons in the atmosphere be banned*), and (2) *despite the Soviet Union's Monday explosion of a nuclear device* (*even though the Soviet Union had exploded a nuclear device on Monday*). Whether the connectors in these instances are truly prepositions (since they have noun objects) or whether they are substitutes for subordinating conjunctions in this act of reduction is a question that need not concern us. In some instances a change of form is obligatory (*despite* for *even though*, *for* for *so that*); in others no change is necessary (*after, before, since* as a time connector). Some of the most subtle redistributions of our grammar make use of extensions of the more usual meanings of prepositions in order to show relations between nominal forms of reduced predications and other units (*He congratulated us on our skillfulness in the manipulation of political forces for the adjustment of differences of opinion among racial groups*). The extent of use of nominal phrases that in one way or another represent reduced predications is one of the principal criteria for distinguishing between one style of expression and another, since it was customary in certain periods of past time to condense and reduce formal predications and render experience so that finite verbs disappeared into abstract nouns, and prepositions and analytic particles replaced conjunctions of many kinds. We may come to believe that ages in which high respect is paid to a surface rationalism, such as the seventeenth and eighteenth centuries, are ages in which the nominalization of predications greatly increases. This belief must be tempered by the realization that the stylistic distinction is as much one between class, status, profession, and speech associated with certain media (a synchronic distinction) as it is a matter of distinction between one period of time and another (a diachronic distinction). Just as absolute constructions are found in current prose as well as in the prose of the past but with a different style of phrasing, so it is with nominal phrasings. The prose of Henry James differs sharply from that of Hemingway because of James's rich and complex use of nominal reductions, but the distinction between James and a modern sportswriter may be found only in the kind of nominal reductions used. The following illustrations may make this point clear:

1. *Valentin's ironic forecast of the secession of Mademoiselle Nioche from her father's domicile and his irreverent reflection on the attitude of this anxious parent in so grave a catastrophe received a practical commentary in the fact that M. Nioche was slow to seek another interview with his late pupil.*—HENRY JAMES

2. *. . . his absence might be a proof quite as much of extreme depression as of a desire to conceal the success with which he had patched up his sorrow.*—HENRY JAMES

3. *Her resolution of refusal only grew more interesting by the addition of a scheme for his subsequent consolation and happiness. His recollection of Harriet . . . suggested to her the idea of Harriet's succeeding her in his affections.*—JANE AUSTEN

4. *"No disease of the imagination," answered Imlac, "is so difficult of cure as that which is complicated with the dread of guilt: fancy and conscience then act interchangeably upon us, and so often shift their places that the illusions of one are not distinguished from the dictates of the other. If fancy presents images not moral or religious, the mind drives them away when they give it pain; but when melancholic notions take the form of duty, they lay hold on the faculties without opposition, because we are afraid to exclude or banish them. For this reason the superstitious are often melancholy, and the melancholy almost always superstitious."*—SAMUEL JOHNSON

(We notice, in this kind of stylistic analysis, that it is necessary to consider the kind of finite verbs used along with abstract nominals. In spite of a general effect of abstractness, Samuel Johnson does not in actuality use as many clear-cut nominal reductions as Jane Austen or Henry James.)

5. *The fleet outfielder of the Phillies climbed to third place last week with a .331 average, with thirteen hits in twenty-seven times at bat for an eight-point gain. He leads the league in base hits with 170.*—*New York Times* sportswriter (1953).

6. *The Cubs touched him for a run in the eighth and followed it up with another in the ninth. (touched him to the extent that they made a run in the eighth, they made another in the ninth)—New York Times* sportswriter
7. *Serena went to second on Clyde McCullough's sacrifice bunt and then sped home on Smalley's two-bagger.—New York Times* sportswriter

By the use of the prepositions *on, in, for, with, to* followed by gerunds or abstract nouns a whole range of syntactical arrangements is created that can be expressed otherwise by clauses or reduced predications of other kinds. A series of contrasts in structures using *with* illustrates significant distinctions:

> *Jonas was arraigned on July 27th for his crime.*
> *with Jonas arraigned on July 27th for his crime*
> *with Jonas's arraignment on July 27th for his crime*
> *with the arraignment of Jonas on July 27 for his crime*
> *with the arraigning of Jonas on July 27th for his crime*

The first is a formal predication; the second is a "with" construction with two nuclei; the third and fourth present nominal forms of reduced predication using *with* as preposition or introductory particle and the abstract noun *arraignment* as headword; in the fifth the gerund form *arraigning* functions as an abstract noun since a determiner is used with it. *Arraign* is a transitive verb; *of Jonas* therefore represents the direct object of *arraigning*. In the first four the forms of *arraign* are presumably passive. Another contrasting pair is seen in

> *with Jonas being arraigned on July 27th for his crime*
> *with Jonas's being arraigned on July 27th for his crime*

The first is a two-nucleus "with" construction in which *being arraigned* is not necessarily a gerund since it is not a nominal headword, for *Jonas* does not signal dependency with a genitive inflection. In the second the subjective genitive is present in *Jonas's,* there is no determiner, passive voice is made explicit in *being arraigned;* therefore, *being arraigned* is a gerund functioning as a gerund. When we consider the delicacy of these distinctions, it is not surprising that they are not always adhered to in our usage, particularly in writing where some of the signals cannot be faithfully recorded. When the ordinary user of English writes *These two guards being so close together gave Jonas no opportunity to escape between them,* he is creating a construction that fails to give signals in speech, for there *guards* and *guards'* are homophonous. The same writer would, however, also say *These two men being so close together gave* . . . , in which case we would have to say that in his dialect some of the usages that we consider standard are not maintained.

The presumption is that a subject-part before an abstract noun is signaled by a genitive suffix. We would not find *with him arraignment* under any circumstances. Gerund phrases, to the contrary, often show the influence of competing structures, particularly when a gerund phrase appears in the predicate part of a sentence. *Did you hear about him shooting his wife last night?* is as common even in the literary language as *Did you hear about his shooting his wife last night?* Since a particle like *about* is in effect part of a verb phrase in countless locutions, the calibration of a distinction between *I don't like him (to be) going* and *I don't like to think about him going* is too fine for the average user of language. A study of Jane Austen shows divided usage a century and a half ago between the two forms for subjects of gerund phrases appearing in the predicate part of a sentence.

Gerunds, like infinitives, can readily function as direct objects of verbs without distinct subjects when the subject of the verb is the ideal subject of the gerund: *She likes arranging flowers.* The same situation is found when oblique relations are to be expressed and a preposition is needed: *She has a talent for arranging flowers.* But again, as with infinitives, the subject of a gerund phrase may be unspecified so that the gerund phrase seemingly is abstracted from finite predication: *Arranging flowers was her delight* (*arranging* picks up an agent only notionally in *her*); *Arranging flowers is a good hobby* (for anyone). In some of these functions either infinitives or gerunds can be used interchangeably; in others usage selects one or the other. We say *rather than go* but *instead of going.* Dependent purpose clauses become changed in the process of reduction to infinitive phrases. Other kinds of the so-called adverbial clauses are reduced to gerund phrases or abstract noun units preceded by prepositions. Some kinds of reduced clauses show merely a foreshortening or elliptical substitution rather than a reduction to either nominal phrase or infinitive phrase: (*Although preferring blondes, he married a redhead* in contrast to *Despite his preferring blondes, he* . . .). In some cases of this kind the ellipsis from a verb of progressive aspect is more apparent (*Although going to the barn when it happened, he was in no position to help*—in which *Although he was going . . . is* suggested).

Thus we can see that the potentialities of reduction of predication through the transformation of clauses to nominal phrases are exceedingly pervasive. So many of the syntactic relations among items in a predication can be expressed within this compass that the grammar of nominal phrases (with a minimum of assistance from copulative and near-copulative verbs) can be almost complete. Time and again in analyzing them we approach the far limits of what can be demonstrated. The essential distinction is that between abstraction as it pertains to derivation from verbs or adjectives—in which assertions or predicative attributes are abstracted—and abstraction as it pertains to class terms for concrete objects. *Mammal* is not the same kind of abstract term as *activity, transformation,* or *serenity.* The headwords of nominal phrases that represent reduced predication must be derivatives from other parts of speech or substitutes for such derivatives (his *idea* of the situation). In a transformational grammar, the establishing of limits is less important than the clarification of the processes by which these nominal reductions are achieved.

MATERIALS FOR EXERCISE AND FURTHER STUDY

Attempt to discover the reduced predications that appear as nominal phrases in the following sentences or phrasings, and reconstruct for each a formal predication from which it could be generated.

1. The knowledge of the usage of the current speech is only important because of the great inconvenience of wanting it.—JOHN EARLE
2. It is but the removal of a disability.
3. In pursuit of heaven he reformed his behavior.
4. Hollywood's cheerful desecration of the arts
    (The next two are taken from Zandvoort, p. 31)
5. absorbed in a scheme of his partner's devising
6. The dinner was of aunt's own cooking.
7. . . . offer hope of at least elementary protection against disregard of individual rights.
8. But his own dexterity, and the discontents of Africa, soon fortified the Vandal powers, by the acccession of numerous and active allies.—GIBBON

9. my generation's view of its own youth
10. His paper presented new evidence for the existence of a second type of nerve activity.
11. his apparent strength of will
12. their seeming audacity
13. his readiness to depart
14. believed in his freedom to control his own destiny
15. our happiness that you could come
16. . . . his achievement was made possible by the availability at the Old Vic of players like . . . .—*New York Times*
17. . . . persistent rumors of a widespread tax investigation in the securities field—(AP)
18. The probe was based on charges of abuse of trading rules . . . . —(AP)
19. could carry the possibility of a fine
20. in Tuesday's air attack on the palace
21. It was Miss Taylor's loss which first brought grief.—JANE AUSTEN
22. Her sister . . . was much beyond her daily reach.—JANE AUSTEN
23. whose resignation in a huff Aug. 25 touched off the prolonged crisis
24. my being taught a lesson
25. at the conclusion of the Eastern meet
26. for the first time since the inception of this annual road race
27. despite the fact his season's play ended on July 7
28. First baseman Billy Goodman dropped Milt Bolling's throw of Minnie Minoso's grounder . . . .—*New York Times*
29. . . . Fox scored on Sam Mele's ground-out to short.—*New York Times*
30. Mele scored on Jim Piersall's bad throw to the plate.—*New York Times*
31. the necessity of his asserting
32. he cried, after a solemn pause
33. . . . in the confluence of the multitude . . . .—EMILY BRONTË
34. I guessed, however, by his irregular and violent breathing, that . . . .—EMILY BRONTË
35. You need not dread a repetition of my intrusion—EMILY BRONTË
36. my presence in his sanctum
37. Under pretense of gaining information concerning the necessities of my establishment, I desired . . . .—EMILY BRONTË
38. exhibition of bad temper
39. his intention of doing nothing
40. repressing the intensity of her delight

41. I never feel hurt at the brightness of Isabella's yellow hair, and the whiteness of her skin; at her dainty elegance, and the fondness all the family exhibit for her.—EMILY BRONTË

42. Heathcliff affirms his principal reason for resuming a connection with his ancient persecutor is a wish to install himself in quarters at walking distance from the Grange, and an attachment to the house where we lived together, and likewise a hope that I shall have more opportunities of seeing him there than I could have if he settled in Gimmerton. He means to offer liberal payment for permission to lodge at the Heights; and doubtless my brother's covetousness will prompt him to accept those terms . . . .—EMILY BRONTË

43. Catherine's exuberance of vivacity

44. his bravery in battle

45. his tallness for his age

46. his towering height above his fellows

47. his prudence in all little things

48. although a boy calls with the intention of asking you out

49. Talk of a steel price increase has been stilled by President Johnson's voiced disapproval.—(AP)

50. He doesn't believe in Negroes running for office.

51. Why are Southern race tracks of better construction and maintenance?

52. the completion of the Fort Adams dam

53. the denial to the Negroes of the right to vote

54. the gift of a watch to the chairman as a going-away present

55. on my re-entrance, he raised his eyes

56. And he made no scruple to speak his doubts of her surviving this second attack, unless she were more submissive to his directions than she had shown herself before.—EMILY BRONTË

57. convinced of his inadequacy for the struggle

58. upon my desiring to hear her reply

59. . . . her first thought on her father's return would be to seek an explanation of the latter's assertion concerning her rude-bred kindred.—EMILY BRONTË

60. the mother's emulation of the young girl's selflessness

13

COMPOSITIONAL PHRASING

COMPOUNDING AS A SYNTACTICAL SYSTEM

There is an almost complete grammar within the confines of the nominal phrase forms of reduced predication. This means that practically all of the syntactical relations that we have been able to describe can be expressed somehow or other within those confines. The implication is that we could, if we so wished, express practically every idea that might come into our heads by using only the machinery of nominal phrasings, together with units that can be made dependent upon them, and copulative verbs in order to make formal assertions and to link up the nominal phrases. And yet we have not called that complex of syntactic devices a separate grammatical system in English. We have not done that because the nominal phrases are a kind of battleground on which the synthetic, analytic, and derivational systems compete for the job of expressing the essential grammatical relations. The grammar of nominalizations is an inversion of competing systems rather than a new system. New kinds of word order come into being in nominal phrasings but most of these are extensions of principles that apply to analysis or synthesis. All languages are more or less polysystemic and we cannot create rigid definitions for discrete systems or determine how many separate systems we use.

We have, however, called the syntactic arrangements by which approximate relations are expressed by compounds a distinct system—the compositional system. The range of the grammar of componding is not as great, actually, as that of nominal phrasings. Complete complex predications find expression in it less easily than in nominal phrasings. The temptation exists to consider the compositional system merely one of the sub-divisions of nominal phrasings, since most of the elaborate compounds in our language have noun-heads. However, as we shall see, some are adjective-headed, some are verb-headed, and some have -*ing* words as heads.

The outstanding weakness of the compositional system of syntax is its lack of devices for specifying relationships among items. In it, we have to understand meanings in most instances without the aid of specifying particles such as prepositions. In a relatively limited number of cases agglutinated prepositions are found in compound structures, often though not always with Latin prepositions instead of those derived from Old English, as in *pre-season game* (*game before the season*), *anti-poverty law* (*law against poverty*), *interstate buses* (*buses between states*), *intramural athletics* (*athletics within confines*), *co-worker* (*worker with me*), *sub-soil tests* (*tests under the soil*), *quasi-mortal development of a normal galaxy* (development of a normal galaxy is like that of a human being), but also *undercover agents, underground workers, outdoor greenery, outdoor pool, uphill struggle, lakeside land* (land at the side of or beside the lake), *roadside cafe* (*cafe beside the road*). When these prepositions are not agglutinated as prefixes, we are more inclined to class them as nonce constructions (not normal structures), as in *beyond gravity levels, an at-ease brewery* (a beer tavern where one can be at ease), *a between-the-acts cigar, an after-the-fact decision.*[1] But in most cases the relationship is not made ex-

---

[1] There is no intention in this chapter to make a thorough study of compounds as such. The intention here is to inquire into the amount and kinds of predication that can be handled in compositional structures. To draw the line between evidence that pertains to morphology and evidence that pertains to syntax is difficult. Compounding of many kinds is involved in the formation of words. Where should we draw the line? Why make mention of *lakeside* and not of *praeternatural* or *superstitious?* Why exclude *manufacture* or *manumission, ingress* or *progress?* Why exclude bahuvrihi compounds like *redcap, sourpuss, tightwad,* or exocentric compounds like *cutthroat* and *pickpurse?* The only answer is that in most of these the predicational force has become inert as the compound has acquired a specialized meaning that pertains to the word as a whole. A compound written as one word is more likely to have predicational force if it is of recent origin, but a test by date of origin is not a sure one. Can we distinguish between *The director is now type-casting* and *Suzy is now typewriting,* between *typewriting* and *broadcasting* or *telecasting?* We shall be concerned with some problems that are

plicit. A pre-positional noun adjunct may express a subject relationship, an object relationship, or a purpose, manner, reference,
respect, time, place, comparison, degree, duration, extent, or
who knows how many other relationships, and all without any
explicit signal. We can find some verbs entering into compound
structures, especially in recent years (to say this is to ignore the
fact that other kinds of verb-headed compounds have always been
in the language), but in most compositional structures the predicators, if there are any, are participles, gerunds, or abstract nouns
derived from verbs, and these are incapable of all the modifications of meaning involving person, tense, number, and modality
that can be found in finite forms. Again the signaling devices
are few. Some signals are given by word order, which is usually
the reverse in compounding of what we expected in other systems. If we create a phrase such as *turtle-dreamy,* the chances
are that something is *as dreamy as a turtle* or that someone is
dreamy for turtle (wants turtle to eat or have as a pet). In the
face of ambiguities cliché phrasings become important. Clichés
can, however, be structural as well as lexical. If we are accustomed to phrases like *dove-gray, mountain-high, new penny-
bright* (all expressing comparisons), we are aware of a cliché
structure and can manufacture instances at will by preceding an
adjective with an appropriate noun assertedly having the attribute specified by the adjective: *reed-slim, ice-cold, needle-
sharp.* Expressions like *girl-crazy* or *honor bright* then upset our
expectations, just as *turtle-dreamy* would if it meant *dreamy for
turtle. Girl-crazy* means *crazy about girls,* not *as crazy as girls
are. Honor bright* is not the same structure at all. *Ten year old*
gives us a degree noun *year* preceding an adjective *old,* the same
pattern as in *blue ice-cold* (except that the stress pattern is slightly
different, and that difference is important). If we recognize the
meaning of *turtle-slow* better than that of *turtle-dreamy,* the
reason is that *turtle-slow* is a lexical cliché, and lexicon supports
structure. Lexical clichés become structural clichés when the
structure of a well-known phrase is applied to another set of

morphological, such as that of *kind-hearted* or *troubleshooter,* but only because
forms like these can be used actively to express syntactic relations. It is, furthermore, important to the analysis of compounding as a syntactical system not to
distinguish categorically among forms that are written as one word, forms that
are hyphenated, and forms that are written as two or more words. These are
matters that lexicographers must decide upon in determining what is common in
current usage; they pertain to style-sheets, not to syntax.

lexical items. These lexical extensions are made one by one until we gradually become familiar with the pattern. One given lexical cliché may also undergo transformation to a related structure. Thus, we may become familiar with a nonce pattern such as *baby-sitter*, an agentive noun with an *-er* suffix. The agentive *-er* suffix is very common in the phrases of compounding and phrases using it can be the starting point for many extensions. One extension is to a participle-headed compound *baby-sitting*, and finally a finite verb form is created, *She baby-sits often.* We can think of parallel extensions: *typewriter, typewriting, typewrites; bird-watcher, bird-watching, bird watches.* The final stage in this progression we tend to resist, for our mainline habit patterns do not involve verbs in compounds in this way. So we can say *housekeeper* and *housekeeping* but only rarely do we say *housekeeps.* As of now. We may well see more of this kind of construction in the future. The Congressional wag who first said "Senator Byrd money-watches in the Senate" was employing an age-old principle of wit and humor, for wit and humor often depend upon linguistic extensions; but the acts of wit of individual human beings also gradually change the structural features of a language. A newspaper columnist writes that so-and-so "horse farms in Connecticut" and a pattern is extended to a new situation. A child says of his friend, "He butterfly catches too." A little later, the same child can be heard saying of a certain "dirty fighter" that "he dirty fights" and now a structural extension has been made. And yet, although we say *housebreaker* and *housebreaking*, we do not yet say *He housebreaks.* Perhaps after the child who has learned new ways grows up, we will. We have little control over semantic shifts. Since the days of the Civil War we have been familiar with the word *bushwhacker*, pertaining to "one who cuts his way through bushes," a frontiersman or guerrilla fighter, and with *bushwhacking;* but only later do we encounter the same base form as a verb meaning "to ambush," as in *He bushwhacked me.* In this kind of semantic shift the predicative sense in *bushwhacker* (*He is one who whacks through bushes*) is lost, and the word has become inert in the compositional system of syntax.

We have witnessed in the past half-century a tremendous growth in the use of compounds and the compositional system of syntax. During the nineteenth century the belief grew strong that the ideal language was one that employed an analytic sys-

tem of showing syntactic relations. Few tears were shed over
the gradually disappearing synthetic devices. Grammarians as
well as rhetoricians advised against using inflected genitives in
their full range and encouraged the substitution of the analytic
of phrases instead. Reflexive datives (as in *They had themselves
a good time*) came to seem to belong to outlying dialects. Compounds were particularly out of favor. For a brief period during
the Renaissance, writers, with Homer's *wine-dark sea* and *white-
shouldered Hera* in mind, made a fashion of using compounds.
Sir Philip Sidney said that he was particularly pleased by them.
Du Bartas in France used them excessively. Shakespeare in his
76th Sonnet says

> *Why with the time do I not glance aside
> To new-found methods and to compounds strange?*

The seventeenth-century French rhetoricians, however, soon led
the counter-attack and banished compounds from their language.
Old English which, like other Germanic languages, had once
been rich in them evolved to the point where compounds almost
completely disappeared.

Now the pendulum swing is in the other direction—for several
reasons, some of which are quite unlike others. Newspaper head-
lines, where much must be cramped into little space even at the
expense of ambiguity, bombard us daily with compound structures that are often exotic. Both newspapers and the weekly
news magazines encourage maximum compression of predication, and the result has been the proliferation of new kinds of
compound structures: *Cuban strongman Fidel Castro said . . . ,
the 73 year old, tattoo-emblazoned, ex-auto mechanic Chairman
of the Board said . . .* The language of technologists has become a jungle of compound structures: *complete-in-one portable
and home four track solid state stereo tape system, with micro-
phones and Sony radial XL-2 stereo sound projection speakers.*
Writers of advertisements, who are highly self-conscious rhetoricians, have aimed at the making of highly energized catch
phrases. The printing on the cartons and containers that line
the shelves of the supermarkets swarms with compound phrases
as thick as bees. Magazine advertisements follow rituals of
liturgy based largely on the rhythms that result from the extension of the system of compounding into new areas. It seems
fairly certain that the kinds of rhythm that occur as a result of

heavy use of compounds account for much of their increased use. The analytic system, with its string of prepositional and verb phrases, tends to an evenly flowing and lulling anapestic rhythm —*the song of the birds that is found in the spring, and the cry of the crickets on hillock and heath.* To the contrary, rhythms in the compositional system are closer to quantitative meters; they are jerkier, more off-beat; there are more abrupt junctures and fewer regularities of flow. Some modern poets feel that such rhythms hold the mirror up better to the kind of world we live in than do the analytic rhythms of the past.

Ours is increasingly a world of compendia of facts and condensed reports. Professors of rhetoric in the schools whose sense of fitness is offended by the rapid extension of the compositional system nevertheless assist in the production of college catalogues that are warehouses of compounds. Sociologists and psychologists have developed a kind of professional language, by means of which they communicate with one another, that is heavy with compounds and closely related syntactical innovations. Verbs are not very important in compositional phrasings; nouns, adjectives, and participles do much of the work. In the bureaucratic and mechanized world we live in nominalizations become the base of our reality. Only someone who is both a poet and a sociologist could continuously indulge in phrasings like *North European and English-speaking farm bred folk with lower grammar-school literacy and a predominantly Protestant world view.* In short, we find extensions of the compositional system all around us. We may react against them as we may react against space probes, superhighway traffic, and the cold war, but these days they are eternally *there.* Some writers handle them with more zest and precision than others.

THE TRANSFORMATIONAL PROCESS

To describe the mechanisms involved in the transformation of predications to compositional phrasings is both very easy and very difficult, because all is anarchy; almost anything goes, partly because some of the tests by which parts of speech are determined in other syntactic systems no longer apply. In general, nouns are the headwords in compositional phrasings even if the noun does not seem at first glance to be a constituent of the compound. This is to say that the compositional phrase in *coffee-producing coun-*

tries is the whole, including the headword *countries* and not merely the hyphenated items *coffee-producing*. The process of reduction here is: *These countries produce coffee > countries that produce coffee > coffee-producing countries*. In this case, in which the participle represents the predicator in the source sentence, the headword of the phrase is the subject of the reduced predication, and the hyphen is found between the verb-representative and what was the direct object of the source verb. Hyphenization is not syntactically meaningful in current practice, beyond indicating immediate constituents. We cannot assume, however, that noun headwords will always represent subjects. When an abstract noun is the headword, particularly, the subject-part will be a dependency if it appears at all, as we shall see. As long as we think in terms of the forms and orders of other syntactic systems, even the determination of part-of-speech in compounds is often difficult. In such phrases as *show and tell time, stop and go traffic, sit-down strikes, high-rise buildings, low-cost housing, take-out orders, a leadoff single by Roberts* we find forms derived from verbs in dependent positions without any derivational signaling, unless we take the very absence of signals to be a kind of signaling. The transformational paths by which we can account for these constructions differ considerably. *Roberts leads off with a single* can be transformed by reduction and redistribution to *a leadoff single by Roberts*, but other sources are possible: *Roberts, in leading off, singles; Roberts led off and singled* (this is the most basic form); that *leadoff* is not a finite form is evident; if its function is that of an adjective modifier of specification, we have to be able to think of a functional shift by which one term modifies its coordinate without any formal change to signal the functional shift. The absence of inflection that distinguishes *leadoff* from the finite *leads off* is typical of a shift to the compositional system. For *low-cost housing* we can find a source in *The housing costs little* or *The housing's cost is low; cost* can derive from either a noun or a verb. *Low* is an adjective that cannot function well if *cost* is a verb in the source: *The housing costs little*. A noun adjunct can be the headword for other noun adjuncts or for adjectives, participles, determiners, or other dependent units (*coffee-producing-country geography:* what part of speech can we assign notionally to *coffee* when it is a modifier of a modifier of a modifier?). In *river boatmen* the first immediate constituent split may be between *river boat* and *men*. A sentence such as *Real breath-*

taking garden beauty can be yours for only a few dollars can be
considered a redistribution of *The beauty of your garden will
really take your breath if you will spend only a few dollars,* but
since we have already described the transformations by which
verbs become semi-predicative participles and then pre-positional
participles (and adverbs become adjectives), only because of
garden and *breath* do we have to think of a phrase like this in
terms of the compositional system; *breath* as object of *taking* is
more troublesome than *garden* if we are trying to maintain a part-
of-speech analysis based on dependency and function. What distinguishes the compositional system is, above all, word order, and,
secondarily, inability to show inflection. Since a participle can be
pre-positional in other grammatical systems, it can be argued that
there are two compositional phrases in *real breathtaking garden
beauty*—*garden beauty* and *breathtaking,* and that the whole
phrase is a combination of compositional and derivational devices.
Garden beauty, in itself, is a reduction of *The garden is beautiful*
and presents a structural contrast to the nominal phrase form of
reduced predication, *the garden's beauty,* in which *garden's* is a
subjective genitive. We have said that pre-positional adjectives
are primarily transformed predicate adjectives but that the form
can be "borrowed" by other functions, such as the subject function
(see p. 104), and that a "modifier" is a dependent unit expressing
some discernible relation to a headword. Thus, if we had in our
dictionaries an adjective form for *garden* with derivational suffix,
such as *gardenish,* we would not have to resort to the compositional system but could express the subject-predicate complement
relationship between *garden* and *beautiful* by saying *real breathtaking gardenish beauty.* Our grammatical systems compete and
interact. For *show and tell time* we can construct parallel phrasings such as *time to show and to tell, time for showing and telling,*
and *time in which we show and tell.* In the compound of *show
and tell time* only hesitantly can we say that *show* and *tell* are
infinitives.

It is possible that *cinema structure, cinematic structure,* and
cinema's structure mean exactly the same thing, but all three are
ambiguous. Is the meaning *the cinema has a structure, this structure is a cinema's,* or *this structure is like that of a cinema?* Not
all of these forms express all of these meanings equally well. Some
modern writers go beyond the limits of our present grammar by
creating structures in which subjects of source sentences are ren-

dered as adjective modifiers. A sociologist writing in a highly respected journal recently presented his readers with these phrasings: *generational styles of life* (*Each generation has its own style of life*), *youthful joblessness of the Depression* (*Young people were jobless during the Depression*), *youthful work economy* (*the work economy of the young, The young have an economy based on their working*), *a youthful response to the mass media* (*Our young people responded on one occasion to the mass media . . .*), *increase in the younger educated groups* (this is a curiously ambiguous construction, since the meaning presumably is *The number of people in the groups comprised of younger and educated people has increased; younger* is a noun adjunct here although it looks like an adjective). Some language of the future may use adjectives in this way. At present, when the pendulum swing is toward use of compositional phrasings, this extension of the normal functioning of adjectives is a compensatory act.

However, if, as we say, anything goes in our compositional system, we should have difficulty in drawing a line between nonce compositional phrasings and standard construction. Nonce constructions abound in compounds. A few examples culled from recent prose are: *the Dr. Jekyll and Mr. Hyde quality of New York Met baseball; a never-to-be-forgotten Lake Placid holiday; hidden extra worries* (worries about extra charges that are hidden in a bill); *the stay-at-homes; out of town newspapers; book-of-the-month club; our Courrèges-looking, college speaking guides* (from an advertisement for clothes for college girls); *the far outs; an American-size luggage compartment; life-of-the-car transmission fluid; infant and first year mortality rate, the bilingual and foreign accent family; an array of class-spaced and sex-separated church goings, sports and other occasions for entertainment; the frontier, rural, hair-on-the chest version of masculinity.* Some of these are more extreme departures from the norm than others, but it is hard to draw a line between what is commonplace in the construction of compounds and what is a bold sally into the unknown and anomalous. *Infant,* in *infant and first year mortality rate,* is a noun adjunct as is *first year* but the two adjuncts are not parallel; *infancy and first year mortality rate* might strike us as a more grammatical expression, for the paraphrase of the original is *rate of mortality of infants and during the first year* while that of the revision is *rate of mortality during infancy and the first year.* Parallelism is a grammatical as well as a rhetorical matter, for we can often derive from the evidence of what we normally allow to parallel a sense of our understanding of grammatical functions. If this particular phrase is an abnormal one, and therefore a nonce construction, the faulty parallelism is perhaps responsible. Would *car-life transmission fluid* be within the normal range of compound structures but a structure in which a noun adjunct is followed by a prepositional phrase, as in *life-of-the-car*, not? The multiplicity of relations that can exist between a noun adjunct and a following noun without their being explicitly expressed bewilders us and can lead us to believe that all compounds are nonce constructions. But some of these relations are encountered more regularly than others even though a sense of ellipsis impinges on most of them. Consider *pioneer days, a pioneer effort, pioneer doings, pioneer traits, pioneer betrayals, pioneer industries, pioneer-bold, pioneer-hater, pioneer imitation, pioneer-exalting spirit*. Lacking explicit signals of connections, most of these are highly ambiguous, but provided that we are conscious that we should look for a relationship, we can usually sort out the right one from all the wrong ones. The context may provide the necessary clues. The intonation contours are not the same for all of these. Does *pioneer imitation* mean *pioneers imitate something, something imitates pioneers, this imitation pioneers in a certain direction*, or *this imitation is like those of pioneers?* It is remarkable that we are not more confused than we are by such constructions.

One notable structural feature of compounds is the loss of inflection in the primary modifiers. This is to say that if a noun is the headword of a compositional phrase it is capable of taking a plural or a genitive form, or an adjective modifying a noun adjunct in such a phrase is capable of comparison, but the adjunct itself, which is a primary modifier, is an inflexible form; thus, we find *early* or *earlier pioneer days*, or *a pioneer day*, but not *pioneers days*. In German, genitives could join compounds. Some remnants of this usage can be found in Modern English, as in *bridesmaid*. In phrases like *bird's nest soup*, *nest* is the primary modifier, and it is indeclinable. A clear distinction can be made between nonce compounds and compounds following established formal principles when phrases showing inflection shift entirely, as a single unit, as in *no-man's-land* or "He is a *has-been*." These become functionally single words no matter how they are marked. Some noun adjuncts inflexibly take a plural form, as in *awards night, securities market, savings account, customs house, sports announcer, weapons carrier.* Lloyd and Warfel (p. 173) cite *a communications situations analyst, a heavy-weapons expert, a sports enthusiast, our rivers and harbors policy, a teachers college.* The principle that these adjuncts are indeclinable is not damaged if certain other speakers or writers would choose to use only the singular forms of some of these adjuncts. Jespersen (*Syntax* 2:33–2:36) in discussing appositional compounds (*lady friends, girl graduates, fellow-travellers,* etc.) notes an exception in *men-servants, women-servants, gentlemen farmers.* In general, however, the existence of some of these exceptions merely heightens our sense of the lack of inflecton in the structures of compounding. When participles are found in compounds they are the headwords of the compounds and so function outside of the compositional system as pre-positional semi-predicatives.

SOME PRINCIPAL KINDS OF COMPOSITIONAL REDUCTIONS

Inevitably, when we ask what happens to basic predicational patterns that make use of the structures of compounds in transformations, some kinds of compounds are going to command more of our attention than others. Most important are compositional structures that contain a unit with some kind of finite predicational force, and this is likely to mean derivatives from verbs such as participles, agentive nouns with *-er* suffixes (*worker, watcher, knocker,* etc.), and abstract nouns of verb origin of the kind that is significant in the formation of the nominal forms of reduced predication. Other kinds of compounds are less likely than these to render full predications, however complex they may be. Copula predications become lost or hidden. In a phrase like *Nazi wartime government machinery* such hidden predications as *These are the machines by means of which the Nazis governed during times of war* may be found, but more obviously we have at hand the equivalent of a series of analytic prepositional phrases —*machinery for government by the Nazis during times of war.* Syntax is ultimately a matter of relationships and the signals for revealing them. In discussing relationships, we found that most of them exist between a nominal and some other unit and are expressed in the analytic system by prepositions. Prepositional phrases can function as predicators to express oblique relations in copula predications. Thus we can say *The machinery was for government. The government was by the Nazis. The government* *was during times of war.* Prepositional phrases like these can function as semi-predicatives. A basic structural ambiguity occurs because prepositional phrases are also seemingly dependent upon nouns, verbs, or adjectives. In the complicating of basic sentence patterns this ambiguity is revealed as the fusion of copula and non-copula predications. As a result, when we look at the expression of predicational forms in the structures of compounds, we should not be surprised that many of them seem to be only segments of predications—sub-assemblies, so to speak. The compound phrase *top quality root divisions* can represent a transformation and reduction of *These root divisions are of top quality* in much the same way that *the good man* represents a transformation and reduction of *This man is good.* The phrase *life income supplement policy* may, since it contains the abstract noun *supplement,* be called a transformation and reduction of *This (insurance) policy supplements your income for (the rest of) your life.* But not all compounds contain so obviously subject-parts and predicate-parts of whole predications.

One of the most frequently encountered kinds of compounds representing reduced predications is that with noun headword with an agentive *-er* or *-or* suffix. An adjunct preceding the agentive noun is usually the object of the verb form converted to a noun by the suffix. Examples are: *weight watchers, newspaper publishers, sword-swallower, second-language learners* (notice how the hyphen is merely a directional signal for determining immediate constituents), *car makers, trouble-shooter, water softener, spot remover, bread baker, underclass advisors, news-world creator, integration regulator, data processor.* The *-er* or *-or* morpheme represents the subject, which, we notice, can be an abstraction. The base to which the suffix is attached represents the verb and the noun adjunct the object. Sometimes, however, the adjuncts do not represent objects and sometimes they are not nouns. *Handicap player = He plays under* (or *with*) *a handicap; lunch counter workers = They work at lunch counters; long-distance runner = He runs for a long distance (extent); early risers = They rise early; late sleepers = They sleep late; a late bloomer = He blooms late; high jumper = He jumps high; far-shooter = He shoots far; city-dweller = He dwells in a city; Indian-giver = He gives like an Indian* (comparison). Further derivations are *car-ownership* and *trout fishermen.*

When abstract nouns are the headwords of compositional phrasings, the noun adjuncts preceding them may stand in a subject relation to the predicate idea in the abstract noun; the indeclinable adjunct is then in contrast to a subjective genitive in the synthetic system. Examples: *race segregation* (*races are segregated*), *adult activities* (*adults are active*), *white supremacy* (*whites are supreme*), *night maid service* (*maid serves at night?*), *youth cynicism* (*youths are cynics;* with an appositive adjunct we would have *cynic youths*), *Negro employment* (*Negroes are employed*). When the verbs in the source predications are passive, we may prefer to equate these subject adjuncts with object *of* phrases (*employment of Negroes* instead of *Negroes' employment*). Verb forms that have undergone functional shifting to nouns may likewise be preceded by adjunct subjects: *price rise* (*prices rise, prices rose, prices have risen*), *London gold-market buying surge* (*buying surges at the London gold-market*), *complete communications breakdown* (*communications break down completely*), *a bus stop* (*buses stop*), *an energy drain* (*energies drain* or *energies are drained*). An assortment of other examples in which adjuncts represent subject-parts in the reduced predication are: *adult behavior, guerrilla operations, dock worker strike, disarmament talk results, today's customer needs, moon glow, sunshine, 20 watts of music power, bank mergers, Negro travellers, labor force participation, the nineteenth century conviction, labor mobility.*

When the headword is a noun functionally shifted from a verb without derivational suffix, the noun adjunct preceding it is often in a direct object relationship with the headword: *border guard, coast guard, old-time revival, treble tone controls, sea-view, free winery tours, fine arts patron, self-concept.* Abstract noun headwords function in the same way: *self-satisfaction, lawn-re-seeding, wedding announcements, air pollution, a .53 percent pass completion record* (object and degree relations).

We have already seen how a noun predicate complement can be transformed first to an appositive, and then to a pre-positional appositive (*that fool man*). Such pre-positional appositives do not differ from compositional noun adjuncts bearing an appositive relationship to their headwords, since the appositive relationship is that of predicate complement to subject. Examples are: *heirloom crystal, guitarist George Smith, loan exhibition, violinist Isaac Stern, robber barons, woman doctor, snap course,*[2] *the youth*

---

[2] The two preceding examples are from R. B. Lees, *Grammar of English Nominalizations* (Bloomington, Ind., 1960), pp. 116–23, which should be consulted for listings of kinds of adjuncts not listed here.

who quickly spent a fantasy four-thousand on a credit-card spree (*credit-card* represents "means" in relation to *spree?*). *A 16-yard pass play* (degree and apposition).

The situation of the relationships expressed by noun adjuncts would be less anarchic than it is, however, if only the non-oblique relationships of subject, object, and noun predicate complement were found among them. But oblique relationships of many kinds are equally common. These are those relationships that usually are expressed by prepositions in analytic phrasings and that are often classed as adverbial in traditional grammar. It is in the expression of these oblique relationships that the system of compounding puts the greatest burden on the interpretive powers of the reader or listener and that the line between established phrasings and nonce constructions becomes hard to draw. Examples, with paraphrases, are:

all star Broadway entertainment (You are entertained by actors who are all stars from Broadway): agent, place

twenty-five mile away Mexico City (Mexico City is twenty-five miles away): *twenty-five mile* expresses extent or measure

exciting Paris Labor Day fiesta (The fiesta in Paris over Labor Day is exciting): place, time

true-life involvement (involved in true life): figurative place

hometown papers (papers from one's hometown): ablative place

in hill-top Jerusalem (in Jerusalem which is on a hilltop): appositional in our paraphrase, but with a place prepositional phrase as predicate complement of the copula predication

to pay the Fair admission (admitted to the Fair): allative place

Wednesday Central Park concerts (concerts in Central Park on Wednesdays): illative place, time

the Town-Hall clock (clock which is on the Town Hall): appositional place

college occasions (occasions at college): place

air hours (hours in the air): place

foreground music (music in the foreground): place

stock investments (invest in stock): figurative place

log cabin origins (originated in log cabins): figurative place

union membership (membership in a union): figurative place

summer festival (festival during the summer): time

night worker, day shifter, night life, night owl, day shift: time

nineteenth-century furniture (furniture from the nineteenth century): time

a June wedding (wed in June): time

three second quarter touchdowns (three touchdowns in the second quarter): time

a two-day swim meet (a swimming meet that lasts two days): duration

six-passenger roominess (room for six passengers): extent or degree

concert form (form necessary for concerts): degree or comparison

twenty-minute headstart (started ahead to the extent of twenty minutes): extent or degree

ten-point handicap: extent or degree

this 60-page catalogue: extent

three-minute, station-to-station rates (rates for three-minute calls that are from one station to another): duration, respect (highly elliptical)

the twenty-minute puppet show (shows puppets for twenty minutes): object, duration

twelve-month service charge (we charge for service for twelve months): purpose, duration

one-day integration (integrated for one day): duration

longtime glories (glory lasted a long time): duration

the last five-year succession of films (films have succeeded one another during the last five years): duration

long-time devotees (have been devoted for a long time): duration

spray mist (mist from spray or mist like spray): origin or comparison

Argentine beef: place of origin

your next American Express statement (from or by the American Express): place of origin or agent

show-music (music from a show): origin

rose-bower mood (mood like that of a rose-bower): comparison

ocean-spray effects (like that of ocean spray): comparison

fairy-tale portrayal (portrays it like a fairy tale): comparison or manner

an eagle eye, rainbow display: comparison

pocket knife (knife to be carried in a pocket): purpose

home laundry size (suitable size for a home laundry): purpose

Purpose and reference phrases are often much alike. Often the even vaguer term of "respect" needs to be assigned to the relationship: *civil rights struggle, a fight sentiment, family vacation package plan, family fun time, play area, excursion boat, nightly entertainment program, tennis courts, style sheet, army provisions, student center, art center, decanter top, engagement party, golf privileges, health baths, credit card plans, cannon fodder, no service charge, fun palace, steel mill, coffee mill* (café), *small fry fashions, tourist bars, dude ranches, gambling tables.* For most of these, whatever the precise relationship is, the particle used to express it in the analytic system is *for.*

part-time occupations (occupied part of the time): time or manner

A kind of "respect" relationship for which the analytic particle is *concerning* or *in respect to* is found in *sports wonderland, absence policies, old clothes dealer, the rest room situation in the South, beauty queens, life story, admissions desk, James Bond enthusiasts, new management plan, band schedule, wool experience, hot water services, suds problem, NATO problem, teen-age problem, dope problem, travel agent, change from a family asset as laborer to a family liability as student-consumer.*

Almost no grammarian who attempts to pinpoint paraphrases like these or to assign exact relationships ever succeeds in satisfying many of his readers. We have stressed the fact that relations are mere approximations. We have resorted to lists because these patterns of structure are all very much alike and we must look for notional differences. These adjuncts are all in a sense modifiers for which the term "specification" can be used, since *eagle* in *eagle eye* or *longtime* in *longtime glories* specifies what kind of *eye* or *glory* is being referred to. The term "specification" is thus a catch-all for all kinds of relationships between noun adjuncts and noun headwords, just as it is between adjectives and nouns. In the absence of clear relationships of other kinds, the term may come to be applied to adjunct-noun headword relationships: *wildlife kingdom, cliff-edge, night life spirit, suspension system, hotel pool, old-world customs, Pakistan pavilion, the Pennsylvania exhibit, amusement industry, arts college, law courts, hotel rates, laggard standards.* The analytic particle here is *of.*

Adjuncts of "material" are common: *steel post, stone wall, silk shirt, cotton fabric. Of* is again the analytic particle used to express equivalents.

In paraphrases the verb *have* is useful in showing the relationship in some cases: *wringer machines* (these machines have wringers), *spinner washers* (these washers have spinners), *cold water flat* (this flat has cold water), *fresh water lakes* (these lakes have fresh water), *5-span bridge* (bridge has 5 spans), *multiple-episode Italian comedy* (Italian comedies with multiple episodes), *full-course meals* (meals with full courses).

A highly particularized kind of coordination is found with adjuncts that are either nouns or infinitives, signaled by a hyphen between the coordinates: *wash-rinse action* (infinitive adjuncts), *a college culture of work-study sociability* (infinitive adjuncts), *cocktail-and-dinner party* (unusual in that the *and* appears), *Edward Albee–Samuel Beckett double bill* (proper nouns unusual as modifiers—indicating much ellipsis), *Beethoven-Hindemith program* (proper noun adjuncts), *alcohol-and-water mix, Hindu-Moslim conflicts, for washer-dryers* (*washer* treated as adjunct by being indeclinable).

When compounds are formed with adjectives as heads, the adjectives function in their usual ways—as predicate adjectives, appositives, pre-positional adjectives, or predicate appositives. In most cases the adjunct to the adjective is a noun that can be paraphrased analytically by a prepositional phrase expressing a limited number of relations—comparison, place, time, respect, etc. One of the commonest compositional forms with adjectives as headwords is that in which the noun adjunct suggests an object of comparison: *pearl gray, rose red, stone hard, sky high, ghost pale, Simon pure, baby soft, iron tough, paper thin, that small, skin-deep, house high, sunshine yellow.* As far back as Ben Jonson we find *They are cream-bowl, or but puddle, deep.* But other relations are also expressed. The degree or extent relationship is frequent: *foot larger, five-year-old trees, ten-year-old child, one third lower, state-wide drives, letter perfect.* Examples of other relationships are the following: *punch-drunk* (drunk from punches), *boy-crazy* (crazy about boys), *world weary* (weary of the world), *travel weary* (weary of travel), *war weary* (weary of war), *world-famous* (famous throughout the world), *homeward bound tourists* (tourists are bound toward home), *Europe bound tourists* (tourists are bound for Europe), *zest-full days* (days are full of zest), *weather-proof roses* (roses are proof against the weather), *winter-hardy perennials* (these perennials are hardy in winter), *bowl anxious football team* (this football team is anxious to play in a bowl game), *pollen-free air* (air is free from pollen), *bacteria-free, bird free* (free as a bird or free from birds?), *trouble free* (free from troubles), *duty-free bargains, adventure mad* (mad for adventures), *heart sick* (sick at heart), *land poor* (poor because of owning too much land), *slap happy* (happy as a result of slaps). Some unusual variations upon this pattern are *hard-to-find items* (carryover in straight order of the construction of infinitive after a predicate adjective), *ready-to-wear clothes, pretty-*

enough-to-eat dolls, good-enough-to-salvage spare parts, dead tired feeling (*dead* as intensifier), *permanently water repellant cotton poplin* (*repellant* functions as a participle and has *water* as a direct object), *wide-open secret* (*wide* as transformed result adjunct: secret opens wide), *the cleanest possible washes.*

A special construction that is used extensively is that by which a phrase including an adjective and a noun is converted to an adjective by the addition of an *-ed* suffix, expressing the notion of *having.* Thus, *the man who has a strong mind* > *the strong-minded man.* The first item in this compound remains an adjective, even though the whole becomes adjectival. Other examples are: *strong-willed, weak-kneed, weak-minded, good-hearted, good-humored, broad-brimmed, thin-skinned, red-haired, good-sized, right-minded, hot-blooded, long-legged.* A form like *right-handed* is superficially the same but with a different structural meaning. *Knock-kneed* is also not quite the same since the paraphrase is *He has knees that knock.* Nouns expressing material or comparison can also be the adjuncts: *bowlegged* (he has legs like bows), *iron-fisted* (he has fists like iron), *potbellied, clubfooted, stone-walled* (material), *ivory-headed* (material), *lion-hearted* (heart like a lion). Further extensions become nonce usages: *censorship-minded, an industrial-minded middle class, silver-tongued* (*tongue like silver* is highly figurative). Ellipses are evident in *far-sighted* and *short-sighted.* Numerical determiners can function as the adjuncts: *two-legged, three-sided, many-headed, four-pronged.* A variant is found in *twin-stacked stern-wheelers.* This construction of noun + *ed* superficially resembles a second participial form.

From the transformationalist's point of view, one of the more significant kinds of compounds is that which has a participle as head, since the phrases in which these constructions occur are capable of rendering full predications (that is, of having both subject-parts and predicate-parts in reduced predication). Since the participles, taken by themselves, function as normal prepositional participles (that is, as further transformed semi-predicatives), our interest in them as compounds comes from the adjuncts that are combined with them and from the noun headword that the participle modifies, since it is the whole phrase that is the reduced predication. Thus, in *sky-brightening explosion, sky-brightening* is the compound, with the participle *brightening* as its headword and the noun *sky* as the adjunct.

The whole, however, is a reduction of *The explosion brightens the sky* or *The explosion makes the sky become brighter*. The adjunct functions as the object of the participle; this construction is a common one. Other examples are: *heart-warming encounters* (encounters warm the heart), *red-baiting politicians,* (politicians bait Reds), *more soil-removing agents* (agents remove more soil), *peace-loving nations* (some nations love peace), *troop-carrying transports* (transports carry troops), *English-speaking guides* (guides speak English), *the sun-swallowing Pacific* (the Pacific swallows the sun), *nerve-tingling adventure* (This adventure tingles the nerves or This adventure makes the nerves tingle), *self-adjusting surface skimmer* (This mechanism skims the surface of your swimming pool and adjusts itself). A closely related kind of construction is that in which the participle is of a copula variant (of such verbs as *seem, look, sound, taste, appear*). The adjuncts in this case are transformed predicate adjectives: *unclean-looking, rosy-looking, gracious-seeming, shrill-sounding, fine-appearing, good-tasting, sour-tasting, sweet-smelling.* These are distinct from *wine-tasting* (he tastes wine), *backward-looking politicians* (politicians look backward), *easygoing* (go at ease or easily). Compounds with participial headwords and adjectival adjuncts representing adverbs or result adjuncts are *free-blooming* (bloom freely), *quick-opening plays* (a football term: *plays open up quickly*), *hard-driving* (drive hard), *hard-hitting* (hit hard), *soft-spoken* (one who speaks softly), *far-reaching* (reach far), *far-travelled* (has travelled far: not a passive), *high-flying* (fly high), *far-shooting* (shoot far), *long-lasting flowers* (flowers last for a long time), *the finest upright flowering red lily* (the finest red lily that flowers upright: result adjunct: a problem in immediate constituents), *well-wishing friends* (friends wish us well), *front-loading washing machines* (machines for washing that load in front: *load* is active in form if passive notionally), *side-loading, top-loading.*

Similar constructions are found with passive participles, but since the subjects are in such instances the ideal objects, the adjuncts are either adverbs, nouns in oblique relations or agent-nouns. Examples are: *the previously-mentioned Negro minister* (this Negro minister has been previously mentioned), *well-written script* (script is well written), *fine-acted movie* (grammatical? the acting in the movie is fine), *tight-knit woolens* (woolens are knit tightly), *fully-fashioned first quality nylons* (these nylons of first quality are fashioned so that they are full), *star-studded holiday arrangements* (arrangements for the holiday are studded with stars), *drought-stricken trees and shrubs* (the trees and shrubs have been stricken by drought), *sun-drenched Pacific* (Pacific is drenched by the sun), *fun-filled vacation* (vacation is filled with fun), *snow-topped Alps* (Alps are topped by snow), *palm-shaded* (shaded by palm trees), *trumpet-shaped flowers* (flowers are shaped like trumpets), *rock-carved city of Petra* (city of Petra was carved from rock). Less usual are the constructions in which the adjunct is the subject of the passive participle and the noun headword is an obliquity: *a service-included price* (the service charge is included in this price), *air-conditioned luxury* (luxury in which the air is conditioned, or air is conditioned in this luxury), *color-matched interiors* (colors are matched in these interiors). A result adjunct is the adjunct in *fine-spun* (is spun fine). Somewhat anomalous are *automatic shut-off sentinel switch* (switch is a sentinel that is shut off automatically), and *American grown bulbs* (bulbs are grown in America: why the adjective?).

The distinction has long been made between gerunds and participles as primary modifiers. A difference in stress pattern is usually found in the two kinds (*dáncing gírl = girl is dancing; dáncing gìrl = girl who is a dancer*). In describing kinds of compositional phrases, we need to make little distinction between gerund-headed phrases and compositional phrases in which gerunds are primary modifiers. In both instances the gerunds behave like abstract nouns. Examples are *color film processing* (color film is processed), *adult buying* (adults buy), *broad-jumping* (jump in breadth), *pole-vaulting* (vault by means of a pole), *extra-strength cleaning* (cleaning has extra strength?), *Monday closings* (they are closed on Mondays), *the next Monday opening of the museum* (the museum will open next Monday), *sun-bathing* (bathe in the sun), *a ten-game winning streak* (the streak of their winning is to the extent of ten games), *deluxe resort living* (one lives in deluxe fashion at the resort), *home-cooking recipes* (recipes for cooking at home), *his eight-hitter pitching* (he pitched a game in which there were eight hits), *nine-fifteen starting time* (the time for starting is at nine-fifteen), *outdoor eating time* (the time for eating outdoors), *hunting lodge* (lodge for hunters), *cooking onions* (onions for cooking), *wholesale selling prices* (prices for selling at wholesale), *qualifying rounds* (rounds for qualifying), *sight-seeing trips* (trips for seeing the sights), *marching music* (music for marching), *losing battle* (appositive gerund: the battle is a losing), *the largest selling lawn sprinkling pump* (a pump for sprinkling lawns that sells the most: *selling* is a participle), *sporting facilities* (facilities for sporting), *cruising revival* (cruising is revived).

From all this we can see that no one would deliberately develop a compositional grammatical system if he wanted to make all relationships explicit and avoid all possibility of ambiguity. The compositional system puts a great strain on a listener or reader. However, if a working synthetic system reduces the number of cases necessary to make all relational signals explicit from fifty to five, and then in further evolution further reduces the distinction to two or three, in conjunction with word order signals, each signal must come to mean almost as many different things as a signal in the compositional system does. Furthermore, if a few prepositions like *with, as, in, on, of,* and *for* each have several different relational meanings in the analytic system, it also can hardly be said to avoid ambiguity. Lacking pluralization and (to a considerable degree) determiners, lacking finite verbs and much of the machinery for showing person, number, tense, mood, and voice in verbs, the compositional system must operate with clusters of cliché structures. At the same time it is evident that nowhere else are nonce constructions so frequent as in compounds. In general, compounding is part of our constant pressing toward nominalization, and suffers from many of the same drawbacks of abstractness that the nominal forms of reduced predications do. It seems to be able, however, to present in highly compressed form a large part of the range of ideas that we wish to express. It is a thorny grammatical system, for tough-minded, adventuresome, or muddle-headed users. We can lament the recent growth of it, but that it has grown we can hardly deny.

MATERIALS FOR EXERCISE AND FURTHER STUDY

Here we have an assortment of compounds of one kind or another. Sort them out according to what kind of headword each has, and then according to difference in relations within each headword column.

night rider	clean-washed windows
that idiot student	red-painted barn

the neighborhood priest
party behavior
cobble-stoned street
clean-shaven face
month-old son
pear blossom
jut-jawed emperor
coffee can
beer can
rain clouds
tablecover
homeward sails in the sunset
cloudbanks
three-legged dog
lemon flavor
upper-West-Side tea dances
bird-life
sweet-voiced
raven-haired
section gang
water-filled pits
stir-crazy
prairie rooster
a what-next
upward-blossoming cloud
life-saver
elm leaves
moon shadows
the living-room air
a discourse-centered rhetoric
window screen
a love-lorn column
jig-saw puzzle
owl king
silk ear
egg-shell
grief-stricken singing
eye-opening events
dinner plate
window-watching smiles
up-soaring bird
pin-tingling hand
black-plated
pumpkinseed
the nightly beginning world

copper-color pinstripe
our first "sandwich" coins
silver-saving dimes
Washington quarter and Kennedy half-dollar
pure-copper core
three-layer coin
all-white edge
80-percent-silver alloy
an overall silver content
the 90-percent silver content of present U.S. silver coins
high-silver coins
silver mines
silverware
silverless or reduced-silver coins
U.S. Treasury's depleted silver stockpile
a non-profit research group
a unique engineering problem
vending machines
pay phones
parking meters
coin-operated devices
a huge 3.5-billion-dollar-a-year business
toll-highway receptacle
sheet aluminum
aluminum coins
play money
bounce test
eddy currents
cupronickel-copper makeup of the new dimes and quarters
silver-saving plans
amusement-hungry
make-believe world
million-dollar spectacle
a fashion-conscious daughter
now-familiar result
stop-loss orders
midnight meeting
quiet-spoken cowboy
milk drivers

account books
grave diggers
vegetable venders
horse dealers
street-car conductors
churchgoers
Easter parade
wholesale grocery concern
football player
August sunlight of a Miami afternoon
mob scene
full dress rehearsal
bull market
gold rush
oil booms
free-land stampedes
newspaper advertisement
heart-sick
seafaring peoples
colt-wild
promotion copy
membership committee
fertile-looking fields
tight-sticking plasters
Florida climate
160-acre tract
coral limestone
family orchards
law school
family estate
fruit and vegetable plantations
real-estate business
railroad connections
hotel chain
a railroad parking lot for private palace cars
electric light plant
water and sewage system
hot water pipes
Georgia pioneer
future resort possibilities
harvester magnate
the coughdrop king
Georgian-style showplace

sometime-politician
sometime-evangelist William Jennings Bryan
income and inheritance taxes
eighteen-hole golf course
small-town banker
subdivision civilization
sales force
dream city
twenty-six-story hotel
Spanish-Italian architecture
woodcarver
interior decorator
prize fighter
off-beat career
society architect
worm-eaten cypress
landscaping experience
subdivision madness
watch towers
"his scape-grace brother, Wilson, a latter-day Sir John Falstaff"
boom spirit
winter-resort economy
boom year
side-show barkers
free-lance orators
Bible-belt gospel shouters
wayside barbeque
office and salesroom space
hotel lobbies
forty-foot mock-up
yacht basin
underwater lots
boom-time hoopla
building lots
the annual reducing-diet fever
industry needs
out-of-towners
the up-the-hill traffic
population explosion
freight cars
mixed-in-transit mortar fleet
soft-ice-cream chain

soup substitute
he double-checked a report
waste motions
administration-sponsored
    demonstration
charming one- and two-bed-
    room suites
a White House fabrication
present administration policy
ground war
mainland China
reception committee
an Air France jet-away holiday
complete tour prices
in the many-weeks-deserted
    parlour
chapel bells
death-like
half-open door
self-denial
misery-maker
the brute beast
self-preservation
ill-treatment
goblin hunter
crooked-legged terrier
well-made youth
narrow-minded
female management
his peace-offering
heather-scented
farmhouse garden gate
low-browed lattices
the whey-faced whining wretch
business visits
faint-hearted venture
morning studies
breeze-rocked cradle
fresh-killed meat
windblown hair
nursery lore
leisure hours
bugbear stories
bad-natured
oat cake

the butcher boy
the slow-heaving polar ocean
ruddy-tinged granite cliffs
peace mission
cloth-of-gold wrought cloud-
    couch
fire-pillar
porch light
shadow hunter
the swallowed-up aeons of time
clay-given mandate
all-subduing sun-splendor
often-repeated doubts
shadow-hunted pilgrimings
battle turning-points
smoke signals
love-makings and scandal-mon-
    geries
many-voiced life
our present century church
    catechism
shoeblack
self-tormenting
soft-bedded
deep-seated disease
sorrow-entangled quests
handwriting
the wild-weltering chaos
rock-formations
spinning-jenny
wonder-working drugs
world-renowned far-working
    institution
paper bag
satire-creating witlings
paste rubbish
Sunday clothes
devil worship
waterproof suit
out-at-elbows appearance
wood nymph haunted glens
the field-circling plane
toil-worn peasant
jewel-studded belt
heavy-laden asses

draught horses
nose-ring
foot-shackles
stripped-off garments
rainbow-dyed aurora
old-clothes market
farce-tragedy
deathsong
fire-whirlwind

steam engine
blood circulation
life-streams
hero worship
court poet
religion-oriented man
world-shaking events
boiling-up emotions

FURTHER READINGS

ALLEN, HAROLD B. (ed.). *Readings in Applied English Linguistics* (2d ed.). New York: Appleton-Century-Crofts, Inc., 1964.

BACH, EMMON. *An Introduction to Transformational Grammars.* New York: Holt, Rinehart & Winston, Inc., 1964.

BLOOMFIELD, LEONARD. *Language.* New York: Holt, Rinehart & Winston, Inc., 1933.

BLOOMFIELD, MORTON W., and LEONARD D. NEWMARK. *A Linguistic Introduction to the History of English.* New York: Alfred A. Knopf, Inc., 1963.

CHOMSKY, NOAM. *Syntactic Structures.* The Hague: Mouton & Co., 1957.

CURME, GEORGE OLIVER. *English Grammar.* New York: Barnes & Noble, Inc., 1953.

————. *A Grammar of the English Language.* Boston: D. C. Heath & Co., 1931–1935. Especially Vol. 3, *Syntax.*

DEAN, LEONARD F., and KENNETH G. WILSON (eds.). *Essays on Language and Usage* (2d ed.). New York: Oxford University Press, 1963.

FRANCIS, W. NELSON. *The Structure of American English.* New York: The Ronald Press Co., 1958.

FRIES, CHARLES CARPENTER. *American English Grammar.* New York: Appleton-Century-Crofts, Inc., 1940.

————. *The Structure of English.* New York: Harcourt, Brace & World, Inc., 1952.

GLEASON, H. A. *An Introduction to Descriptive Linguistics* (rev. ed.). New York: Holt, Rinehart & Winston, Inc., 1961.

HALL, ROBERT A., JR. *Linguistics and Your Language.* Garden City, N.Y.: Doubleday & Co., Inc., 1960.

HATHAWAY, BAXTER. *Writing Mature Prose—The Mastery of Sentence Structure.* New York: The Ronald Press Co., 1951.

HILL, ARCHIBALD A. *Introduction to Linguistic Structures.* New York: Harcourt, Brace & World, Inc., 1958.

HUGHES, JOHN P. *The Science of Language.* New York: Random House, Inc., 1962.

JESPERSEN, OTTO. *Essentials of English Grammar.* New York: Holt, Rinehart & Winston, Inc., 1933.

————. *A Modern English Grammar on Historical Principles.* Vols. I–IV, Heidelberg: C. Winter, 1909–1940; Vols. V–VII, Copenhagen: E. Munksgaard, 1940–1949.

————. *The Philosophy of Grammar.* London: George Allen & Unwin, Ltd., 1924.

KRUISINGA, ETSKO, and P. A. ERADES. *An English Grammar* (8th ed.). Groningen, Djakarta: P. Nordhoff, 1953.

LEE, DONALD W. (ed.). *English Language Reader.* New York: Dodd, Mead & Co., Inc., 1963.

LEES, ROBERT B. *The Grammar of English Nominalizations.* Bloomington, Ind.: Research Center in Anthropology, Folklore, and Linguistics, 1960.

————. "A Multiply Ambiguous Adjectival Construction," *Language,* XXXVI, 207–21.

LLOYD, DONALD J., and HARRY R. WARFEL. *American English in Its Cultural Setting.* New York: Alfred A. Knopf, Inc., 1956.

LONG, RALPH B. *The Sentence and Its Parts; A Grammar of Contemporary English.* Chicago: University of Chicago Press, 1961.

NEWSOME, VERNA L. *Structural Grammar in the Classroom.* Milwaukee, Wis.: Wisconsin Council of Teachers of English, 1961.

NIST, JOHN. *A Structural History of English.* New York: St. Martin's Press, Inc., 1966.

OHMANN, RICHARD. "Literature as Sentences," *College English,* XXVII (1966), 261–67.

POUTSMA, HENDRIK. *A Grammar of Late Modern English.* Groningen: P. Nordhoff, 1914–1929.

PYLES, THOMAS. *The Origin and Development of the English Language.* New York: Harcourt, Brace & World, Inc., 1964.

QUIRK, RANDOLPH. *The Use of English.* New York: St. Martin's Press, Inc., 1964.

ROBERTS, PAUL. *English Sentences.* New York: Harcourt, Brace & World, Inc., 1962.

————. *English Syntax* (alternate ed.). New York: Harcourt, Brace & World, Inc., 1964.

————. *Patterns of English.* New York: Harcourt, Brace & World, Inc., 1956.

————. *Understanding Grammar.* New York: Harper & Row, 1954.

ROGOVIN, SYRELL. *Modern English Sentence Structure.* New York: Random House, Inc., 1964.

RYCENGA, JOHN A., and JOSEPH SCHWARTZ. *Perspectives on Language— An Anthology.* New York: The Ronald Press Co., 1963.

SAPIR, EDWARD. *Language: An Introduction to the Study of Speech.* New York: Harcourt, Brace & World, Inc., 1921.

SAWYER, JANET B., and LOUISE C. LUBBE. *From Speech to Writing.* New York: Holt, Rinehart & Winston, Inc., 1966.

SLEDD, JAMES. *A Short Introduction to English Grammar.* Chicago: Scott, Foresman & Co., 1959.

THOMAS, OWEN. *Transformational Grammar and the Teacher of English.* New York: Holt, Rinehart & Winston, Inc., 1965.

TRAGER, GEORGE LEONARD, and HENRY LEE SMITH, JR. *An Outline of English Structure.* Studies in Linguistics, Occasional Papers 3, 1951. Reprinted, Washington, D.C.: American Council of Learned Societies, 1957.

WHITEHALL, HAROLD. *Structural Essentials of English.* New York: Harcourt, Brace & World, Inc., 1956.

ZANDVOORT, REINARD WILLEM. *A Handbook of English Grammar.* London: Longmans, Green & Co., Ltd., 1957.

GLOSSARY

ABLATIVE—A relation denoting "motion from" or "separation"; the name of a case in the inflection of Latin nouns, pronouns, or adjectives, functioning in expressing not only this relation but also others.

ABSOLUTE CONSTRUCTION—A reduced predication containing two nuclei—a subject-part and a predicate-part—without a finite verb and without any formal connection with the unit on which it is dependent. See Chapter 10.

ABSTRACT NOUN—a noun derived from a verb or adjective, so that it does not signify a concrete object—*collision, strength, vacation, frailty.*

ACCUSATIVE CASE—In a synthetic language showing inflectional endings for nouns, pronouns, and adjectives, this is the case for direct objects and other nominal functions. In Modern English, distinct accusative forms are found only in certain pronouns. Sometimes referred to as the "objective" case, except that in Modern English "objective" means any case except nominative, genitive, and vocative.

ADJECTIVE—One of the three main form classes of words, bordering on substantives in meaning and sometimes easily convertible into substantives, but predicating qualities, attributes, or describable attributes of substantives: *red, kind, energetic, improbable.*

ADJECTIVE CLAUSE—So-called in traditional grammar; here called a "relative" clause; a formal predication related and subordinated by a relative pronoun (which may be deleted if the relative pronoun functions as other than subject of its clause) to a substantive upon which the clause is dependent.

ADJUNCT—In Otto Jespersen's grammatical terminology, an adjunct is a word or unit that modifies or is grammatically dependent on a primary word or unit. Primaries are usually nouns; hence adjectives (and verbs) are the principal kinds of adjuncts, but nouns functioning as dependencies are also called adjuncts. In modern grammatical terminology this term is merely a relic from a disowned system and is usually used to designate a noun used as a dependent unit in a compositional phrase: *stone* wall, *building* fund, *football* game, his *idiot* son. But *see also* RESULT ADJUNCT.

ADVERB—One of the four main form classes of words as these are usually described. These words are usually conceived as modifiers of verbs, adjectives, or other adverbs. Here adverbs are treated as if they form a specialized sub-class of adjectives, since *-ly* adverbs are derivatives of adjectives or participles, and only a few words can be called base adverbs (a limited lexicon is a sign of a function group). A source of confusion is that adverbs are too often defined in terms of the relational functions that structures of all kinds perform rather than in terms of a form class.

ADVERBIAL CLAUSE (so-called)—A dependent formal clause of any one of the kinds traditionally called "adverbial" either because they seem to be dependent upon verbs, adjectives, or adverbs, or because they express relational notions that are often thought to be adverbial functions, even though terminology should not mirror a confusion of forms and functions. Expressing "cause," for instance, is said to be an adverbial function, but a relative clause or an appositive adjective does not become an adverb if it happens to express a "cause." See Chapter 8.

ADVERBIAL COMPLEMENT—A very hazy concept, since only by extending the definition of "adverb" from form to a group of functions can most of the units functioning as so-called adverbial complements be interpreted as adverbial units. Prepositional phrases and "adverbial" nouns are two such kinds of units said to function as adverbial complements (i.e., "completers" of a predicate). These are complements that express a relational obliquity in addition to their being "objects" of some predicational motion. *I placed it* is incomplete. *I placed it on the shelf* is complete. The preposition *on* expresses the obliquity—the notional relation of place. It is necessary to account for the presence of "adverbial" nouns and some prepositional phrases in basic sentence patterns. If they cannot be explained as transforms, an additional basic sentence pattern must be constituted to dispose of them. See page 79.

ADVERBIAL NOUN—A noun that usually appears in the predicate part of a sentence, in an oblique relation (time, place, degree, extent, duration, etc.), but with zero inflection or without an explicit preposition to signal the relationship.

ADVERSATIVE—A conjunction or some similar relating word that expresses opposition or antithesis between the units that it connects: *but, however, although,* etc.

AFFIX—A bound form attached to a stem of a word. "Affix" is a term that includes prefixes, suffixes, and superfixes.

AGENT—The word that denotes the "doer" of the action of a verb or a form derived from a verb—if it does in actuality denote an action. Gerunds and infinitives that denote generalized action have no specified agents. When finite verbs are active, their agents are usually identical with their subjects. In passive transforms the agent may appear as the object of the preposition *by* or may not appear at all. The agent of an active participle is usually the substantive that the participle is said to "modify."

AGENTIVE NOUN—A noun made from a verb with an *-er* or *-or* suffix that denotes agency—*singer, jumper, maker, collector.*

AGENTLESS VERB—A verb for which no agent or "doer" is specified, whether or not an agent is implied. When a verb is passive, the direct or indirect object of its active form may be its subject and the agent may or may not be explicit elsewhere in the sentence. Subjects of predications are not necessarily agents.

AGREEMENT—A verb should agree with its subject in person and number, as should a pronoun with its antecedent.

ALLATIVE—The relation of "motion to"; in Latin and Greek this relation is not assigned a separate case.

AMBIVALENCE—In syntax this term applies to a construction that has more than one syntactic function, so that it has more than one "valence" or "value." *See* DOUBLE VALENCE.

ANALYTIC SYSTEM—The syntactic system in which relationships between words or functional modifications of concepts are expressed by free function words such as prepositions or verb-auxiliaries, in contrast to a synthetic system in which the relationships are shown by bound (not free) inflectional affixes. The general drift of modern European languages has been toward the analytic system. In Modern English, nouns that have lost distinctive inflections without requiring prepositions to express their functions are still to be considered within the synthetic system, with zero inflections.

APPOSITIVE—The headword of a phrase that is the transformed predicate-part of a copula predication with the copula deleted. An appositive unit thus can take any shape that a predicate complement can take—predicate noun, predicate adjective, prepositional phrase as predicate complement, the so-called adverbial noun as predicate complement. See Chapter 9.

APPOSITIVE NOUN ADJUNCT—A construction that is possible in the compositional system in English, in which a predicate complement noun is transformed to a pre-positional noun adjunct: *that fool man, fellow Americans.* See page 269.

ASPECT—A qualification of a verb's meaning either in terms of duration in reference to a specified time or of completion in reference to a specified focal point, or of emphasis. The principal aspects a verb can reveal are thus the progressive, the perfect, and the emphatic aspects. These are expressed analytically in Modern English, by means of auxiliaries: *I am going, I have gone, I did go, I have been going,* etc.

BASIC SENTENCE PATTERNS—The basic patterns of formal predication; kernel sentences; sentence patterns that contain no included predications, no transforms; the simplest forms of predication, from which more complex statements can be generated. The three basic patterns are: 1) subject-part + intransitive verb (sometimes with so-called adverbial complements), 2) subject-part + transitive verb (+ indirect object) + direct object (sometimes with adverbial complement), 3) subject-part + copulative verb (or copula variant) + predicate complement (sometimes with adverbial complement).

CASE—A pigeonhole or category in the inflectional paradigm of a synthetic system of syntax, not necessarily signaling any given relationship since a single case can be the repository for semantic relationships of various kinds. Some names for cases commonly encountered in grammars of Latin, Greek, and similar languages are nominative, vocative, genitive, dative, accusative, locative, ablative, instrumental.

CLICHÉ STRUCTURE—A customary and set use of a given phrase structure or principle of structure within a given range. An extension of this range is a *deviant.*

CLOSE APPOSITION—A term used by traditional grammarians. Since these forms do not arrive at their present shape by a common transformational road or process, they do not comprise a real class for the transformational grammarian. See pages 165–66.

COMPARISON OF ADJECTIVES AND ADVERBS—The ability of words of these form classes 1) to be inflected by suffixes showing comparative (-er) or superlative (-est) degrees of the characteristic denoted by the word, or 2) to show these degrees by the analytic degree particles more and most. See page 60.

COMPOSITIONAL SYSTEM—The syntactic system of signaling relationships between words by making compound phrases of them; the adjoining of free forms in a pattern in which a headword usually comes last in a string. It consequently functions primarily with sub-assembly of predications and is not a complete system. The term "compound" as used here applies more to the word order in a compound phrase than to the creation of one word (hyphenated or not) out of more than one free form.

COMPOUND—A construction in the compositional system in which words are juxtaposed without inflectional, derivational, or analytic signals of relationship, and usually in reverse order from the normal predicational word order of other systems.

CONJUNCTIVE ADVERB—The traditional grammarian's term for a Sequence Word; a word whose function is to show the relationship between two clauses but that is not a conjunction. The term "adverb" may not strictly fit words of this class, which should instead form a function group. Examples are however, nevertheless, therefore. These appear in the second of the units to be related, but their position within the unit is not fixed. See pages 148–52.

COORDINATING CONJUNCTION—A word that connects syntactic equals whether these are words, phrases, or clauses: and, but, or. And is an "additive" conjunction, but an "adversative," or an "alternative." These form a function group.

COPULA VARIANT—A verb that is followed by a predicate noun or predicate adjective, not a transform, so that its behavior is much like that of the pure copula be: become, remain, get, stay, etc. Predications having seem and look as verbs are not quite in the same class, since these verbs represent transforms of impersonal verbs: That seems good. < It seems that that is good. Verbs followed by predicate appositives and verbs that are hybrids of copula and intransitive verbs also differ from copula variants. See Chapter 5.

COPULATIVE VERB—The verb be in its various forms (am, is, are, has been, was, were, was being, might have been, etc.) when it simply signals a predication together with tense, number, aspect, and mood, and does not mean exist. Copulative verbs are followed by predicate complements of some sort. See Chapter 4.

COUNT NOUN—See Pluralizer noun.

DANGLING PARTICIPLE—See pages 175–76.

DATIVE CASE—An inflectional constant in the paradigm of a noun, pronoun, or adjective in a synthetic language such as Latin. Since we have no dative inflections in Modern English distinct from other "objective" inflections, we can use the term only by a shifting of meaning from the form the inflectional suffix gives a word with the implication of the set of relationships the form can express to the set of relationships themselves. By using signals of word order and zero inflection, we can, however, identify some nouns and pronouns as datives (indirect objects, datives of reference, reflexive datives, etc.).

DECODING—A speaker or writer who finds expression for an experience by giving it a syntactic form is said to be "encoding" the experience. The listener or reader who catches the meaning of the expression is said to "decode" it.

DEMONSTRATIVES—A class of determiners or near-nouns that point a reference to some unit that has already appeared: *this, that, these, those, such.*

DEPENDENT CLAUSE—A formal predication that has been included in a matrix sentence in some way in a dependent status. See Chapter 8.

DEPTH GRAMMAR—One of the ways of referring to a generative or transformational grammar, since a grammar of these kinds adds a third dimension to a description of the immediate constituents of an utterance by inquiring into the process of change by which the resulting form has come into being.

DERIVATIONAL—A term applying to a word or morpheme that has been derived from a word or morpheme of a different part of speech, usually by the addition of a bound affix.

DESCRIPTIVE GRAMMAR—That kind of grammar in which the grammarian is content to describe a language's structures as he finds them to exist without unduly asking himself whether they ought to exist or not. A transformational grammar is not necessarily either a descriptive or prescriptive grammar since a structure is not really a structure in such a grammar until the process of its generation is worked out.

DETERMINER—A function word that can be used as a signal that its headword is a noun; the making of that signal is not necessarily the whole function or even the primary function of the word. Some determiners are *a, the, this, that, his, her, its, John's.*

DIRECT OBJECT—About the hardest construction in grammar to define and yet one of the commonest and most easily identifiable. A direct object is a nominal of some kind that directly receives the predicational force of a transitive verb. Its existence makes the verb transitive, so that it is hard to define the one without defining the other at the same time. The direct object is a necessary nominal complement of a transitive verb in an active predication. It can become the subject of the sentence in a passive transformation. It is often said that a direct object receives, either literally or figuratively, the "action" of the verb. Semantically, we may sometimes reason that the movement designated is from the object to the subject, as in *I see the cat* (The light waves from the cat impinge upon my eyes), but formally this experience is rendered as if *seeing* is an action that can have *cat* as its object. When we say that verbs express action, we most often mean predicational, not physical, movement.

DO AS FUNCTION WORD—See Chapter 6.

DOUBLE-OBJECT CONSTRUCTION—The construction frequently called the object-objective complement construction in traditional grammar. In this treatise the double-object construction is treated as a two-nuclei infinitive phrase in the direct object position (with the infinitive *to be* often deleted). See pages 220–29.

DOUBLE VALENCE—Two syntactical values or functions exhibited in a single unit. In a sentence like *I asked him to go, him* stands in the relation to direct object to *asked* and in the relation of subject-part in a predicational nexus with *to go.*

ELLIPSIS—The omission of words or phrases that need not be duplicated and so are "understood"; found often when one unit parallels another: *He likes candy very much, she cake.*

ENCODING—See DECODING.

EXCLAMATORY NOUN CLAUSE—See page 154.

FACTITIVE VERB—A verb expressing notions of causing, forcing, usually followed by an object that is a reduced predication: He *made* me go.

FINITE VERB—Any verb or verb phrase that shows a tense distinction and that can conceivably show person and number distinctions. That is to say, if the situation can be adjusted so that a third person, present tense form would be called for if the construction demanded a finite form, would the finite form be possible. The structure of *I see the boys run* is ambiguous, since it can be seen as *(that) the boys run* or *the boys to run.* Test with a singular boy: *I see the boy runs.* In this interpretation of the structure the verb is finite. Only finite verbs are verbs functioning as verbs; forms derived from verbs can function as predicate-parts in reduced predications.

"FOR" CONSTRUCTION—A two-nuclei reduced predication using an infinitive as its predicate part, having its own subject, and introduced by *for;* used in a variety of functions. See pages 227–28.

FUNCTIONAL SHIFT—The moving of a word from functioning as one part of speech to functioning as another, with or without the addition of a derivational affix: *run* as verb to *run* as noun; *cash* as noun to *cash* as verb; *choler* to *choleric.*

FUNCTION WORDS—Words performing relational functions, denoting relational concepts, or signaling structures. We use them repeatedly, but the list of them is quite short; they are outside the main form classes: *in, and, since, with, do, not, can, would, the, this,* etc.

GENITIVE CASE—The only relic of the original inflectional paradigm for nouns in Old English. The name POSSESSIVE CASE can be used as well, so long as we realize that not all substantives with "possessive" inflection express "possession," since that relation is only one of several that this case can express. To avoid that confusion of nomenclature, the term "genitive" is used here for the case, and "possession" remains the name of a relation.

GERUND—An *-ing* or *-en* derivation from a verb functioning as a nominal in nominal reduced predications in a way that some of the properties of the verb are still present, such as the ability to take complements without periphrasis and to be modified by adverbs. The passive *-en* forms are found in gerund use only in the progressive or perfect aspect forms (*his being chased, his having been chased*). Gerund forms can, however, function as abstract nouns. Only by differences in function in certain constructions can gerunds be kept distinct from participles, and sometimes even difference of function is not clearly evident: *Going away, he . . . , After going away, he . . . , After his going away, he . . . .* Differences between gerunds as noun adjuncts and prepositional participles can usually be made by differences in stress pattern.

GRAMMAR—A grammar of a language is an account of the structures for the putting of words together to create meaningful utterances. These structures are created by the users of a language. They may be bad or good structures—or seem so to us if we judge them according to our taste or upbringing. If, however, they are the structures that we actually use as members of a speech community, they are part of the grammar of our language. A "depth" grammar of a language is a description of its devices for forming predications and combining them into complex predications.

HEADWORD—The constituent in a phrase structure upon which the other constituents are grammatically dependent. (It is a mistake to try to determine for an analytic verb phrase—such as *has been thinking*—which word is the headword, since to do so would be tantamount to deciding which word in the phrase carries the important meaning, and this kind of question is not one of grammatical dependence.)

HIDDEN PREDICATION—A predication that is "sneaked" across sentence boundaries when in effect a nominal in a subsequent sentence acts as a predicate complement in relation to a nominal in the sentence preceding it. See pages 106, 112–13.

ILLATIVE—The relation of "motion in" or "into"; not assigned a separate case in Latin or Greek.

IMMEDIATE CONSTITUENT ANALYSIS—A method of analyzing phrase structures by which layers or levels of modification can be determined. In *our little old house*, the first cut removes the determiner *our*, and then in order *little* and *old;* in *our old father's house*, to the contrary, the phrase must first be split into *our old father's* and *house*. This is binary division. In binary division a construction is divided into two constituents at any given step of its analysis. This kind of immediate constituent analysis cannot get at the processes by which transformed structures are generated.

INCLUDED PREDICATION—The structure that results when a source sentence is transformed by reduction or not into a dependent unit and made part of another predication called the "matrix" sentence. The matrix sentence can, of course, be transformed to an included predication within another sentence that becomes a matrix for it.

INDIRECT OBJECT—A nominal unit (including pronouns) that appears after certain kinds of verbs that have a meaning allowing for the movement of something (the direct object) "to" or "for" or "in reference to" something else (the indirect object). Indirect objects are usually animate beings but not always. Indirect objects usually appear in the company of direct objects. In their synthetic forms (with zero or objective inflection), they precede the direct objects; in analytic forms (most often with *to* or *for*) the prepositional phrase usually follows the direct object. Indirect objects can become subjects of passive words in transformed structures.

INFINITIVE—Often thought of as the base form of a verb, but infinitives are not finite verb forms. They can be part of finite verb phrases, but their chief uses are in reduced or included transforms of one kind or another. The *to* sign or marker of an infinitive is often not present. See Chapter 11.

INFLECTION—The alteration of a word, usually by the addition of a bound suffix, in order to express such things as plurality, relationship, or modality. Old English once had more inflections than Modern English now shows—particularly for nouns, pronouns, adjectives, and determiners. Inflection can be by internal change as in *goose-geese, man-men*. Most verb specialization in Modern English is done by analytic auxiliaries rather than by inflection, but in the third singular, present tense, and in the change of form to past tense inflection is still present.

INITIAL APPOSITIVE (INITIAL PARTICIPIAL PHRASE)—Included, non-restrictive reduced predications of the semi-predicative kind that appear at the beginning of the matrix clause. These often, but not always, convey a sense of causality: *Proud to be in the army, Jonas would not listen to their slanders. Wanting to become the first-string tackle, he never missed practice.*

INSTRUMENTAL—The inflectional case bearing the relational concept of "means" limited to the "instrument" by means of which something is done. According to some Old English grammars, that language had a separate instrumental case.

INTENSIFIER—A word in a function group in which words like *very, quite, rather, pretty,* etc., indicate the intensity of the quality denoted by an adjective or adverb.

INTERROGATIVE NOUN CLAUSE—A transform in which a question has been converted into a clause functioning nominally. The question is itself a transform usually involving an inversion from basic sentence word order. In the interrogative noun clause, word order reverts to basic sentence order, and the *do* used as a function word in the question transformation is deleted. See pages 153–55.

INTERROGATIVE PRONOUN OR ADVERB—A word functioning in the formation of a question in which the answer is not "yes" or "no": *who, what, when, where, how, why,* etc.; the same function words are found in a question transformed into an interrogative noun clause.

INTONATION CONTOUR—The profile (i.e., shape or contour) of a spoken phrase or sentence noted in terms of pitch changes, stress changes, and juncture or pauses. A large part of meaning in utterances is derived from differences in contour.

INTRANSITIVE VERB—A verb the meaning of which is such that it is not followed by a direct object. A passive form of an intransitive verb is impossible, unless a particle is added that makes the verb transitive: *Home was arrived at early.*

ISOLATING—A language, such as Chinese, is called an isolating language when words do not change form when they change parts of speech. Word order is all-important in such a language.

It TRANSFORMATION—The creation of the construction using a dummy "it" to delay the appearance in a sentence of a noun clause, nominal infinitive phrase, "for" construction, or other nominal. See pages 122–26.

JUNCTURE—The pauses, rests, glidings, or dying falls of sound between words or units. These function together with stress and pitch signals to form the intonational contours of utterances. By means of them many structural or syntactical meanings are communicated. In this book not much attention is paid to degrees of juncture.

LEARNED PHRASES—Inflexible phrases that a speaker has learned to use in a given situation. A door-to-door salesman may ask, "Is the lady of the house at home?" The child who answers may think that "lady of the house" means simply "mother." The salesman may not care what it means so long as an adult female comes to the door.

LEXICAL MEANING—The meaning of words or part-words that we normally learn from a dictionary. Since words are not the things themselves but are only symbols for them, we have to learn the relation between symbol and thing or symbol and concept, item by item.

LINGUISTIC LEVEL—Level of subordination, starting with the top level of subject and predicate of the matrix sentence. Modifiers are on a lower level than their headwords, but subject-part and predicate-part (at least in any two-nucleus construction) are on the same linguistic level. In a semi-predicative construction, however, subject-part and predicate-part of the reduced predication are on different levels.

MASS NOUN—See QUANTIFIABLE NOUN.

MATRIX SENTENCE—A sentence into which another predication, formal or reduced, is inserted or included by a transformational process.

MODAL AUXILIARY—A particle in the analytic system such as *can, may, must, will, should, ought* denoting modality as it assists in the formation of a verb phrase.

MODIFICATION—In traditional grammar it has been customary to define "modification" notionally—that is, a modifier is said to change the meaning or scope of reference of a general term by specifying, qualifying, or describing. The term is, however, used in this book only to signify grammatical dependence of one unit upon another. In a basic sentence pattern, a finite verb does not modify its subject, nor a direct or indirect object its verb, even though units with these functions may become modifiers when basic patterns are transformed.

MORPHOLOGY—Study of the internal structures of words: how segments within words fit together to signal both lexical and relational meanings.

MORPHOPHONEMICS—This is a high-level term that cannot be defined here adequately. Morphemes are small families of forms (words or part-words) that function more or less identically. Phonemes are those small families of sounds within which slight variation is unimportant in the communication of meaning within a given language or dialect. Morphophonemic principles are those that deal with the interplay of morphemic and phonemic principles.

NEAR-NOUN—A term introduced here to designate a class of function words

that have been called by various other names in former grammars—
"pre-determiners," "demonstrative pronouns or adjectives," "numerical
pronouns," "partitive pronouns." A phrase like *this man* represents a
substantive (near-noun) *this* alongside and in close apposition with
another substantive, *man,* either one of which could act substantively
in this position. See page 52.

NEGATION TRANSFORMATION—See pages 96–100.

NEXUS—A syntactic bond or connection between two items. Here the term
is used principally in connection with the phrase "predicational nexus."
A predicational nexus is an imputed connection between two items by
which an included predication is expressed, one of the items acting as
subject-part, the other as predicator, usually without any formal signal
of predication. In *I found it all dried out,* there is a predicational nexus
between *it* and *all dried out.*

NOMINAL FORMS OF REDUCED PREDICATION—See Chapter 12.

NONCE CONSTRUCTION—Unusual, unhabitual, anomalous usage. See pages
66–67.

NON-RESTRICTIVE MODIFIER—A dependent unit that does not notionally restrict, limit, or narrow the scope of reference of the unit on which it is
syntactically dependent.

NOUN—A member of one of the three main form classes—the class that
names entities conceived as substantives. Most nouns will respond to
some or all of the formal or functional tests for nouns: They are capable
of being marked by determiners; they are capable of plural inflection;
when they are in subject slots, verbs are in agreement with them; they
may end in known nominal derivational suffixes; they are capable of
assuming genitive inflectional suffixes. Not every noun will pass all of
these tests. We may call words or phrases *nominals* if they function
as nouns but lack the basic formal characteristics. The lexicon of nouns
is large and almost infinitely expandable.

NOUN ADJUNCT—A noun in a structure of modification before another noun
(*chicken thief*), functioning in the compositional system of English syntax. In *chicken's head, chicken's* is not a noun adjunct because it is a
genitive functioning in the synthetic system.

NOUN CLAUSE—A formal predication included in a matrix sentence in a
position usually filled by a substantive and functioning as a substantive.
See Chapter 8.

OBJECTIVE COMPLEMENT—The predicate-part of a reduced copula predication the whole of which functions as a direct object (sometimes with
double valence or obliquity) of certain factitive verbs or verbs denoting mental activity. In the reduction the copula is deleted. See pages
81–83, 220–23.

OBJECTIVE GENITIVE—When a formal predication having a transitive verb
is transformed into a reduced predication having a noun as headword,
the verb becomes an abstract noun and the object of the verb becomes
either an inflected genitive in the synthetic system (*his removal*) or the
object of an *of* prepositional phrase in the analytic system (*the removal
of him*). The inflected form is an objective genitive. The prepositional phrase form is its analytic counterpart.

OBLIQUE PREDICATOR—The unit in a reduced predication (usually a semi-predicative construction) from which has been deleted not only a copulative verb but also a signal of an oblique relation. Thus, for *He painted the barn red* we can re-create as source sentences *He painted the barn* and *The barn is now red*. The need to supply the word *now* in reconstituting the second source sentence indicates the obliquity of the predicational nexus between *barn* and *red*. The word *red* can thus be called an oblique predicator in this sentence.

PART OF SPEECH—See Chapter 4.

PARTICIPLE—A derivative of a verb that can be used as a constituent in a verb phrase or can be used in structures of modification, in semi-predicative structures, or as the predicate-part in two-nucleus reduced predications. These forms can be active or passive (*-ing* or *-en* forms; not all *-en* forms are passive). They can also express aspect (*having gone, being counted*) and to some degree modality (*being able to go*). Participles can take direct objects and be modified by adverbs when they have not been shifted to pre-position. See Chapter 9.

PARTITIVE—A relationship found usually with near-nouns of number or quantity (a few *of my friends*, several *birds*, much *of the time*). In Modern English the relationship is expressed usually by *of*. In highly inflected languages this is usually expressed by an inflected genitive.

PASSIVE PARTICIPLE—A derivative from a passive verb form having a suffix that can take many forms: *-ed, -d, -t, -en*. These are called *-en* participles (to have one name for all these forms) or second participles. Since these second participles do not show tense (in one function they are used in forming verb phrases of perfect aspect—not a tense), they are not appropriately called past participles.

PASSIVE TRANSFORMATION—A transformation in which a sentence with an active verb becomes a sentence with a passive verb (constructed with the appropriate form of *be* and the *-en* derivative of the verb). A direct or indirect object of the source sentence becomes the subject of the transformed sentence. See pages 100–103.

PERIPHRASTIC EQUIVALENT—A phrasing in the analytic system, usually using prepositions, that performs the same function as an inflected form in the synthetic system. The analytic form is a *periphrasis* of the synthetic form: *the surrender of Napoleon* (analytic periphrasis); *Napoleon's surrender* (synthetic genitive inflection). See page 244.

PHONEME—The term for a given sound within a slight range of differences that do not lead to significant differences in the signaling of meaning within a given language. This is a complicated matter and the term is rarely used here.

PHONEMICS—The study and classification of phonemes.

PHONETICS—The physical description of identifiable sounds. A phonetic alphabet is not identical with a list of the phonemes of a language.

PHRASE—A group of words with some sort of identity that does not make a formal predication; that is, that does not contain a subject-part and a finite verb. Some kinds of phrases are: prepositional phrases, verb phrases, nominal phrases, infinitive phrases, *with* and *for* constructions, absolute constructions, participial phrases, appositive phrases.

PITCH—The heightening or lowering of tone by which many structural meanings are signaled, especially distinction between one kind of predication and another. The ordinary pitch level is designated as 2; a raising of pitch above this level can be to the 3-level or the 4-level; at the end of declarative assertions there is a drop below the 2-level to the 1-level. The normal pitch pattern for a declarative utterance is thus 2–3–1:

$$2 \quad\quad 2 \quad 3 \quad 1$$
I bought a house.

At the end of included predications a rise to the 3-level is usually found, but the pitch returns to the 2-level rather than to the 1-level:

$$2 \quad 3\ 2\ 2 \quad\quad 3\ 2\ 2 \quad\quad 3 \quad 1$$
My cousin, who was a pirate, came to see me.

See pages 92–93.

PLURALIZER NOUN—One that is capable of being conceived in the plural; the kind of identity in which individual members can be counted.

POLYSYSTEMIC GRAMMAR—A grammar that is a somewhat disorderly *mélange* of two or more systems of syntactic arrangement. In actual practice, the important question is whether the grammarian attempts to cramp all the grammatical facts within one system or whether he assumes that the rationalization of one system cannot be carried over completely to another. Modern English is a polysystemic language.

POST-POSITIONAL RESTRICTIVE ADJECTIVE—The normal position for a restrictive adjective in English is before the noun it modifies (the result of a "prior" transformation); sometimes, however, restrictive adjectives appear after the nouns, either because they are headwords in cumbersome phrases or because they are part of phrases borrowed from French or other languages. See pages 169–72.

PRE-DETERMINER—A name sometimes used for a sub-class of what are here called "near-nouns." Examples: *all* the boys, *half* the pie. In using this term, one slights the three-cornered partial similarity between *all the boys, all of the boys,* and *all boys.*

PREDICATE—That part of a sentence that is not part of the subject or a dependency of the subject. In transformed structures items from the subject-part are sometimes found intermingled with items from the predicate-part, but not in basic sentence patterns when they follow normal word order. Predicate appositives, for instance, may be dependent on the subject-part even if physically they are found in the predicate-part. The predicate part of a sentence includes the verb phrase, any modifiers of the verb (even if they precede the subject-part, any objects of the verb or modifiers of the objects, and any adverbial complements.

PREDICATE APPOSITIVE—An appositive construction in which the predicator part of a copula predication is reduced and included in the predicate-part of a matrix predication; the subject-part of the appositive (a semi-predicative) is the subject of the matrix predication, but the verb of the matrix occurs between subject and predicate appositive:

1. He died *rich.*—adjective as predicate appositive
2. He died *the richest man in the county.*—noun as predicate appositive

3. He arrived home, *in a hurry to settle his business.*—prepositional phrase as predicate appositive
4. The dog lay in the dusty road, *dreaming of bones.*—participial phrase as predicate appositive (or at least as predicate semi-predicative).

PREDICATE COMPLEMENT—Whatever completes a predication after a copulative verb (*be*) or a copula variant (*become, remain, stay,* etc.). Same as *subjective complement.* Most predicate complements are nouns or verbs, but other kinds of units are possible—nouns in oblique cases (I am *home,* The meeting was *yesterday*), or prepositional phrases (The phone call is *for you*). Complements after transitive verbs (not predicate complements) are called direct or indirect objects, after intransitive verbs adverbial complements unless the predicational nexus is directly with the subject and not with the verb.

PREDICATE-PART—The part of a predication (formal or reduced) that asserts or predicates something about the subject-part. The predicate-part of a clause always contains a finite verb or a finite verb-phrase. In reduced predications the predicate-part is whatever the predicate-part of its source sentence has been transformed into.

PREDICATION—An assertion; one that is in fact asserting something. In real or implied form, a predication has a subject-part and a predicate-part. A predication that has the full form of a predication—a *formal predication*—has a subject and a finite verb. Any clause is thus a formal predication whether it is independent or dependent. According to this definition, a declarative sentence is taken as the base form of a predication, and questions are transformations of declarative sentences. In their transformed state they are of course still predications. Reduced predications, which are not formal predications after being reduced, are dependencies.

PREDICATIONAL NEXUS—The connection between a subject of some sort and a predicator of some sort. In *I fought a wildcat* the predicational nexus between *I* and *fought a wildcat* is very obvious. Less obvious are those cases in which the very existence of an included predication is not immediately evident. In certain reduced predications we have to ask "*What* does *what?*" or "*What* is *what?*" In *I knocked him silly,* it is *he* who is *silly,* not *I.* The predicational nexus between *silly* and something is with *him,* not with *I.* An expansion into source sentences could be: *I knocked him. He became silly.*

PREDICATIVE ADJECTIVE—An appositive adjective.

PREDICATOR—The unit that semantically does the predicating in an assertion or predication when the verb has been deleted or is a mere signal of predication. When a copulative verb *be* is merely a formal signal of predication, plus tense and mood, the predicate complement is the semantic predicator. Normally the verb is the formal predicator. Sometimes it is impossible to say just what word or phrase is the predicator.

PREFIX—A bound morpheme attached at the beginning of a word: *in* + *valuable, re* + *ject.*

PREPOSITION—A word belonging to a function group analytically making explicit a relationship between a noun or pronoun (usually called the "object" of the preposition) and some other word or unit: *by, from, before, to, with, according to,* and many others.

PRE-POSITIONAL ADJECTIVE—An adjective that immediately precedes the noun it modifies unless another pre-positional adjective intervenes (*good* man, *intelligent* good man). Most pre-positional adjectives are transformed predicate adjectives; those that are not are "borrowers" of the structure. It is sometimes asserted that, as transformed predicate adjectives, pre-positional adjectives are appositive adjectives that have undergone one further transformational step.

PRESCRIPTIVE GRAMMAR—A grammar in which rules are made for grammaticality on the basis of what the maker of the rules thinks the arrangement of constructions *ought* to be in a sentence, in accordance with his ideas of what is logical, tasteful, systematic, or agreed upon by educated and right-thinking people.

PRIOR TRANSFORMATION—A sub-assembly of parts that creates a unit functioning as a whole in a later transformation. See pages 105–6.

PRONOUN—A proxy for a noun: a symbol to be used in place of the name of something in order to represent it. The true pronouns are the personal pronouns *he, she, it, they, him, her, them.* This leaves out *I, me, we, us,* and *you* because these are not proxies for nouns but refer to things outside the verbal framework. This distinction is not, however, important, and for all practical purposes these can be called pronouns, as can the relative pronouns *who, which, that, whom,* and the interrogative pronouns *who, whom, what, which.* Demonstratives and numericals should be classed as near-nouns—ambiguously functioning as substantives, as determiners, or as pre-determiners in close apposition with substantives.

PROPER NOUN—The name of a particular person, place, organization, or entity.

QUANTIFIABLE NOUN—The name for the kind of identity that is a mass, the parts of which are uncountable—hence incapable of pluralizing: *mush, water.*

REDISTRIBUTION—A term for a kind of transformation that is a rearrangement of parts within a basic sentence pattern, a conversion of one basic pattern into another basic pattern, or the intermingling of parts from two source sentences so that they seem to make one sentence. See Chapter 7.

REDUCED PREDICATION—A predication transformed to less than a clause for the purpose of including it within, or attaching it to, another predication. This term is usually used here to refer to a dependent unit containing both subject-part and predicate-part without a finite verb, but some semi-predicatives (participial phrases and appositive phrases) can be structures of reduced predication even though they exhibit within their limits only the predicate-parts of the predications of which they are reductions. See pages 189–207.

REITERATION—The rhetorical device of repeating or picking up a word already used in a sentence in order to begin a new line of development that is not coordinated with the first and not parallel to it. See pages 178–180.

RELATION—The nature of the notional connection between two morphemes, two words, or two parts of a sentence: the way in which they are related to one another. The structural relation is not always identical with the notional relation, and one notional relation can often be signaled by more than one structure.

RELATIVE CLAUSE—A dependent formal predication in which a relative pronoun refers to the substantive or predicational unit on which the clause grammatically depends. Traditionally called an *adjective clause*. The relative pronoun may sometimes be deleted. See Chapter 8.

RELATIVE PRONOUN—*Who, whom, which, that, as, whose*. A relative pronoun is unlike the *that* particle introducing a noun clause in that it functions in a substantive position in its own clause. It is necessary also to distinguish between relative and interrogative pronouns, even though the same lexical items (like *who, whom,* or *which*) can serve both functions. Interrogative pronouns appear in questions and in interrogative noun clauses. The transformational process for the two kinds of clauses is dissimilar. *See* PRONOUN and pages 136–43.

"RESPECT" REDISTRIBUTION—See pages 126–27.

RESTATEMENT—The recasting of an idea in a construction that is parallel to the first statement of it but not coordinate with it. In restatement there is no predicational forward movement. See pages 178–80.

RESTRICTIVE MODIFIER—A modifier that reduces the area of reference or application of the term it modifies. Restriction applies most obviously to adjective modifiers, but by extension it applies also to some specialized functions of adverbs. Thus, *awkward movements* is related to *move awkwardly*.

RESULT ADJUNCT—A construction found in the predicate somewhat resembling an objective complement but with an obliquity of relation. *Clean* in *We made the windows clean* is an objective complement. In *We washed the windows clean* it is a result adjunct. In both instances a predicational nexus is found between *windows* and *clean*, but the source predication for the result adjunct is *The windows are now clean*. Here the *now* reveals the obliquity. The predicational nexus of a result adjunct is with the direct object, not with the subject, unless the verb in the clause is passive.

RESULT SENTENCE—The sentence that results when one predication (a source sentence) is included within or dependently attached to another predication (the matrix sentence).

SECOND GENITIVE—Forms like *mine, ours, theirs, yours, John's, the men's*. Only in some pronouns is the form of the second genitive different from that of the first genitive (*my* as opposed to *mine*, etc.). These second genitive forms are used substantively.

SECOND PARTICIPLE—The *-en* participial forms, often in the past called the *past participle*. *See* PASSIVE PARTICIPLE.

SEGMENTAL MORPHEME—One of the segments into which words or utterances can be separated, down to base forms. Segmental morphemes are distinct from suprasegmental morphemes (signals from stress patterns, pitch patterns, or juncture). Segmental morphemes are basic lexical symbols.

SEMI-PREDICATIVE—A structure that represents the inclusion of the predicate-part of a predication in a matrix sentence when the subject-part of the included unit is already present in the matrix. The chief kinds of semi-predicative structures are participial phrases, appositive phrases, and certain kinds of infinitive phrases. The transformational paths have to be separately described for each of these, but in all cases the semi-predicatives are dependent on their detached subject-parts. See Chapter 9.

SENTENCE—An autonomous syntactic government: an independent predication together with any units that are syntactically dependent upon it. If in some systems of punctuation or some schools of style agreement cannot be reached concerning what is or what is not a sentence, we need not as grammarians be much concerned. We start with the assumption that a sentence has a noun phrase and a verb phrase that together create a formal predication that is not dependent on anything. A formal predication is not necessarily a sentence since dependent clauses also are formal predications, but all sentences contain at least one formal predication.

SENTENCE MODIFIER—A term used by some modern grammarians to apply to dependent units that seem to modify whole predications (formal or reduced) rather than individual words such as nouns or verbs. The term has, however, been loosely used.

SEQUENCE WORD—Traditionally called *conjunctive adverb;* a kind of function word that expresses a relationship between clauses without being a conjunction: *however, nevertheless, therefore, otherwise,* etc. See pages 148–52.

STRESS—A speaker can, by increasing or decreasing the force of the breath stream, give meaningful signals of syntactic relation as well as of emphasis. Four degrees of stress can be noted: ´, ^, `, and zero: *Whíte Hòuse, a white hóuse, a little bírd's nêst.* These are called primary, secondary, tertiary, and no stress.

STRUCTURAL LINGUISTICS—The approach to grammar used by a school of modern grammarians in which much stress is put upon the spoken language since most of the structures that signal meaning are sound structures. The structuralist has been, however, in no position to pay much attention to the generative processes by which sentences are formed, so that the structuralists and the transformational grammarians have seemed to use oppositive approaches. Ideally it should be possible to combine the two.

SUBJECT—The word or group of words about which a statement is made or a question is asked. In normal word order in Modern English the subject of a sentence comes first and the predicate follows. In copula predications it may sometimes be difficult to tell which is subject and which is predicate complement since they may appear in reverse order: *A mighty big river is the Mississippi.* The scope of reference made by a predicate complement is presumably as broad as that of its subject or broader—a broader class or at least one of the same size. In *Those men are cowards* the class of *cowards* contains more members than the class of *those men.*

SUBJECT-PART—The part of a formal or reduced predication about which something is asserted or asked. When a predication is reduced, the subject-part usually remains intact.

SUBJECTIVE GENITIVE—In a noun-headed reduced predication, the subject of the transformed source sentence may appear with a genitive inflection: *Beethoven's creation of the Seventh Symphony*. *Beethoven's* is a subjective genitive in such a construction. See page 243.

SUBORDINATING CONJUNCTION—A connecting word in a function group that lexically specifies the relationship between a dependent clause and a superior unit. In traditional grammar a subordinating conjunction introduces adverbial clauses. By our definition, relative pronouns and the *that* introducing noun clauses are not subordinating conjunctions since they do not specify relationships. Subordinating conjunctions are words like *although, because, after, if,* etc. Their position is rigidly fixed at the beginning of the dependent clause.

SUBSTANTIVE—A class term for any word that can do the work of a noun: noun, pronoun, near-noun, or nominal.

SUFFIX—A bound morpheme attached to the end of the stem of a word to perform some inflectional or derivational function.

SURFACE GRAMMAR—A grammar that concerns itself only with immediate constituency in explaining constructions and that does not concern itself with the generative process by which the constructions have come into being.

SYNTAX—That part of grammar concerned with the ways in which words are joined together in a significant word order or by other ways of signaling to create communicable meaning. Syntax is only indirectly involved in the way in which the segments of a word are put together; that is the province of morphology.

SYNTHETIC SYSTEM—The syntactic system by which relationships between words are indicated primarily by symbolic inflectional affixes. Derivational affixes, which serve mainly to convert words from one part of speech to another, resemble inflectional affixes in part of their range, but as signalers of functional shift rather than of semantic relation, they are not directly instruments of a synthetic system. Synthetic systems contrast most markedly with analytic systems, which use particles or isolated counters to express the relations expressed by inflectional affixes in synthetic systems.

TENSE—The "time" of a verb's content. "Present" and "past" are the only inflected tenses of Modern English. If we truly have a future tense, it is expressed analytically, not synthetically. "Tense" must be kept distinct from "aspect." The distinction between the "imperfect" and the "perfect" is one of aspect, not tense. Similarly, the French "conditional" is a mood distinction, not one of tense. Non-finite forms deriving from verbs are incapable of showing tense.

There TRANSFORMATION—See pages 120–22.

TRANSFORM—A unit that has undergone a transformation.

TRANSFORMATION—An alteration of a basic sentence pattern that can be described with some precision, so that the sentence takes on a non-basic form (as in the change of an assertion to a question or negation), or so that it can be subordinated to or included in another basic sentence (called the "matrix" sentence).

TRANSFORMATIONAL GRAMMAR—A grammar like this one in which the process of describing the nature of complex forms is to work out the steps by which they are generated from simple or basic sentence forms. A transformational grammar is thus a three-dimensional, or depth grammar, in contrast to a static, or immediate-constituent grammar, which contents itself with indicating layers of dependency as they can be represented two-dimensionally. A transformational grammar may more aptly be called a "generative" grammar up to that point at which basic predicational forms cease to be generated and these basic forms begin to be transformed—that is, altered into other forms.

Two-Nuclei Construction—A unit (usually a reduced predication) having a subject-part and a predicate-part on the same linguistic level: absolute construction, *with* construction, *for* construction. Clauses are also obviously two-nuclei constructions—so obviously that the term makes no significant distinction in respect to them.

Unit—A term deliberately left vague and general so that it can refer to an identity of any sort—a single word, a phrase, or a clause.

Verb—*See* Finite Verb and pages 55–57. A word or phrase that notionally predicates something about a subject, unless it is a copula, which merely signals predication. In form a verb can show tense, person, number, aspect, mood, and voice by adding inflections or auxiliaries. By this definition only finite verbs or finite verb phrases are called verbs. Forms such as infinitives, participles, gerunds, and abstract nouns derived from verbs—which are derived from verbs but lack the formal attributes of finite verbs—may function as predicators in reduced predications, but are not verbs.

Verbal—A term that has been avoided in this text. Some modern grammarians have adopted a dual set of terms, with distinction in the pairs according to definition by form and definition by function: noun, nominal; adjective, adjectival; verb, verbal; adverb, adverbial. According to this scheme, a verbal is a word or phrase that functions as a verb but is not a verb in form. This definition cannot be made to apply to participles, infinitives, gerunds, or abstract nouns, since these have usually undergone functional shifts and so do not function as verbs—certainly not as finite verbs, although even as nominals they may still have some force as predicators.

Voice—A term that in English can apply only to analytically constructed verb phrases that show a relation of their subjects of "active" or "passive." This is a question of forms primarily and only secondarily of meanings. Basic sentence patterns contain active verb forms. Predications with passive verb forms are transformations from predications with active forms.

Word Order—In Modern English, as in most languages, many of the structural signals that make meaning possible are derived from the order in which words appear. These signals, however, form only a partial system for indicating relationships, and they must be correlated with signals of other kinds. Consequently, only imperfectly can we speak of a word-order system of syntactic signals.

Zero Inflection—An inflectional difference that has actually been lost in the evolution of a language but that can still be said to exist because the word from which it has disappeared still behaves as if it were still present. This behavior may be seen in word order or from the possibility of a competing structure. Thus, *John* in *I gave John an apple* can be said to have a zero dative inflection (representing its indirect object relationship), even though the relationship is actually discovered from word order or from the possibility of using the contrasting form *I gave an apple to John*.

ZERO MORPHEME—A signaling form that is not actually made explicit but that can be inferred by pre-supposing an ellipsis or ideal conformity to a paradigmatic scheme.

INDEX

305